BRAWN

BODYBUILDING FOR THE DRUG-FREE AND GENETICALLY TYPICAL

Stuart McRobert

CS PUBLISHING LTD.
NICOSIA - CYPRUS

WARNING

Every effort has been made in this book to stress the importance of proper technique and safety when using a bodybuilding or strength training program. Check with your health practitioner to ensure that it's appropriate for you to follow such a program. Follow the instructions carefully. Neither the author, nor CS Publishing Ltd., will be responsible for any physical injury that may result from following the routines and advice given in this book.

You'll benefit from this book in direct proportion to how seriously you study it, how thoroughly you understand the contents, how well you make the understanding one with you, and how resolutely you apply it.

Before thinking something important has been missed out of this book, please wait until you've studied *every* paragraph of *every* page.

Where it has been cumbersome to use both genders of a pronoun, the male gender has been used. This is *not* to imply that **BRAWN** only applies to males. With the exception of the goals given in Chapter 3, **BRAWN** is aimed at both sexes.

Published by CS Publishing Ltd., P.O. Box 390, CY-2151 Nicosia, Cyprus
Printed in Cyprus by Zavallis Litho

First published in November 1991
Reprinted in April 1992 (with a new cover and minor corrections)
Reprinted in September 1992 (with minor changes)
Reprinted in March 1993 (with minor changes)
Reprinted in July 1993 (with minor changes, and together with the first hardback edition)
Reprinted in October 1993
Reprinted in April 1996 (with minor changes)

ISBN: 9963-7838-0-5 (softbound)   ISBN: 9963-7838-1-3 (hardback)

Contents

Preface

The extraordinarily genetically gifted – the potential championship winning material – usually compound their physical advantages by using anabolic steroids. The combination of genetic advantage and drug use puts these bodybuilders in a class of their own. They are the antitheses of role models for drug–free and genetically typical bodybuilders.

This book is dedicated to genetically typical bodybuilders who have the *good sense* and *strength of character* not to take anabolic steroids. In other words, **BRAWN** is dedicated to the great mass of bodybuilders – dedicated to those who need advice that originates from drug–free and genetically typical sources.

Training drug–free and genetically typical bodybuilders, to realize their genetic potentials, is a whole different (and *far more* difficult) activity than that of training champions or potential champions.

While this book doesn't describe everything about training the drug–free and typical bodybuilder, it describes more than enough to take all who are willing and dedicated – both male *and* female – a darned long way. It can take them to a level of development that will put them in a very privileged bracket. Such achievement will impress everyone except the few who have first–hand experience of fully developed, genetically gifted and drug–assisted (or *drug–built*) competitive bodybuilders.

Don't think that the methods in this book will only help the genetically typical. The methods that pack size and strength onto typical bodybuilders will pack even more size and strength onto genetically blessed bodybuilders, and do it in less time.

BRAWN is crammed with substance, providing – for the drug–free and genetically typical – an in–depth bodybuilding education.

Read – Understand – Apply – Persist – Achieve

Acknowledgements

Charles A. Smith, over the time I knew him before his death in January 1991, used to remind me that what we have today we owe to the past. How right he was. As Chas used to put it, "It's upon the pioneers' shoulders that we have to stand in order to be as tall as they. We're merely the heirs of those who have gone before us."

My biggest debt of gratitude is owed to Peary Rader. He taught me a lot of what I know about training, and published my early work thus enabling me to get a foothold in the world of bodybuilding journalism.

My understanding of bodybuilding and strength training has accelerated over the years I've been publishing HARDGAINER magazine. Working with readers and contributors has been invaluable in garnering the understanding needed to write this book.

Without the consistent publicity HARDGAINER has received through IRONMAN and MUSCLEMAG UK, and the crucial initial contacts given by Dr. Ken E. Leistner, there would neither be HARDGAINER nor this book. Particular appreciation for help with publicity over the last two years goes to IRONMAN for publishing my monthly column.

I want to thank individually the following for their feedback on draft chapters of this book. In alphabetical order, they are: Richard G. Abbott, Jan Dellinger, Dr. R. Keith Hartman, Tony Rose, Randall J. Strossen, Ph.D., Mike Thompson and Stephen Wedan. Special appreciation goes to Dr. Hartman for giving Chapter 11 a professional stamp of approval, and to Mike Thompson whose scrutiny of all the final draft chapters provided suggestions that helped to hone the book into its final, more comprehensive form.

Dr. Strossen, with the rigorism of his academic background, and his expert knowledge of the training world, provided valuable comments on the final draft chapters. His unwavering support and encouragement helped to get me through the final stage of this work.

Without the generosity and thoughtfulness of Paul O'Hara, my library of bodybuilding and strength training material would be much depleted. Thank you, Paul.

The artistry on the front cover comes from Stephen Wedan. Thank you, Steve.

Years ago, when I changed my training frame of mind, the investigation of "alternative" training methods opened a *vast* area of study. This book is a summary of much of this whole area of study.

As long as we maintain a mentality of, "That's not how Arnold did it," or, "That's not how Lee Haney does it," then we'll get nowhere but into a well of frustration and despair.

The imitating of inappropriate models has been responsible for so much of the futile training methods that are so prevalent in gyms worldwide.

1: The Need

Bodybuilding literature is dominated by the achievements of those who are most suited to bodybuilding. These genetically gifted few make up a very tiny minority relative to the great mass of bodybuilders.

The great mass of bodybuilders doesn't share the genetic advantages and drug assistance of the few who reach the highest level of the modern bodybuilding world. So, what practical use – for most gym members – are the achievements and methods used by the top-liners?

It can be argued that the achievements of top contestants inspire the rest of us. While this may be so for some of us, it's easier to argue that using a gifted minority as role models for the genetically average majority is nothing but a recipe for frustration.

Unless we have the constitution, genetic propensity for the development of astounding muscular mass and strength, and almost unlimited time to train and rest, what chance do we have of dedicating ourselves to the life of a professional bodybuilder? Furthermore, what chance do we have of benefiting from such dedication? No chance, no chance at all.

Many of the top achievers (whether international, national or regional) are, simply put, drug-built. Not only do they not know about how to train without drugs, they rarely if ever train "seriously" without pharmaceutical assistance. Right from the early months of their training they used drugs. Together with being genetically gifted, the heavy drug use enabled them to win a big title within just a few years. When you read about a "great" achiever who has taken the bodybuilding world by storm after just a few years of training – due to his dedication, hard work and good genetics – add on your own postscript: "Of course, don't forget that heavy and consistent use of steroids was the bedrock for the development of the 'great' physique."

Typical bodybuilders don't have the genetic advantages needed to build huge muscles, and shouldn't be foolish enough to tamper with drugs. We're light years removed from those who dominate the bodybuilding press and so strongly influence the mass of bodybuilders.

The failure rate among aspiring bodybuilders is enormous. Attend a gym for a few months and watch the change in the clientele. A hard core remains, but the others come and go. Of course, many people lack the application and resolve needed to do justice to a training program. However, *so many* people are given inappropriate training routines and so have no chance of obtaining satisfactory results, irrespective of their degree of application. Of the hard core that maintains its membership, how many make progress from year to year? Very few.

Appropriate role models

As long as we maintain a mentality of, "That's not how Arnold did it," or, "That's not how Lee Haney does it," then we'll get nowhere but into a well of frustration and despair.

I know more than a bit about this well of frustration and despair. I've been in it, and stewed in it, for years. I spent the second half of my teenaged years, together with later years, utterly consumed by bodybuilding. If following the dedication, resolve and training methods of the champions was the key to success, I'd have been up there competing with the best of them. I never was, and never can be.

The use of the word "champion" is misleading. Many "champions," despite their genetic advantages, wouldn't even be close to where they are, or were, without heavy steroid use. Such physiques are pseudo–champions. The "real" champions are those who built themselves up from runts – without drugs and without divorcing themselves from everyday life. Though not entering any contests, and getting no publicity in magazines, these are the real champions.

The genetically gifted and drug–assisted (or drug–built) top achievers belong to a different species than do the rest of us. It took me years of frustration and misery before I grasped this fundamental point, not to mention the thousands of hours spent poring over magazines and books dominated by the top competitors.

Had I been an isolated example of the folly in following the advice and activities of an astonishingly gifted minority, then my example would have no value. However, in every gym I've been to I've seen the great majority of members being either akin to me in physical potential, or, having even less bodybuilding potential than I.

As publisher and editor of HARDGAINER I receive a constant pouring in of letters from readers, reporting their failure when using popular training methods. Only a resort to rational, appropriate and abbreviated methods yielded the gains they craved. *What a shame abbreviated training is usually seen as the last resort rather than the first resort.*

Despite all of this, the achievements, opinions and training methods of the genetically blessed and drug–assisted (or drug–built) continue to dominate the minds of the huge majority of bodybuilders.

The time has long since come for bodybuilders to adopt appropriate role models.

Let's keep our own expectations down-to-earth, and then keep our training methods realistic. Only by keeping our training methods in the "land of reality" will we actually derive substantial benefit from training. There's no loss of potential achievement from adopting a realistic and appropriate approach to bodybuilding. It's all gain.

Bodybuilding results follow from the use of practical and appropriate training methods. Such methods follow on from a realistic set of expectations. Such a set of expectations doesn't come from imbibing the achievements and training lifestyle of the drug-using and genetically gifted top-title contestants.

Realistic achievements *don't* mean paltry achievements. Far from it. The achievements of a successful typical gym member – a successful hard gainer – are extremely impressive. Though modest relative to the professional bodybuilders, they are fantastic relative to untrained people and bodybuilding neophytes.

In fact, a successful hard gainer has climbed a bigger mountain than has a successful easy gainer. Though the latter develops greater size and strength than the former, it's the hard gainer who has far greater obstacles to surmount.

It's easy, and, at least for beginners, understandable to conclude that bodybuilders with the biggest muscles know the most about training. It's true that they know a lot about training as it applies to those with extraordinary genetic potential, and especially when in combination with anabolic steroids. However, how much do they know about training someone who isn't damaging his body (and integrity) with drugs and who only has an average or less-than-average genetic potential?

It would be too generalized to say that all top physiques know nothing about training that could help the typical bodybuilder. However, it *is* accurate to say that not a single easy-gaining top physique can possibly put himself in the shoes of the genetically typical and drug-free bodybuilder.

While the leading physiques might have many insights that can help us, they have no personal experience of the gaining difficulties of the typical person. No personal experience of the *substance* of the matter for typical bodybuilders. Without the nitty-gritty personal experience of actually struggling themselves to get even 15" arms and a 300 pound squat they are at a loss that can never be compensated for.

The top physiques *have* done things we all need to copy, especially *building up to using big poundages in the big basic exercises.* However, the methods they used to achieve these desirable things are usually in a different world to the methods our bodies will respond to. We need to take a radically different route to get to the same objective.

The imitating of inappropriate models has been responsible for so much of the futile training methods that are so prevalent in gyms worldwide. Young neophytes – beware of imitating your idols.

> What works for a gifted few who have an astonishing
> natural ability to grow muscle is often almost the
> antithesis of what the rest of us need.

What is a hard gainer?

A hard gainer is someone who finds making gains in size and strength hard to come by. It's a broad category encompassing almost all bodybuilders and lifters. Who doesn't find gains difficult?

Though almost all of us lack the genetics needed to tolerate and respond to almost any training and nutritional regimen, and to build huge size almost regardless of methods followed, we're not all identical in severity of "hard–gainingness."

Some hard gainers find gains more difficult to make than do others. Just how "hard" a hard gainer you are, only you can know. The harder you find gaining to be, the more thought you need to give to the interpretations of training needed to get you to gain.

The opposite of a hard gainer is an easy gainer. Exist they do, though in small numbers. All gyms have one or a few of them, though very few easy gainers realize their potential for growth and strength. I've seen people come into the gym with arms bigger than just about everyone else's in the gym despite never having formally trained their arms. These blessed few find gains so easy that they often attach little value to muscular development and don't sustain hard training.

There have been, and continue to be, bodybuilders at the top of the world of competition who eat poorly, constantly dissipate themselves, have been drug–addicts, have been alcohol–dependent, have private lives that are chaotic and stress riven, and yet are able to build astonishing physiques. Their extraordinary genetic superiority and constitution, in combination with anabolic steroids, get them through all of this. The price they will pay in the long–term, and even are paying in the short–term, is often very heavy indeed. All of this is shunted to one side as their photographs and achievements astound onlookers.

Compare this with the hard gainer who trains, eats, rests and sleeps with absolute dedication – for year after year – and yet, after ten years, still hasn't got 16" arms and a bench press close to 300 pounds.

Easy gainers who have reached, or almost reached the limit of their muscular size *do* have problems adding the final finishing touches. The slow progress they might make at this stage of their development doesn't qualify them to be hard gainers. That some of the supermen started out very thin doesn't qualify them as hard gainers either. In their skinny bodies they had far greater capacity for growth than do the rest of us. That it might take them ten years to get 19" arms and the like isn't hard gaining. Spending ten years and yet still having not developed 16" arms, or perhaps not even 15" arms, despite dedication (though misdirected), is hard gaining.

The easy gainers get their size with no problems at all. It's the "finishing off" and contest preparation stage that presents them with difficulties. How fortunate they are to be able to get to the point where they have such problems of luxury. How many hard gainers get big enough to be able just to concern themselves with maintaining size while concentrating upon adding the finishing touches?

Of course the top physiques have trained hard (at least some of the time) and with dedication. Such easy gainers have the comfort of knowing that results are, simply, about putting in some effort in the gym and then, as sure as night follows day, the muscle will follow. Not so with hard gainers. Effort in the gym is only part of the picture. It's correctly applied effort in an integrated package of factors that's the key.

The range of maneuver within the bracket of "productive effort" for the easy gainer is vast. Just about anything will deliver results. In fact, at least during their building years, easy gainers may have experienced unlimited room for error. The muscle just piled on. Dreamland.

For the hard gainer, the range of maneuver within "productive effort" is drastically reduced. Hard gainers need to get the whole package of size and strength–related considerations in extremely good order – *all* things correctly in place. Correctly in place according to hard gainers' standards, not easy gainers' standards. For hard gainers, a single thing not in good order – be it food, rest, sleep, training frequency or number of exercises in a routine – can ruin the productiveness of everything else that *is* in good order. Compare this with the easy gainer who can break many of the hard gainers' "rules" for productive bodybuilding and yet still packs on the muscle.

A typical hard gainer

I've spent years and years embroiled in completely *dedicated* but fruitless toil in the gym. Looking back, it's incredible to think I could have maintained my resolve despite such colossal frustration and failure. I discovered through painful experience that dedication, effort in the gym and food supplements are only a part of the picture. Only when they are put into an integrated and thoroughly comprehensive and appropriate whole can they deliver the goods.

As an archetypal hard gainer I intimately know about the misery of achieving nothing while using traditional training programs – the very same programs that dominate the bodybuilding literature today. I have dragged, I mean *dragged* my protesting and barely receptive body from that of a runt to respectability by normal gym standards.

I know what it's like to be as dedicated – if not more so – than a Mr. Olympia contestant, but yet I had sticking points that lasted for years. I diligently and conscientiously followed popular size building routines only to *lose* size.

I've been so miserable at the sight of so little reward for so much effort and dedication that, in my early years of training, I've wept.

Hard gainers of average height who have battled through years of frustration, before "clicking" with what they need to do to gain, and who finally made it to the 300 pound bench press, 400 squat and 500 deadlift bracket, or thereabouts, and shorter or taller bodybuilders who have made comparable achievements, know what the score is. Ultra–extreme hard gainers who have achieved a lot less than the 300–400–500 example have still made herculean achievements. They had more stacked against them both from the start and during their journey.

Though all such successful hard gainers don't know everything, *myself included*, they *do* know tons about what does and doesn't work for fellow hard gainers. Just because these people haven't won bodybuilding titles, and don't have photographs of their physiques in magazines, is no slight against their effectiveness as trainers.

That I've made it to this 300–400–500 bracket (without drugs, wraps, lifting belt or lifting suit), and have added over sixty pounds of muscle to my thin (6–3/4" wrists) 5'9" frame – and I've not finished yet – has taught me much about what to recommend to other hard gainers. While what worked for me may not work for you, we're in the same locality.

Years ago, when I changed my training frame of mind, the investigation of "alternative" training methods opened a *vast* area of study. This book is the summary of much of this *whole area* of study.

> This is the book I wish had been available to me when
> I first started bodybuilding, the one I wish I could
> have made an integral part of me.

It's one thing to have a book available, and to buy and read it. It's another thing to become one with the book and to put its advice into sustained, practical use. Had I been able to do this with this book, when

I was a teenager, within a few years I would have developed almost all the size and strength that I realistically could have.

I would have done this without having become fanatical about training, without having marred my academic achievements, without having given up a social life, without having spent huge sums of money on training literature and food supplements, without having given up sports, without having sustained any lasting injuries, without having been miserable at having no gains for long periods, and without having wallowed in the frustration and misery of not being able to emulate the top physiques.

I know intimately of the desperation and frustration of slaving away in the gym and living the dedicated bodybuilding lifestyle, and yet still make no progress. I know of this through long personal experience. Nothing abstract or theoretical about this understanding.

I'm a typical gym member – an archetypal hard gainer. I see lots of people like me – people who can't grow unless on an unadulterated hard gainer's routine. I see very few people who can grow on the routines that the top contestants have used and recommend. That the top contestants have never trained like a hard gainer needs to is in no way a criticism of the hard gainers' training methods.

The easy gainers never get so desperate for gains that they need even to consider the radical methods the hard gainer must use. They never need to turn to the last resort approach of very abbreviated training. *Extreme* hard gainers may *never* be able to respond to anything else. For them, the last resort way is the only way. Other hard gainers can work into less abbreviated training *once they have developed the necessary substantial foundation.*

Had I been an easy gainer I wouldn't have genuine sympathy with the plight of the hard gainer. Had I been an easy gainer, my recommendations would be academic and hollow.

Successful hard gainers don't have the physiques to convince those who need a mega–star's physique to be impressed. However, it's vital to judge people on what they have developed relative to what they had to work with and relative to the obstacles they had to overcome.

On top of my personal and observational experiences in the gym, are my experiences publishing HARDGAINER. This is a magazine devoted to the promotion of training methods totally geared to meeting the needs of typical bodybuilders and lifters. I've learned much from readers and contributors.

The distillation of knowledge in this book provides the typical bodybuilder with a *very* powerful tool. Seize the tool and put it to work.

Never, *ever*, forget that the overriding factor responsible for the phenomenal success enjoyed by so few bodybuilders is genetic advantage compounded by drug assistance. *Never* let anyone kid you otherwise.

Even genetic superiors have genetic flaws. These flaws are but a *drop in the ocean* compared to the bodybuilding limitations and difficulties imposed upon the majority of us by average genetic endowment.

Once you're big enough and strong enough from having followed the advice in this book, then, *and only then*, can you graduate to "finishing" routines and work to hone the mass into its final form.

2: Genetic Variation

Just what are the advantages that separate the mass of us from the minuscule minority of bodybuilders who were born with the potential for building phenomenal size and strength?

Do genetics *really* matter?

There's a bodybuilding opinion that fosters the notion that the world's top physiques are made, not born; that unfavorable genetics only slow down muscle growth, while never actually preventing the development of huge muscles. This opinion urges the disregarding of genetics. So, with a lot of commitment, Woody Allen could have matched Lee Haney on the posing dias, Stan Laurel could have held his own with Eugen Sandow and Bing Crosby could have kept pace with John Grimek. After all, genetics don't matter.

Such opinion lives in domains that have no contact with truth. It's the opinion that encourages bodybuilders, especially young neophytes, to live their lives up in the clouds of unrealistic expectations while simultaneously following the training routines of the top physiques.

It's the opinion that leads millions of bodybuilders down the road of utterly inappropriate and ineffective training programs.

It's the opinion that encourages the excessive attention upon supplements and, ultimately, the dangerous use of anabolic steroids and other nocuous substances.

It's the opinion that causes so much heartache, frustration and pain because it promises something it can't deliver and so moves the falsely guided to extreme measures. However, even *with* drugs the genetically typical can never emulate the achievements of the genetically gifted.

This "genetics don't matter" opinion believes that work and application build huge muscles, irrespective of genetic inheritance. (The importance of drugs is casually forgotten.) Of course how well you realize your potential is a reflection of your application, dedication, desire and type of program used; but ultimate muscular size is determined by genetic endowment.

To state, or imply, that all serious and determined hard gainers didn't develop spectacular size merely because they haven't trained hard enough and long enough, and because they didn't have a sufficiently positive attitude, is a gross insult. I'm but one of the countless number of typical bodybuilders who have applied themselves to bodybuilding with dedication and diligence enough to match any winner of a top title. Don't tell us that we didn't try hard enough or seriously enough. My God, don't tell us that!

We tried all right. We tried, tried and tried some more. And we tried with utter and complete – no, fanatical – dedication. We lived, slept, ate and drank bodybuilding, with our self–esteem and goals way up in the clouds. We gave our ton of flesh. But *we* never looked like Arnold, Lee, Sergio, Casey, Rich and the others.

What's particularly galling, for typical bodybuilders, is to have a drug–using genetic superior lecturing about how, while genetic variation plays a role, it's a small role relative to application and know–how. Even more infuriating is when a prominent physique moans about how hard he found it to bring up a lagging body part. He neglects to say that the "lagging" body part was already well ahead of even a successful hard gainer's, and that he built massive muscles throughout most of his physique before he was 30, 25 or even 20, and that he used (uses) drugs. (There's a connection with reality when at least some top bodybuilders acknowledge the role of heredity in endowing them with the necessary talent for elite achievement.)

As I've already said, the genetically gifted (though of course flawed in some way) simply *can't* understand true hard gaining. No matter how much they try, they *can't understand*. If I had a magic wand I would put some writers and title winners in the shoes of a genetically typical hard gainer weighed down with family, financial and employment concerns. After he's struggled to build just a 230 bench and 315 squat, after years of determined effort and many setbacks, then he might begin to understand what I mean. If I could then wish him into the shoes of the ultra–hard gainer, he would, when feeling suicidal, finally get the full message that genetics matter *one heck of a lot*.

Having "perfect" genetics isn't necessary to become a professional bodybuilder. All the genetic superiors have "faults" they try to correct or hide as best they can. I'm aware of the high calves of Tony Pearson, Robby Robinson and Shawn Ray. Just as I'm aware of the narrow shoulders that Larry Scott had to live with, the flat biceps of Sergio Oliva, the wide hips of Mike Mentzer, and the weak calves that Arnold *used* to have.

These men made the best of their shortcomings. However, bear in mind that, because they had so much going for them outside of the shortcomings, they could make a good job of coping with the weaknesses. They could make a far better job than can hard gainers with the same shortcomings but in a genetically typical body. Plus, the championship–level bodybuilders use drugs. It's just a different world for them. Let's just stop comparing drug–assisted and drug–built easy gainers with hard gainers. (Let's also dismiss the training methods of hard gainers who have built themselves up using drugs. While surrendering their integrity and self–esteem, and damaging their health, they have nothing to teach us about training.)

The "imperfections" of the top competitors are but *a drop in the ocean* compared to the bodybuilding difficulties and limitations imposed upon the majority of us by average genetics. I wish I just had the "shortcomings" of Oliva, Arnold, Scott, Mentzer or any of the others. They were so generously blessed with advantages that their shortcomings could be overlooked.

Relative to the limitations that average genetics impose on our ultimate bodybuilding success, every single one of the top competitors *doesn't know the meaning* of genetic limitation.

All of us can transform ourselves, and develop physiques and strength levels that make us true super–beings relative to the untrained person. However, we can never, *ever*, compete with the tiny minority that is extraordinarily genetically favored. This might not be a palatable truth, especially for beginners, but it's the truth nevertheless.

Grasp this key point right from the very beginning. Don't devote yourself to becoming a professional bodybuilder. Spare yourself from having your life nigh–on destroyed by the obsession.

Easy gainers and hard gainers, proportions of

What proportions of bodybuilders belong in each category? The genetic mega–superiors of the ilk of Casey Viator, Lee Haney and Tim Belknap are extraordinarily rare. (In no way am I criticizing their natural talent for bodybuilding. I've spent years of my life wishing I had their same "freak" genetic condition.) Let's be generous and say 1% of a sample of bodybuilders have the potential to be super–achievers should they put in the work and dedication, and take enough drugs.

I would say that over three quarters of a random sample of bodybuilders (not from an elite group or elite gym) are typical bodybuilders – hard gainers – varying from extreme hard gainers to just "regular" hard gainers. All these get nowhere using the orthodox training methods. This leaves a balance of bodybuilders who are neither typical hard gainers nor phenomenal easy gainers. They are, however, easy gainers to some degree. Some of them are capable of developing very big muscles, though not in the fantastic category.

Bodybuilders in this group can make progress using the orthodox training methods that are so vigorously promoted in the bodybuilding literature. While they could grow faster using more hard–gainer type routines, they make enough progress to demonstrate in gyms that progress can be made using the popular routines. Though they aren't genetic mega–superiors, they still have sufficient advantages relative to the majority of us for them not to be fit role models for us.

The focus of this book

This book is aimed specifically at the majority of bodybuilders – typical hard gainers. My concern is with developing the substance needed before you even think about concerning yourself with the detail and "finishing off" (advanced) work that so many trainers and writers concern themselves with. My criticism of this latter aspect of bodybuilding is that it's stressed in the literature way out of proportion to the percentage of bodybuilders who are sufficiently advanced or genetically gifted to benefit from it.

I don't doubt that this or that aspect of a muscle can be stressed, to provide "balance" and "finish." As there's so much emphasis upon this "finishing" aspect of training, I don't need to deal with it here. Once you're big enough and strong enough from having diligently and conscientiously followed the advice in this book, irrespective of genetic starting point, then, *and only then*, can you graduate (should you be interested) to the "finishing" routines and try to hone the mass into its final form. Just don't start to hone the mass into its final form before you have enough mass in the first place.

Once you're as big or bigger than the measurements given in the next chapter, then you can experiment, at least some of the time, with the "other" routines to see if they can do some of what they claim they can do. (You may still find these methods unproductive even when you're big by hard gainers' standards.) The rest of your time, devote yourself to more advanced hard–gainer type basic routines that use more volume, possibly more frequency, and substantial use of the power rack. Continue with getting bigger and stronger, while throwing in periods of "finishing" type work to keep the body in good proportion.

Few typical bodybuilders get to this stage, so this book's focus is on getting you big enough to qualify for the advanced routines.

The *fine–tuning* of supplements and diet, the ins and outs of exercise selection, the training attire to be seen in, the gossip in the training world, contest results, the political wrangles, top–liners' personality stories, and all the rest of it, are irrelevant to your progress in the gym. While it all has interest value to some people, and certainly sells magazines, it has no value where it matters most – in the gym and in satisfying the requirements that determine your progress.

What you read in this book, and in HARDGAINER, isn't concocted just to fill pages. What you read here is the opinion in the bodybuilding world that gets minuscule mention in the mainstream literature. That it gets so little mention there in no way detracts from its importance.

This book, and HARDGAINER, are devoted to the minority opinion because it was *only* this opinion that had the chance of building me – and *countless other* typical bodybuilders – from runts to fair specimens. The only opinion that could deliver the goods. That it hasn't delivered the goods of spectacular development isn't significant. What's important is that it got us out of "runt–land" and into "respectability–land" for people not favored by genetics.

> Don't let anyone deflect you from priorities: Substance, not detail. Basics, not the frills. Progressive poundages, not gym attendance records. Effort and seriousness, not acting and frivolity. Determination to improve yourself, not the imitating of the gifted minority. The sanity of cycling training intensity, not beating your body into stagnation. Experimenting with the radical, not sticking with the conventional methods. Being open–minded, not being the mouthpiece of those who are so genetically superior that they can no longer be called homo sapiens. The worship of rest and recovery, not the worship of the utterances of drug–using mega–achievers.

How we differ

Though we're all physically similar in basic physical structure and metabolism, the characteristics that govern ultimate strength and muscular development vary hugely.

No amount of genetic advantage matters unless it's combined with effort, persistence and good coaching. At the same time, all the effort, persistence and good coaching in the world can't alter basic genetically endowed characteristics.

Bodybuilding rests far more upon genetically determined physical factors than do predominantly skill and practice orientated activities such as sailing and horse riding. The more an activity depends upon physical factors, the less that achievement there is affected by pure practice and application.

There's a lot to be said for selecting at an early age the

activities most suited to an individual's natural make–up. This is the starting ground for ultimate high individual achievement.

We shouldn't have to have our eyes set upon championship winning achievement to motivate us to take up an activity. Even modest achievements (relative to the achievements of the extraordinarily genetically blessed) are astonishing achievements relative to the physical standard of what almost the entire population ever achieves. Taking up an activity with the purpose to compete internationally isn't a recipe for the life–long bodybuilding activity that enhances life in all respects.

Woody Allen could have transformed his physique and strength levels, and produced an impressive physique. However, no matter what he could have done for himself, he could never have gotten even close to Sergio Oliva, Casey Viator, Lee Haney or any other of the most genetically favored bodybuilders.

Now for a look at some of the genetically determined attributes that are responsible for the differences between genetically gifted and genetically typical bodybuilders. (The outline of these attributes is based on Daniel P. Riley's article on genetic factors in Strength Training by the Experts.) While you read these attributes, keep in mind that it's their total that matters. There are some astonishing physiques that have been less than generously blessed in some areas, but sufficiently blessed in the other areas to be still left with an outstanding package.

For example, bone structure alone isn't the be–all and end–all to indicate bodybuilding potential. Sure it's an important indicator for ultimate size and strength, but some very big and powerful bodies have been built on medium to light frames. While muscle length counts a lot in influencing ultimate size, strength and power, it's not omnipotent. Power, for example, depends, among other things, upon coordination, muscle fiber type, bone length and nervous innervation.

1. Bodytype

Bodytype, or somatotype, depicts a clear–cut body structure. It refers largely to the bone structure and the amounts of muscle and fat that cover the body. Regarding the bone structure, for adult males of average height, 6–7 inch wrists indicate a small bone structure, 7–8 inch wrists show a medium bone structure and more than 8 inches belongs to a large bone structure. While wrist measurements usually correlate with ankle structure – the latter typically being about 2–2½ inches thicker – this isn't always so. Some people have a heavier lower–body structure than upper – for example, a wrist of 6½ inches and an ankle of 10. Some have a heavier upper–body structure than lower – an ankle nearly the same size as the wrist.

Though there are three basic categories of bodytype, many, if not most people, possess characteristics from more than one of the divisions. By dietary and training measures it's possible to change drastically the appearance of the body, and its *apparent* bodytype, but with the removal of the training and dietary discipline the body would revert to its natural type. (There are personality traits that can be generalized according to bodytype, though there are plenty of exceptions.)

Whatever you have, you must make the most of it. Rest assured that you can transform yourself, no matter where you started from. The most important body part is the mind. With the will and know–how you can perform near miracles. Here are the three elementary categories of bodytype, as described by the theories of Dr. William H. Sheldon:

a. The mesomorph is distinguished by a musculature that is naturally – without training – hard and visible, with little fat. The body is square and rugged. Bones are large and muscle is thick. This is the bodytype most suited to building large and strong bodies. How aesthetic the developed physique is, is another matter, but the potential for muscular size and strength is great. There are ectomorphic mesomorphs, and endomorphic mesomorphs, so not all predominantly mesomorphic bodies have the potential for developing the largest lean physiques. They all have a potential for size and strength far greater than have predominantly ectomorphic bodies. However, only a few of these mesomorphs are the extreme easy gainers that have the potential to become internationally competitive bodybuilders.

b. The archetypal endomorph has a round and soft body, with a lot of fat. He usually shows very little potential for any type of physical activity. Those endomorphs who want to transform their bodies usually have some non–endomorphic characteristics. Endomorphs are usually hard "progressers" but not as hard–gaining as archetypal ectomorphs. In some ways, the endomorphic bodybuilder has a more difficult time obtaining satisfaction with physique changes than has the ectomorphic bodybuilder. The former needs to get rid of a lot of fat *and* build muscle and strength. Though the skinny ectomorph is what probably comes to mind when thinking of the struggling bodybuilder, there are plenty of struggling endomorphic trainees. The fat–loss strategy for the endomorph is given in Chapter 14.

c. The ectomorph is characterized by a thin and long bone structure, apparent frailty, little fat and thin muscles. The extreme ectomorph is the hardest of hard gainers. Archetypal ectomorphs, though not uncommon, don't fill gyms. A greater number of ectomorphs found in gyms, trying to transform themselves, have some non–ectomorph characteristics and so have a less difficult time putting on the mass than do the archetypal ectomorphs.

2. *Insertion points*

A muscle produces movement by being connected to two bones. For example, one end of the biceps is fixed to the upper arm – at the shoulder – and the other end is attached to the forearm. When the biceps contracts, it pulls the forearm to the shoulder. Where the muscle is attached to the more moveable bone – the lower arm in this case – is called the insertion point. The other attachment end is called the origin of the muscle.

While the origins of muscles vary little, the points of insertion can vary from individual to individual. Following on with the biceps example, the farther down the lower arm the biceps has its insertion, the better the mechanical advantage. Only a small difference in insertion can make a big difference in the mechanical efficiency that results.

Generally, typical people have insertion points very near their joints. Genetically blessed athletes have insertion points farther from their joints. Assuming same sized muscles and same length of bones, the athlete with the more distant insertion points will be able to lift more weight. No amount of effort and application (other than surgical) can change your points of insertion.

3. *Neuromuscular efficiency*

This is the ability to employ muscle fibers through the signals that come from the nervous system. The greater the efficiency, the greater the number of muscle fibers that can be called up to work. The more fibers you have laying dormant, the less force you can apply relative to the total muscle mass. If the body could miraculously increase its neuromuscular efficiency, there would be a large increase in work output from the same level of effort as before the "miracle."

Though the size of muscles is a major factor determining strength and work output, it's by no means the only one. Neuromuscular efficiency determines just how well your body can call upon the muscle to do what it wants the muscle to do.

4. *Muscle belly length*

Skeletal muscles are attached to bones by tendons. Tendons are bundles of connective tissue – sinew – that fix the muscle on to the bones. Cut off the entire tendons from the "body" of the muscle and you're left with the muscle belly. The muscle belly is the "meat" part of the muscle, the part that provides the rounded mass of the muscle.

While muscle cross–sectional area can be considerably increased, muscle length can't be. The longer the muscle bellies, the greater the potential for cross–sectional area and overall volume, other considerations being equal. If short muscle bellies have been inherited, then ultimate size is vastly reduced relative to long bellies.

Those with huge muscles, or the potential for developing them, have short tendon attachments and long muscle bellies. Stocky people have long muscle bellies and short tendons and so have thick arms and legs even if they don't train.

The length of the belly of the calf muscle is a dramatic example of the importance of belly length. Some people have short calf bellies – the so-called "high calves." No matter what they do, their calves will always be behind the rest of their physiques. Larger calves they can develop, but the ultimate size is proportionately much less than for the other muscles that have long bellies. Generally, whether or not you have longer than average bellies is true throughout the body. However, there are many bodybuilders who are eloquent testimony to a variation throughout their physiques. Some have upper arm bellies that are disproportionately large relative to the rest of their bodies. Their arms can become huge and rounded, while other body parts remain much more flat, regardless of what is done for the latter.

Great generosity of genetically endowed muscle belly length throughout the body, together with a single example of an unusually short belly, is seen quite often. Of the top bodybuilders over recent years, Brian Buchanan and Bill Grant are examples of men extraordinarily blessed with long muscle bellies and other advantages, everywhere except in their calves. Some who have this same incongruity have resorted to calf implants.

5. *Muscle fiber type and number*

Muscle isn't made up of a single muscle type. The percentage of each type can vary from individual to individual. Some fibers are more suited to size and strength development while others are more suited to endurance activities. If you're endowed with an unusual generosity of the growth and strength fibers, your muscles – if properly and appropriately trained – will have a greater ultimate size and strength potential than muscle that is endowed with a greater percentage of endurance biased fibers. Some bodies are more suited to endurance activities while others are more suited to strength activities.

Muscle grows by the myofibrils that comprise each muscle fiber increasing in size and number. The number of fibers each muscle contains is generally thought to be genetically determined, though there's a minority opinion that says some splitting of fibers may occur with some types of training. If you have tricep muscles that were given to you with an average or below average number of muscle fibers in them, you're at a huge disadvantage relative to someone who inherited an above average number of fibers in the triceps.

The initial size of an untrained muscle isn't an automatic indication of the number of fibers. A very thinly muscled person, due to a very inactive life, may have muscles before training that are of similar size to those of an active ectomorph. However, once both start to train with the weights, the differences in fiber numbers will become apparent very soon. For the ectomorph, the muscles will fill out slowly. For the mesomorph with a plentiful supply of fibers, the muscles will visibly swell with growth for month after month after month.

Assembling the genetically blessed

Put together these five contributions to genetically endowed variation and you quickly see why the typical hard gainer is in a different universe of existence relative to the rampant easy gainer. It's rather like considering that hard gainers have inherited small sized balloons with only a moderate degree of elasticity. The muscles can be made to grow all right, but only so far. Enormous muscular size is simply out of the question. For the genetically gifted, larger balloons with great elasticity were inherited. These balloons can be made to grow very large.

Imagine a full-blown mesomorph endowed with muscle insertions an unusual distance away from the joints, long muscle bellies throughout the body, unusually profuse numbers of muscle fibers throughout the body, and great neuromuscular efficiency, and all of this in an aesthetic package. Combine all of this with the will to achieve and you get a genetic mega-superior who can take the world of bodybuilding in his stride.

In practice, even the most superior of genetic superiors don't fully satisfy the optimum for each of the five factors, but nevertheless they get quite near. However, even having the five factors well satisfied (in an aesthetic package) is only part of the story – though of course for an aspiring title-winner it's the most important part. Contest preparation and contest presentation, together with influence developed through reputation, are only three of the other factors that greatly influence contest success, irrespective of physical advantages.

The bodybuilders who have gotten the closest to getting a full measure of the five genetic attributes are those who have achieved at a level that makes the rest of us stare, and want to weep. They include people of the ilk (in no particular order) of Casey Viator, Sergio Oliva, the Mentzer brothers, Tim Belknap, Bertil Fox, Lee Haney, Rich Gaspari, Danny Padilla, Eddie Robinson, among others.

When their genetic good fortune is given assistance by the use of drugs, they are taken light years farther from the realm of role models for genetically typical and drug-free bodybuilders.

All of this doesn't even consider the other advantages that the rampant easy gainers so often have – unusually strong constitutions and efficient digestive systems, and extraordinary recovery capacities and tolerance of exercise.

As an additional bonus, the most extraordinarily favored can find sponsors to support a professional or semi-professional bodybuilding lifestyle. Progress becomes even easier to make.

Take heart

Understanding that genetic variation is the biggest factor determining how far you can go in bodybuilding doesn't mean, "I can't get to the top so I won't bother training in the first place."

Neither does it mean, "I know I can't go very far but I'll go through the motions." If you expect nothing you'll get nothing. A high self-esteem and a positive attitude are vital.

Expect a lot of yourself – "a lot" in terms of the goals of the next chapter, not "a lot" in terms of the mega-achievers.

No matter how limited your genetic potential may be for size and strength, with effort and determination you can transform yourself. That's more than enough incentive to train as if your life depended upon it. Who knows just how limiting your genetic potential is? You'll never know unless you train intelligently and consistently for many years. Even modest achievements relative to the most extraordinarily developed physiques are still spectacular. Such achievements will have people ogling you when you're in your trunks at the beach or swimming pool, and have beginners and intermediate bodybuilders in the gym thinking you're some sort of "star."

Many hard gainers, while not having the genetically endowed factors that contribute to huge muscular size, do have aesthetic bodies and some are exceptionally aesthetic. Bodies that have fine proportions, narrow hips and waists, small joints and natural leanness. These factors combine to present a package that, if well developed throughout, will create a physique of extreme impressiveness though of small size relative to the top professionals. This type of structure is, of course, a result of genetic good fortune. Getting huge is absolutely *not* necessary to achieve an impressive physique.

Other hard gainers don't have an aesthetic structure. Whatever you have, you have to live with. That's the frank reality. You can only make the best of what you have. However, the joy of bodybuilding is that no matter how unsuited your body may be for bodybuilding, you can still make spectacular progress relative to where you are now. You only have one body. Make the most of it!

The important thing is to make progress for yourself, no matter how fast or slow. No matter where you are now, you can progress, and progress a lot. Stop comparing yourself with others, especially with the drug-using genetically gifted. You can never be like them, even if you stuff yourself with steroids. Stop fantasizing being one of them. It may hurt having to accept this reality, but this book is about reality.

Compare yourself with how you were a few months ago. Then look to comparing yourself now with how you're going to be a few months from now. Little by little you can achieve your own metamorphosis. That's miles more interesting and relevant than being concerned with the achievements of others. Concern yourself with yourself.

All of this reality of the huge disparity between the "haves" and the "have nots" – as far as bodybuilding potential is concerned – isn't given to foster negativism and defeatism. It has been presented to instill a hefty understanding of the reality of the advantages we don't have. All of this is of paramount importance when establishing realistic goals and adopting practical training methods that are appropriate to typical people. Now you can see why what works for the genetically gifted is nearly always irrelevant and inappropriate for the rest of us. The genetically gifted are different creatures to us.

The genetically blessed rampant easy gainers (and probably drug–assisted too) simply can't truly understand the lot of the rampant hard gainer. (Most of them couldn't care less about the struggling hard gainer anyway.) The more easily something comes to you, the harder you find putting yourself in the shoes of someone who finds things the opposite way round. Generally speaking – easy gainers are the antitheses of the models that hard–gaining bodybuilders need to depend upon in order to realize their modest potentials.

I'm *not* saying that all easy gainers have absolutely nothing of value to say to hard gainers. Many of the famous pre–steroids easy gainers had much to say of value to hard gainers. While out of reach for the average person, their physiques are inspiring because they are "real," not drug–built achievements.

To avoid getting confused, ignore – once and for all – the training methods given by the drug–using genetically gifted. Instead, accept your genetic normality and follow the recommendations of successful hard gainers. These are people who have been through the mire of frustration and failure arising from following the methods used by those with extraordinary physical (and chemical) advantages, and can spare you undergoing the same "torture." This book gives you a summary of many of the findings of successful hard gainers.

The biggest lie I ever swallowed is the one that says anyone can become a top physique if he adheres to a certain training program, diet and combination of supplements, and follows so and so's guidance.

If you realize something around the goals given in this chapter, you'll have developed a physique that will stand you apart in just about all company.

3: Expectations

Measurement claims

Before comparing ourselves with easy gainers, let's take a look at some measurement claims of top contestants.

What about farcical claims of forearms taping 17–18" on bodies of 220 pounds or so? Such claims exist – comb through enough of today's bodybuilding magazines and you'll find them. Consider that Bill Kazmaier, at 340 pounds, had his forearms accurately measured at 17½" by David Willoughby. Bear in mind that Willoughby didn't measure goose–necked forearms with a slack tape and a heavy dose of fiction.

Actual forearm girths of more than 13", for hard gainers, are impressive. (Willoughby regarded a clenched forearm of slightly less than twice the size of the wrist as outstanding, measuring the forearm with the arm *straight* and without bending at the wrist.) Dishonest claims, even from the elite of the training world, that add inches to the real measurements serve to dishearten hard gainers who are unaware of the fiction involved. It also makes a mockery of the claimants in the minds of those who know of the dishonesty in print.

What about claims of 21" and above for upper arm girth? Arthur Jones is a man renowned for his "telling it like it is" attitude. In his <u>Bulletin Number Two,</u> he cites Sergio Oliva's upper arm measuring 20-1/8" "cold" and Arnold Schwarzenegger's slightly pumped arm filling the tape to 19–7/8". Arnold and Sergio – two of the easiest of easy gainers bodybuilding has seen – were famous for their massive arm development. Their development was visibly greater than that of many if not nearly all the modern day competitors who claim larger measurements.

Jones also measured the arms of other genetic superiors in their best condition: Casey Viator at 19-5/16", and both Mike Mentzer and Bill Pearl at 18–5/8". The difference between an 18" arm and a 14" arm is enormous. An 18" arm is *huge*. Those who claim arms of 22" are, in effect, saying that the difference between theirs and Pearl's and Mentzer's is as clear as the difference between a 14" and an 18" arm. Unless they are around 300 pounds of muscular bodyweight, who do they think they are kidding?

These illustrations are necessary to clear the way for honest measurements to be given as a guide for the sort of development that most resolute and determined hard gainers can realize or at least get very near to. When comparing these down-to-earth measurements with the fiction promulgated by many of the top contestants (or their ghost writers), the successful hard gainers' measurements pale away. However, when these measurements are compared to the *actual* measurements of the top physiques, they command respect, especially when the gaining difficulties of the typical bodybuilder are borne in mind.

Urging realist expectations doesn't mean accepting mediocrity. Far from it. If you realize something around the goals that follow, you'll have developed a physique that will stand you apart in just about all company. The only company you'll feel "normal" in will be that of a crowd of competitive and genetically superior and/or drug-using bodybuilders.

The development of the following standard of physique, and even a physique of a slightly lesser standard, is magnificent. The stuff of dreams for most people. The sort of development that would have won big competitions a couple of generations ago. How many people have such a physique? Virtually none. That the physique is still a long way short of that of a professional bodybuilder doesn't matter. We can all get good physiques, darned good physiques, but only a minuscule number can develop the staggering development of a top contestant.

Age

Your age is a tempering factor. If you're starting training and are already middle-aged, reduce the following expectations. If you've been training for a long time, and are in good condition, you may be able to realize the following sort of development though you're no longer in your twenties or thirties.

What follows is a guide – malleable, of course – aimed at healthy males between the ages of 18–35. All healthy males between these ages, even if new to weight training, can realistically expect a spectacular metamorphosis following a few years of determined adherence to rational training methods. Those of you in the 35–45 age group, and experienced with the weights, also can achieve along the same lines. Those of you in this 35–45 age group who are new to training should, at least initially, moderate your expectations.

Those of you who are older than 45 can achieve a metamorphosis, but of a much more modest extent to that of the young man. However, relative to the condition of the typical untrained 50 year old, a hard training 50 year old bodybuilder can achieve near miracles. Temper your goals, priorities and activities according to your age. The older person shouldn't adopt the heavy diet that the younger person can productively use. The older person needs to give more attention to cardiorespiratory fitness than does the very young man – this will divert some energy away from pure bodybuilding.

The older you get, the more careful you have to be to avoid injuries. What the very young person can "get away with" the older person can't. While everyone should pay attention to proper exercise performance and sufficient rest between workouts, it's the older person who pays the price more immediately and more severely if adequate care isn't taken. Heed this warning!

An important point about older trainees is that age is by no means the limiting factor untrained people make it out to be. The limiting factor is in the mind. There are enough genetically typical bodybuilders around, in their middle to late years who have astonishing physiques and strength levels. Expect little from your body, and that's what it will deliver. Expect a lot from it, and that's what it will deliver. Not "a lot" compared to the later–in–life incredible achievements of, for example, John Grimek, Sergio Oliva or Albert Beckles, but huge achievements relative to the untrained person of later years.

Twenty reps with 220 pounds in the full squat might not impress a 20 year old, but if it's a 55 year old that can do it, that's impressive. If you're a life–long trainee and have carefully looked after yourself, 220x20 in the squat at 55 should present no problem. If you're extremely determined, and don't let age curtail you, you could be squatting more than 220x20 at 55 or older.

John McCallum's formula

One of the best formulae I've come across for providing a challenging yet realistic guide for hard gainers is that provided by John McCallum. McCallum, in the sixties and early seventies, wrote an arresting, instructive and entertaining series of articles for Strength & Health, a magazine then put out by Bob Hoffman's York Barbell Company.

McCallum's formula is based on wrist measurement and has been given a new lease of life in Super Squats, a first–rate book written by Randall J. Strossen, Ph. D. The formula (used with permission of IronMind® Enterprises, Inc.) runs like this:

    1. 6–1/2 times your wrist gives chest girth.
    2. 85% of the chest girth produces the hips.
    3. Take 70% of the chest girth for the waist.

4. 53% of the chest gives the thigh girth.
5. The neck size is 37% of the chest.
6. 36% of the chest produces upper arm girth.
7. The calves come out a little less at 34%.
8. The forearms get 29% of the chest measurement.

Everyone won't neatly fall into the set of measurements produced by this formula as it assumes that wrist size directly correlates with bone size throughout the body. With some people, this isn't so. However, genetically typical and drug–free male bodybuilders will, generally speaking and when at or very near the limit of their development, be remarkably close. Many people have a body part that responds better than the rest of the body, producing a measurement an inch or so more than the projected one.

Some people have a lower–body that has a structure bigger than their upper–body – large ankle relative to the wrist. Some people are the other way around. This means that some people find their lower bodies easier to develop than their upper, or vice versa. If the difference between upper and lower–body structure is striking, care has to be given to prevent the musculature differences from becoming too exaggerated and putting the physique way out of proportion.

Using the McCallum formula, a 7" wrist will produce a chest of 45.5", hips of 38.7", waist of 31.9", thigh of 24.1", neck of 16.8", upper arm of 16.4", calf of 15.5" and a forearm of 13.2". At a height of 5'9" this development will come out at around 190 pounds (solid but not "ripped"). Such a development, for a typical bodybuilder, is some going. Forget the claims of 55" chest, 22" arms and 19" calves of some competitive bodybuilders. Remember that their real measurements are more likely to be in the 50", 18–1/2" and 17–1/2" bracket respectively.

The appearance differences between the physiques of the successful hard gainer and the competitive easy gainer come about only partially as a product of pure size. Hardness, definition and vascularity, together with skin color and photographic and lighting assistance are major contributing factors.

A wrist measurement under 7" will produce smaller guide girths, and a wrist measurement above 7" will produce a larger set. John McCallum advised that the wrist be measured just above the protruding bone. If the wrist is measured below the protruding bone, it will likely be a little less and so produce a slightly reduced set of muscular girths.

Another formula

This set of guidelines isn't based on wrist measurement but on height, producing a range of measurements for each different height. The range gives, as its minimum, goals for the typical male to shoot for that will produce a physique a little lighter than that given by the McCallum formula. The upper end of the measurement range is for those with genetic endowment greater than that of the typical person but still below that of the extraordinarily blessed.

Start with a height of 5'2" and arms, calves and neck of 14", "relaxed" chest of 38", thighs of 21" and waist of 28". To produce the "minimum" measurements, for every additional inch of height you add 1/4" to the calf, arm and neck measurements, 3/4" to the chest, 1/3" to the thighs and no more than 1/2" to the waist.

Using this formula, the "minimum" measurements produced for a 5'9" male will be arms, calves and neck of 15-3/4", chest of 43-1/4", thighs of 23-1/3" and waist of 31-1/2". To produce the upper range of the measurements, keeping the waist where it is, add 1" (or a little more) to the calves, arms, neck and thighs, and add 2-3" to the chest.

The set of "minimum" measurements for a 5'9" male very nearly equals that of a 6-3/4" wrist using the McCallum formula.

Comparing the possible achievements of typical, good and great genetic potential the arm measurements would be 16", 17½" and 19" respectively. Of course, many hard gainers fall short of even the "typical" classification and may never be able to develop a hard 16" arm.

Beyond measurements

The single measurement of the waist makes a dramatic difference to the appearance a set of measurements provides. In the example set of girths given using the McCallum formula, if the waist is 33.9" the physique will be dramatically different to if it's 30.9", with all the other measurements being the same.

Don't just pile on the weight by adopting a long-term very heavy eating program. You want to have a firm physique, not a soft one. 16.4" arms that are hard – say accompanying a 30½" waist at 5'9" – are very impressive by normal standards. 16.4" arms that go with a 34" waist are *far* less impressive. Lesson to be learned – keep yourself on the hard side.

This doesn't mean striving for the leanness of a competitive bodybuilder, but it does mean keeping a physique that's firm and at least showing some of the lines of the muscles. An unusual degree of definition can be sought, if it interests you, once you already have substantial muscular mass.

Calculate the measurements that both formulae (the McCallum and the "minimum" version of the other one) produce for your wrist size and height. Write the two sets down. Pick one of them, or work out the average of the two, and regard it as the goal to aim for. If or when you attain the goal, only then should you consider looking for bigger girths. Do remember, however, that a physique has its impact according to how it looks, not how it measures. Of course, the two are related, but not so closely that you should concern yourself with measurements pure and simple.

You want balance in your body, from neck to calves. You want strength and development in parts of your body that don't have dramatic effects upon girths – lower back, trapezius and thickness throughout the back rather than just width. You want size to be muscular, not fat. Perhaps you don't want to get as large as the formulae compute for you, or maybe you wish to be larger still. Perhaps you're more interested in strength than size. Look deeply into what you want in relation to your age, genetic endowment, willingness to work in the gym, determination, and so on.

Decide what you realistically want, and then set out to get it. Be determined, make your plans, knock off short–term goals, knock off the medium–term goals and then you'll get to the long–term goals.

Strength

Developing large muscles demands developing the ability to move some large poundages. Though the two aren't 100% related – it *is* possible, for example, to get a lot stronger without getting bigger – the relation between the two is very strong. This is especially so for novice and intermediate bodybuilders. As long as you concentrate on striving to keep upping the poundages moved, primarily for medium reps (and higher reps particularly for the lower–body) while always using good form, your muscles will increase in size in correlation with the increase in poundages used. Low rep work, including singles, has its uses and can be very productive, but not for cycle after cycle.

Once in the advanced category of bodybuilding and lifting, strength and power increases can be made without increases in size. There are many examples of competitive weightlifters and powerlifters who have been top–class lifters, even world champions, over many years within the same bodyweight class. Since they maintained low levels of body fat over these years, and were highly skilled in lifting technique throughout, a major part of their ability to lift more poundage each year is due to a learning effect within their nervous systems.

Nervous system control of the muscular contraction has a major effect on the tension created in the muscle and, therefore, the strength of the muscle. This is the domain of the advanced lifter and of the strength–minded bodybuilder. Once you're already big and strong, and then want to get a lot stronger still, then you can explore the methods needed to make you stronger while changing you little in size. The detail of how to do this is out of the scope of this book.

What sort of poundages tally with the 5'9", 190 pound, 7" wrist "typical" and successful hard gainer given earlier? Only approximations can be given because of the great variations there are among bodybuilders in the routines they use, leverages (limb and torso lengths) and other genetically determined factors, speed of rep cadence, length of rest periods between sets, and other considerations.

There can be a great difference in what a bodybuilder with a 24" thigh can lift compared to another with the same measurement. Maybe one has much longer thigh–bones than the other. Perhaps one always does high reps, the other low reps. Perhaps one concentrates more on explosive (but no cheating) power work while the other uses a much slower rep cadence and so uses much reduced poundages.

However, here's a guide for those of you wanting to get an idea of the sort of poundages our typical 5'9", 7" wrist and 190 pound successful hard gainer will be moving at that degree of development. The lifts (given in pounds) consider that the lifter *isn't* moving the bar in a pre–determined slow cadence but in a "regular" style of cheating–free lifting.

> Regular squat – a single with 375–400, 10–15x300.
> Regular deadlift – a single with 450–500, 10–15x350.
> Stiff–legged deadlift – 10x275.
> Bench press – a single with 280–300, 6–8x250.
> Press behind neck – a single with 165, 6x130.
> Barbell curl – 8x100.
> Close–grip (about 15" between thumbs) bench
> press – 8x220.
> One–leg–at–a–time heel raise – 20 with a 50–pound
> dumbbell.

To construct goals to accommodate both the hard gainer who is less suited to bodybuilding than the "typical" hard gainer (or who is quite a bit older), and the hard gainer who is better suited then the "typical" trainee, consider a 10% leeway either way. For the regular squat, this gives 10–15 reps with a range of 270–330 (10% either way of 300), stiff–legged deadlift for 10 reps with 250–300, bench pressing 6–8 reps with 225–275, and so on. Aim for the *lower end* of the poundages first. Only once you're there should you look to achieving even bigger poundages. Hard gainers who build up to the lower end of the range have made wonderful accomplishments. Those of you who build up to the upper end of the range have made astonishing accomplishments. Some of you will be able to go even further and qualify for advanced training. More on this is given in Chapter 10.

These targets don't consider variations in physical structure that can account for one or more movements that is/are especially weak or strong. Your body structure – limb and torso length – may be well suited to deadlifting but poor for bench pressing. It's possible you can do stiff–legged deadlifts with more than you can squat, for the same repetitions. As long as you're putting the *same effort and seriousness* into all your exercises, you'll soon discover whether you're better suited to some exercises rather than others. More on this can be found under *Something special,* later in this chapter.

To repeat myself, these are guide figures only, not a statement of what you need to lift. These lifts assume no powerlifting paraphernalia. A belt may be used when doing low rep work in the squat and deadlift if you prefer. With correct use of the gamut of powerlifting paraphernalia the powerlifts would be increased considerably.

If you train "two seconds up, four seconds down" your poundages will be much reduced. If you train in very slow style – perhaps "ten seconds up, five seconds down" (super slow) – then your poundages will be greatly reduced. The above lifts are given for the bodybuilder who lifts in what might be considered the traditional manner – lower under control and then drive the weight up quickly, just "braking" in the final stage of the rep, and without cheating it up. Do understand there's a huge difference between driving the weight up quickly, and so using momentum but in good form, and cheating the weight up. Using momentum does *not* have to mean cheating.

As described in detail by Randall J. Strossen, Ph.D., in the tenth issue of HARDGAINER, cheating–induced momentum means using muscles other than the exercise's target muscles to help the target muscles out, and is so often injurious. If the momentum is delivered purely by the exercise's target muscles, that's a different situation. So long as you're conditioned to driving the weight up quickly you shouldn't experience injuries from it so long as you're not cheating and your form is sound. Also, if you're doing a ten rep set, you don't drive the weight up as quickly as possible during the early reps of the set. You hold back or else you may injure yourself. As the reps become difficult you start to drive the weight up as quickly as you can. However, "quickly" isn't really quickly because the weight has become hard to move. When actually doing maximum singles, you must drive the bar up as quickly as you can.

All of this is very different to maintaining a given rep cadence of, for example, "two seconds up, four seconds down." Different rep cadences have their uses, according to the needs of variety, physical condition of the trainee, training purposes and other considerations. For those learning how to exercise, and possessing very weak bodies, a slow rep cadence is the safest way to go. Ellington Darden, Ph.D., has reported some very impressive results when supervising trainees using a very slow rep cadence. Of course, very impressive results have been obtained with other training methods.

If you've been training with a slow rep cadence and then decide to try a maximum single, with maximum explosiveness, you're asking for trouble. Get conditioned for low rep and explosive work first. Of course, near limit poundages done for very low reps move slowly even when done explosively. This is totally different to deliberately keeping the cadence slow.

Never forget that if you want to build considerable size, reckon on – when using "traditional" rep cadence – building up to using substantial poundages, substantial for hard gainers. *This is the bottom line*. If you're using roughly the same poundages you were handling two months ago, a year ago or three years ago – as most bodybuilders are – then you can't expect to have grown much, if at all. Unless of course you're using the same poundages but at an appreciably slower rep speed. Progressive poundages, never forget, are at the core of bodybuilding.

Many of you will aspire as high as these lifts, while some of you will aspire much higher. Get as high as this list first, then look higher. Bite off a bit at a time. Decide what you want, ensuring that it's realistic, and then plan accordingly. Many of you may be content with poundages somewhat less than those given. Fine. To be content with more modest achievements is no small thing – it's a matter of individual desire, age and value judgement.

Something special

Many people, regardless of how hard–gaining they are, have a lift or two they can do much better than the other lifts. Their physical structure gives them a bias towards a certain type of movement. Once you're trained for a while you'll likely notice this. Perhaps you can easily stiff–legged deadlift more than you can squat. Perhaps you can bench press nearly as much as you can squat, despite working hard at the squat. Perhaps you have a terrific grip and can comfortably hold anything you can deadlift. Perhaps your calves grow quite easily and you can't understand what all the fuss is about building calves.

Whatever individual "strong" movement you may have, if you want to take a single lift close to if not beyond what a genetically gifted bodybuilder of comparable size can lift, then make sure you make the absolute best of that "strong" movement. While it means you'll exaggerate the differences between your "strong" lift and your other lifts, you'll enjoy holding your own in a single lift. Don't keep a "strong" lift intentionally behind your other lifts if you really want to mark yourself out as outstanding in one area even among genetically superior and even drug–assisted (or drug–built) fellow gym members.

Monitoring progress

Poundage progression in the exercises you use should be a clear sign of progress. However, if you loosen up your form as the weeks go by, and take ever–increasing rest periods between reps and sets, you can increase the poundages you use but without actually increasing your true strength. For poundage progression to be a barometer of your progress, the testing conditions must be the same. You must maintain good form and only compare the poundages in the same exercises done in the same form, with the same number of reps, and with the same length of pauses between reps and rest periods between sets.

Keep accurate records of your bodyweight and body girths. You can then objectively monitor your progress rather than just leave it up to your eye. Now that you know where you're going, you need to find out where you're at now and then be able to watch your progress as you slowly move towards your long–term goals.

Record your bodyweight weekly, and do it at the same time each week. For example, record it immediately before a workout.

Take your measurements at the same time of day each time you do it – say first thing in the morning. Don't "pump up" first, take the measurements "cold." Avoid measuring yourself every few days. Let enough time pass so you can measure a difference. At the end of each training cycle is a good point.

Record your neck, upper arms, forearms, shoulder girth, chest, waist, hips, upper thighs and calves. Also, measure the thickness of a pinch of skin and fat taken from the mid–point between your navel and hip bone. Make sure to "dig" as deep as you can each time you do this, and to "dig" at exactly the same site.

Make a written note of the precise location you choose for each measurement. Measure at the same location each time you get the tape out. If you don't, you might – for example – raise the tape measure around your chest a little each time you measure, not replicating the first location. As another example, if initially you measured your hips at the largest point with your buttocks contracted, don't change later to a lower location and relaxed buttocks. If you don't write down exactly how you initially measured each site, you won't be able to replicate the locations at subsequent measurement times.

While waist measurement and the thickness of the waist pinch of skin and fat will show body fat changes, you can be more thorough by using accurate skinfold calipers. You need to follow carefully the directions supplied with the calipers.

An optional method of monitoring progress is to use photographs. Have photographs taken periodically under the same conditions of lighting, attire, setting, skin color and poses. Have the prints sized so the image size of you is always the same. Being the same height in the comparison prints, you can compare yourself accurately.

How far can you go?

When you've come to a stop, to the point where you can't gain more size and strength, it can have one of two explanations. You've either genuinely reached your limit of genetic potential, or, *far* more likely, you've reached the limit of the productiveness of the training methods you've been using.

How many bodybuilders reach their absolute limit of genetic potential for muscular size and strength? I'll answer with another question: Is there anyone who couldn't get just a few pounds stronger?

Few people are fortunate enough to come across the most effective training methods immediately upon starting training. Most people get buried under the mountain of distractions and training nonsense. Those who manage to extricate themselves take years to get a thorough understanding of the training methods needed to sustain progress for many years. If you take too long to get this understanding, you'll no longer have age on your side for realizing your absolute lifetime potential for muscular size and strength.

There are no tests you can undergo that can say, with full assurance, when you're at the absolute limit of your size and strength potential. So how can you know? You can't.

Very few typical bodybuilders get close to realizing their absolute potential. So, rather than underestimating your limits, err on the side of expecting more from your efforts. However, don't get so greedy that you fail to see the wonderful achievements you may have made already.

The price tag of impressive muscular development and strength is a very high one – extraordinary commitment, desire, mental toughness, motivation, application and intelligence. Dig deep, and start paying your dues.

BRAWN

No other consideration matters – be it coach, equipment, smart clothing, food, supplements, mental aid or literature – until you've absorbed into your being the absolute importance of simple progression.

Search out for the smallest discs you can get – quarter kilogram or half pound. You can add these to your barbell time after time, even once you've hit the full-bore stage of a cycle.

No matter how hard the going gets, keep at it. Life is no picnic and neither is bodybuilding. *Persist!*

4: PPP

The bedrock of success in the gym is the triumvirate of progression, performance and persistence:

Progression

Simple progression is so much the essence of successful bodybuilding that its importance shouldn't need stressing. Today's world of distracting hype has placed simple progression on the sideline of training considerations. It's usually added onto a training article as an appendage, as an afterthought. So many other factors tend to dominate the written and spoken word of bodybuilding.

The need for simple progression should be embossed upon the gym clothing of every bodybuilder, especially neophytes, and emblazoned in every training facility and upon every training–related product.

Simple progression is about marching into new ground, going into areas you've not been in before, pushing yourself harder than you've been pushed before, demanding more of yourself than ever before.

At its simplest, and best, it's the "one more rep" principle. The adding of a rep each workout to each "work" set, and the adding of a little iron to each exercise once the rep goal has been achieved.

How often do you see the achievement of "one more rep" be the all–dominating force behind a workout? How often do you see someone push his body beyond what was thought the last rep, to grind out that last, painful, slow, gut–wrenching and oh so productive rep?

That you don't see much of this sort of application of the simple progression principle is eloquent testimony to the paltry results that so many bodybuilders get. No other consideration matters – be it a coach, equipment, smart clothing, food, supplements, mental aid, literature or whatever else – until you've absorbed, into your being, the absolute importance of simple progression.

The "one more rep" simplicity of simple progression, and the adding of some iron (as little as half a pound made up by a few large washers) to each exercise every week or two or three, isn't the only way to increase progressively the load upon your muscles. However, for the hard gainer, it's by far the most important means of progression. Grasp

– with life–long and irrevocable understanding – that simple progression is the name of the game, and that simple progression is about effort – unadulterated and belligerently determined effort.

It's neither possible nor desirable to drive yourself to a new limit every workout on a permanent basis. The body of a drug–free and genetically typical bodybuilder can't take such a battering. (More on the need to cycle intensity of effort is given later on.)

In the initial stages of bodybuilding, the neophyte usually gets to grips with simple progression because, at that stage, progression is easy. There's no need to push yourself to failure to keep the progression coming along. This is the easy stage of training. This assumes the use of a sensible routine that's neither too long nor too frequently done.

Things start to go wrong when the easy poundage progression of the initial months of training grinds to a halt. Now you have to earn the progression by putting in extremely determined effort. However, it's *now* that training routines are too readily expanded, split routines adopted and the attractions of the distractions ruin progress. Effort gets spread thinly, recovery time is decreased, volume of work increased, and marginal concerns of bodybuilding are treated as major concerns.

Tiny discs

When maintaining poundage progression, avoid the mistake of making the increments too big. When you're in the stage of a cycle that has you training *nearly* flat–out, and then flat–out, keep the poundage increments very small. Search out for the smallest plates you can get – get a pair of quarter kilogram plates. Hunt around for a specialist supplier of Olympic weightlifting gear. Using these you can add a mere 1.1 pounds to your barbell. When the sets are hard to eke out, progressing 1.1 pounds is realistic and the bar doesn't feel any different. If five pounds is the minimum you can add to your barbell, that can make the bar feel a lot heavier when you're getting towards the end of a cycle. This will "kill" the gaining momentum. Haste makes waste. *Keep the momentum going as long as you can.*

These tiny discs can lengthen a cycle a surprising amount. Your body can adapt to 1.1 pound increases every week or two. Strength can easily be built at that rate. (Perhaps you can get half pound discs rather than quarter kilogram discs.) You can add these discs to your bar time after time after time without the bar feeling any heavier, even once you've hit the full–bore stage of a cycle. If you can't get hold of quarter kilogram or one pound discs, find *any* way of tying (or taping) a half pound load to each side of the barbell. A metal–worker should be able to rig up something for you. Get the discs (or substitutes), and use them!

When doing 20-rep squats, for example, suppose you just eked out the full twenty in Monday's workout and it demanded more than you've given to an exercise before. Don't put another ten pounds on the bar for your next workout. Don't even put five pounds on the bar. Just put 1–2 pounds on or, perhaps better still, repeat the poundage and put on the additional pound or two at the following workout. Once the workouts are very hard, keep increments small but maintain them for as long as you can. The quickest way to "kill" a training cycle is to pile on the poundage too rapidly. Don't be impatient and ruin your progress.

To be able to sustain the principle of simple progression, there are three factors you must get in sound order:

a. *Volume of work*

The more work you do, the more work over which you have to spread your effort and energy. The briefer your workouts, the more concentrated is your effort. Think it through. The more multiple-set work you do, and the more exercises you use, the more you conserve on your effort levels to make it through the whole schedule. No one can train flat-out for long workouts. No amount of grimacing and noise making can convince to the contrary.

There's no single combination of numbers of exercises, sets and workout frequency that's universally appropriate for all hard gainers. More on this point later. The general rule is to do fewer exercises rather than more, do fewer sets rather than more, and do less frequent workouts rather than more frequent ones.

b. *Choice of exercises*

As effort can only be applied at full force in small quantities, and as the recovery capacities of hard gainers are in short supply, the volume of work must be very limited. It's necessary to concentrate effort on the most basic and most demanding exercises. This causes the most growth stimulation from as few exercises as possible. This means the priority selection of the major basic exercises, or variations of them. No need to get locked into the same set of exercises all the time.

This means squats, not leg extensions; bench presses or dips, not flyes or crossovers; deadlifts, not hyperextensions; overhead presses, not lateral raises, et cetera. The most productive exercises are the ones that "hurt" the most when done in *good form*. The more an exercise "wipes you out" the more growth it can stimulate. The "comfortable" exercises are the most unproductive ones. I must qualify this to say that isolation exercises done with real effort "wipe you out" too and certainly aren't "comfortable." However, the discomfort from the latter is mostly local rather than local *and* throughout the body as with the big multi–joint exercises such as squats, deadlifts, bench presses, dips, et cetera.

Hard gainers have *much* more limited recovery capabilities than do genetically superior easy gainers, especially if the latter are using drugs. This exaggerates the stress we need to place upon the use of the major basic exercises. We need to get the absolute most out of as little exercise as possible. The extreme interpretation of this produces routines of only 1–3 exercises. Absolute heresy it is, absolute growth stimulation it can be. Never short–change abbreviated routines.

Look at what some powerlifters do to their bodies. Some powerlifters don't do much, if anything, in the way of assistance exercises. They just pour themselves into the three powerlifts, sometimes only training each lift hard *once* a week, but they grow all over. Sure the overall physique balance isn't perfect, and the pure aesthetics are lacking (by *advanced* bodybuilding standards), but they have little or no interest in that. All they want to do is to get stronger.

You can adopt similar principles and, once plenty of mass has been built, then the balance and "finish" can be worked on. While the heavy lifters aren't renowned for their definition, the under two hundred pound lifters are usually hard and defined, though lacking the "chiselled" look of an advanced bodybuilder. Don't worry about the details of the "finished" look until you're so big they become significant.

> This brings us to one of the most striking differences between typical hard gainers and genetically gifted and/or drug–using bodybuilders. The latter can build mass and work on detail simultaneously. The former can only build mass if they focus on that for several years. Once they have enough mass, then they *may* benefit from a scaled–down interpretation of the latter's detail work.

Drug–free and genetically typical bodybuilders don't have enough training energy and recovery ability to be able to recover and respond to what the easy gainers can. It's a different world. While the easy gainers can get to the targets in Chapter 3 very easily, the typical bodybuilder can't. Just to get to those goals is a major task, involving almost total focus upon those single goals.

Easy gainers have far fewer problems getting big than they have with getting all the detail, "chiselling" and fullness of development so necessary to win competitions. They have the luxury of being able to concern themselves with something the majority of us never can.

For hard gainers, getting even moderately big is such a mighty task that detail work is not only a distraction but it's an utter irrelevance. Even once at the Chapter 3 targets – after having climbed the Everest – many typical bodybuilders still won't have the ability to grow *and* work on the detail. Just what *you* can productively use *you'll* have to discover yourself *once you're already at* the goals of Chapter 3.

> It's a million percent true that the top bodybuilders, and even those not right at the top, couldn't have developed their full, balanced and detailed physiques without a variety of exercises, both multi–joint and single–joint. A single basic exercise can*not* fully develop size *and* detail in a single muscle.

This doesn't mean that you should rush out and start using a multitude of exercises to get the full and detailed development you want. What it does mean is that you should set about getting the development in a way appropriate to a drug–free and genetically typical bodybuilder. Size and overall strength first, even if it comes with physique imbalances and lack of detail.

You may be able to alter, at least in a small way and at the appropriate time, the apparent shape of a muscle by focusing on a single "aspect" of it. This doesn't mean you can do anything about genetic shape limitations. You can only make the best of what you've got. Of course, that "best" is always terrific relative to where you started from and fantastic relative to the untrained person.

The most striking need, visible in all typical gyms, is the absence of enough muscular mass. The best way to get better "shape" is simply to get bigger muscles. (More size with the same amount of body fat makes you appear more defined too.) Focus on size and strength first. Build the foundation. Work up to being advanced – by drug–free and genetically typical standards – and then pay attention to the detail, supposing you think you have enough mass to do that. It may be that you still feel that your focus should be on mass for another year or few.

Even on an abbreviated routine, so long as the calves and neck get direct work, and you don't pile on the mass too quickly – mistaking fat for muscle – everything else has to come along in size while maintaining satisfactory hardness. If you pour yourself into a short set of basic exercises such as squats, stiff–legged deadlifts, a row, an overhead press, and dips or bench presses, together with calf and neck work, (not all done at every workout) what major structure of the body isn't going to respond? Apply yourself for a few years to these exercises, or variations, building up to big poundages, and you'll see what so "little" exercise can do.

Forget once and for all the myth that lots of exercises and lots of sets are needed to build size. A variety of exercises is important, but a variety of the major exercises *over time*, not a variety of anything and everything at the same time.

For example, do barbell bench presses on a horizontal bench for a cycle. Next cycle, do bench presses on a low incline. Later, following another cycle of regular bench presses, you could do dumbbell bench presses or dips.

Variation is not only good for your body, to prevent it getting in a rut, but it's good for your mind too. It helps to keep motivation and interest high. Just make sure that the variations are variations on the basic movements. For other ways of introducing variety while maintaining the focus on the big, basic lifts, see Chapter 13.

This isn't to say that all isolation exercises should be shoved aside, and that some interpretation of a split routine can't be used effectively. It *is* to say that isolation exercises should play, *at most*, only a minor role for hard gainers struggling to reach their size potentials. It *is* possible to get big and strong without ever using a small isolation exercise. For some hard gainers, it's the *only* way to get big and strong.

If all isolation exercises were to disappear from the face of the earth, then all bodybuilders other than competitive ones in the advanced "finishing" stage would benefit greatly. There would be more stress on the "building" exercises and the great mass of bodybuilders would have a much greater chance of getting what they need the most – substantially increased muscular mass and strength.

The traditional split routines are a waste of time for the vast majority of hard gainers. However, there *are* interpretations of split routines – nothing like what you usually read though – that can be very helpful.

c. *Absolute progression versus relative progression*

Linear progression can't be sustained for year after year. Linear progression *can* be maintained for individual cycles. Don't even try to increase your absolute best rep and poundage achievements every workout you do. It can't be done.

You must structure your cycles so that most workouts, or even every workout in each cycle, show progress relative to the previous workout, but only the workouts in the final weeks of the cycle will show absolute progress – new personal bests of rep and poundage achievements. Detail on cycling is given in Chapter 7.

Performance

The emphasis upon progression doesn't mean a disregard for proper style of performance for each exercise. Every rep and poundage increase has to be earned through effort and real strength and muscle increases. No mere loosening up of style to get out the extra reps. This is dishonest and ineffective training.

You can keep ten pound a week increases going for a long time in the squat so long as you keep cutting the depth of the squat. Eventually you'll be doing next to no squatting but there will be a heck of a lot of iron on the bar. Your actual strength and muscle mass won't have changed much though.

Proper style of performance matters, matters a lot. What is correct style of performance? A lot of opinion here. I don't recommend counting seconds during reps. This will distract you from doing what you're supposed to be doing – getting out as many reps as possible (on your "work" sets, that is). Every rep you do that's entered into your training diary must be performed strictly, *without cheating*. (See the previous chapter for the distinction between cheating–induced use of momentum and cheating–free use of momentum.) Reps *can* be counted without the counting becoming a distraction. Once you're experienced in training you can almost subconsciously count reps. Counting reps is a powerful device for training harder so long as you have a target to beat.

The first few reps of a set are easy to do – very low rep work excluded – so you don't give forth of full effort at this stage. If you do, you'll be throwing the bar, setting yourself up for injury. Once the reps become hard, you use as much force as you can, without cheating, to get the bar up. The bar is always lowered deliberately, with no dropping. Following the early reps of a set, you'll be trying to move the bar rapidly but, in practice, the bar will be moving slowly.

Between reps there's a deliberate pause. It's very short early in a set – perhaps one second pauses. It will lengthen as the set progresses, to the point of taking a breath or few between reps to set yourself up for the next rep. Rest–pause training exaggerates the rest between reps, but that's only for certain exercises at certain times.

At the end of a set, once all your strict reps have been gotten out, *then* you can do a rep or two extra with the aid of a prudent amount of cheating, but only in some exercises. Don't do cheat reps in the squat and deadlift, for example. Forced reps in these exercises can be done instead, so long as you have proficient spotters. When doing bench presses, you may do a final "cheat" rep by arching so long as you have no problems with your back. Use forced reps using a training partner if you have back problems. Don't get carried away with forced reps though: 1–2 in the final set of each exercise no more than once a week is enough for general purposes during the full–bore stage of a cycle.

The manner of rep and set execution just described is orthodox. However, it's not the only way to do it. Rep cadence can be slowed down. "Two seconds up and four seconds down" is promoted by some, and sometimes promoted as if it's the *only* way to train, which of course it isn't. Another method is super slow training (see Chapter 13) in which each rep takes fifteen or more seconds to perform.

Rep cadence variation can help keep variety in your training. Don't get locked in one fixed pattern. At the same time, don't go chopping and changing so much that you never "milk" any single interpretation dry. Stick to one (rational) interpretation of exercises, rep cadence, sets and rep scheme for a whole cycle before passing judgement.

Productive bodybuilding is about a number of unified factors. Take one factor out of the whole, and the productivity of training will evaporate. Stressing simple progression is an absolute must, but only in combination with sound exercise form and satisfaction of all the other factors of bodybuilding.

When starting a new training cycle, the training intensity has been slackened off. Now is the time to apply yourself to perfect exercise performance (see Chapter 11). Do the exercises properly, and keep doing them properly as the intensity picks up over the course of the cycle. Always slow down the poundage increments and lengthen the cycle. If you hurry the poundage increments you'll slacken your exercise style, incur the chance of injury and reduce the effectiveness of the cycle.

Persistence

Putting the requirements of successful bodybuilding onto paper is straightforward. It's the putting into practice that's the difficult bit. *Hard gainers always need to adapt given routines to fit their own uniqueness.* Some of us need to adapt things more than do others. This business of testing, experimentation and trial and error takes time. Some people find what works for them early on. Some take a long time to find what delivers the goods, even though they've been moving within the range of sound, sensible and basic training. *There are so many interpretations.*

Some bodybuilders get so distracted by the ineffective alternatives that dominate popular bodybuilding that they can take years before coming around to finding what actually works. Some take so long that they never find what delivers substantial size and strength.

Even when training is going well, gains don't flood in on a long–term basis. You'll experience short periods of quick gains, but you'll have long periods of little or no gains. Keep at it. Never give up. Every mistake is a lesson learned; a useful lesson. So long as you don't keep repeating mistakes, mistakes are fine to make.

Keep a training diary and record all your workouts. You need a written record of what you've done previously in order to determine what you need to do later on. Be diligent and serious about the whole matter of training. Huge success in the long–term is about little bits of success in the short–term. Chart the success and record the little bits of success by using a training diary.

A bite at a time, a step at a time, brick by brick, piece by piece. Think of some of the huge man–made structures. They were built by one little bit being placed on top of another little bit. This is how it is in bodybuilding. Just work at adding the next 2½ pounds (or 1¼ or even half a pound) to your barbell, then the next, then the next and on and on. Just work at adding the next 1/8" to your arms, calves and everything else. Add up all the eighths of an inch, and add up all the bits of iron; then you get many inches over your body and hundreds of pounds on the bar. Persist.

Frustrations, setbacks, disappointments, injuries (not necessarily caused by training) and unsuccessful experiments are all part of life. Come they will. When they do, then you'll be tested.

There will be times when you'll have to content yourself with keeping regression to the minimum; progression is then but a mere dream. There will be wonderful times when everything clicks for the good and you can really forge ahead.

No matter how hard the going gets, keep at it. Life is no picnic and neither is bodybuilding. Persist.

Life is a continuous challenge. Rise to it. See every setback as a challenge. Let nothing get you down. Ignore negative influences. Stay true to what you know is the way to go. Persist.

"Stickability" is one of the biggest factors in bodybuilding. Successful hard gainers aren't built overnight. They need time, sometimes lots and lots of time. Pound by pound on the bar, eighth of an inch by eighth of an inch on your muscles. Persist.

Workout after workout, week after week, month after month, year after year. Persist.

Not only should you never give up, you should never even *think* of giving up, not ever. Relish the satisfaction of persistence and achievement. The only people who don't have the satisfaction of rising to challenges and overcoming setbacks are the ones in the coffins. Persist, persist and persist some more!

We can all gain insight and knowledge from others, but only you can train yourself. This book will give you insight and knowledge, but it's up to you to use all this in the most appropriate way for you.

Misdirected enthusiasm is at the root of so much bodybuilding failure. What a shame so few learn this lesson. Of those who learn this lesson, they often take so long to learn it that they lose many of their most productive years.

5: Variations on a Theme

There's no single universally effective training program that will cater for all individual needs and purposes. There are, however, sound guidelines that can and must be applied to all routines if hard gainers are to prosper on them.

Though we're all basically the same, we're all different. On top of the genetic variations described in Chapter 2, are a multitude of other factors involved when designing effective training programs. Genetic variations influence both ultimate levels of achievement and the likelihood of responding positively to a given routine. Other factors have a big say in the design of a training routine. These factors include capacity for work, age, structural toughness, health, mental discipline, history of injuries, individual preferences, equipment available, dietary habits, economic considerations, working hours and conditions, family obligations, time available for training, quality and quantity of sleep.

Unalike identical twins

Suppose we have a pair of equally motivated and healthy identical male twins, aged twenty-five. Both have identical genetic inheritance and so have no variation in physical make-up. Suppose that one won a lot of money in a lottery and is single, with no employment concerns. He has access to a gym with a first class variety of quality equipment. He can eat "perfectly" and can have restful days outside the gym and undisturbed nights of sleep.

The other twin works shifts at a job of manual labor and lives on a very tight budget. He trains in a garage with only an Olympic barbell, plenty of plates, a bench and a pair of safety racks and squat stands. He has two young children and barely any spare time to train, and no time for leisure and rest. If he's not at work he's at home fulfilling family obligations, working on the house or car, or training in the garage. He never gets an undisturbed night of rest. His daily routine is regularly disturbed by the shift work. The children never leave him alone when he's at home. Food over the needs of an average person is difficult to fund, and supplements are out of the question. Life just seems to be struggle on top of more struggle.

What the first twin can gain from will be very different to what the second twin can, despite sharing identical genetically endowed potentials, limitations and advantages. The second twin can't emulate even his genetically identical brother, let alone emulate a professional bodybuilder. The second twin will be lucky if he can grow on half the exercises, sets and training frequency of his brother.

What you can productively use in the gym is greatly influenced by the quality of rest, nutrition and sleep that are available to you out of the gym. You can't battle away in the gym without any regard for out–of–the–gym but non–genetically determined factors.

Of course, even with the optimum equipment, routine, rest, sleep and dietary factors, there will be no progress in the gym if the individual hasn't the will to sweat his dues in the gym. However, once this will to work is present, then progress is all about how you let this enthusiasm manifest itself in the gym and how well you meet recuperation needs when outside the gym.

To make a routine specific for you – tailor–made – the general sound advice has to be modified to fit your individual circumstances. Only you can do this. Only you know how you react to a given routine. Only you know your lifestyle and its effect upon bodybuilding progress.

This isn't permission to experiment with anything and everything, in any manner you choose. That would be an undisciplined, lazy and frivolous approach – useless. What *is* needed is experimentation and variation within a sound general framework, and the will to try some radical approaches. The onus is upon you to refine and perfect what you select so it suits you fully and maximizes your progress within the confines of your genetic endowment and lifestyle constraints.

When experimenting, the key rule is that what matters is what works. If something is working for you, stick with it. It's when something doesn't work, despite being used diligently and conscientiously, that it needs changing. Perhaps some of what you do is only good in short spells. It's the *timing* of different types of training that can determine whether or not they are productive.

To satisfy the range of individual needs and lifestyle variations, while keeping within the confines of realistic training, there are many ways of modifying programs. These include:

1. Set and rep schemes and interpretations
2. Choice of exercises and equipment
3. Volume of work
4. Training frequency
5. Intensity of effort

It's by manipulating these variables that a variety of training programs can be designed, providing all typical bodybuilders with the tools for progress. Out–of–the–gym variables – rest, sleep and nutrition – can so often determine the productiveness of a training program.

You'll need to adjust the training variables according to changes in your everyday life. You can't continue your usual bodybuilding program, without modification, once you have children and you need to work longer hours and perhaps establish your own business.

For the typical person, individual adjustment of training should nearly always be on the side of less work and/or less frequent workouts. Adjustments on the side of more work per workout and more frequent workouts will usually be unproductive, at least for average–type bodybuilders. Such ineffective adjustments are the popular way to go. Such misdirected enthusiasm is at the root of so much bodybuilding failure in gyms throughout the world. What a shame so few learn this lesson. Of those who do learn this lesson, *they often take so long to learn it that they lose many of their most productive years.*

An example of modification according to circumstances

Suppose you productively used to follow a routine of warmups plus two or three hard sets of squats or deadlifts (alternating workouts), donkey calf raises, bench presses, pulldowns, press behind neck, barbell curls, parallel bar dips and neck work. You productively did this twice a week. You'd train in cycles of ten weeks – a week's layoff, two easy weeks, two medium weeks of training and then five weeks flat out. You did this for the last eight months, adding sixty pounds to your deadlift, fifty to your squat and forty to your bench press. These gains accompanied a gain of fifteen pounds of muscle.

In the following month you became a father of twins and took on a part–time second job to make ends meet. You maintained your twice per week training but gains dried up immediately. Training became a drag, disturbed nights the rule, meals were skipped as the second job squeezed out a few hours of most days.

Adjust your training because of the changes in your life outside the gym. Reducing training frequency to three times every two weeks improves things, but gains still don't happen. More adjustment needs to be done. Gaps provided by missed meals can be filled by using drinks from out of a blender, enabling quality nutrition to be consumed quickly. Reps in the gym are reduced from the usual 10–12 to 7–10. Only one or two hard sets are done per exercise, rather than the previous two or three. Workouts now only use 2–3 big exercises plus calf and neck work. Deadlifts are done only alternate weeks. Less work is done, done less often, and nutrition – care of the blender – is got back in good order. The gains return.

If there's a family crisis and you don't feel in the mood for the planned Friday workout, postpone it. Taking an extra day or two between workouts can be beneficial. *We must rid ourselves once and for all of the mentality of wanting to accumulate gym hours just for the sake of an addiction to the gym.* We want results, not gym attendance records.

Be 100% sure not to miss or delay workouts for the wrong reasons. There's an enormous difference between intelligent delay of a workout and the skipping of workouts due to lack of seriousness. Training must become a habit if it's to be productive. The gym must have a very important place in your life, something not to be treated lightly.

You're your own guide and trainer. We can all gain insight and knowledge from others, but only you can train yourself. This book will give you insight and knowledge, but it's up to you to use all this in the most appropriate way for you.

To-failure versus almost-to-failure

Manipulation of the variables that make up sensible training can involve a lot of trial and error. Mistakes will be made. Perhaps you didn't cut back enough, or, you've cut back too much for a less than 100% level of training effort. Perhaps you've cut out the most important exercises in favor of the little exercises. Perhaps you simply aren't consuming enough nutritious food to gain on any program. Perhaps the amount of work is fine, and so is the intensity of effort, but the training frequency is still too much. Perhaps you simply aren't, at present, capable of responding positively to single or double set to-failure type training. However, perhaps you can gain on 3–5 sets of almost-to-failure training on each of only 3–4 exercises per workout.

While you may find that some increase in training volume can compensate, at least partially and temporarily, for a drop in training intensity, don't overdo it. Effort and intensity of effort are the names of the game, but sometimes you can't lift yourself to the heights needed to train flat-out. Some people don't have the will and tolerance of pain needed to train to absolute failure on only one or two sets per exercise.

Alternating cycles of the one or two sets to-failure training with 3–5 sets of almost-to-failure work per exercise is something worth trying. Each stresses the body differently – physically and psychologically – and alternating the two approaches may be beneficial. Alternating a pure power-based cycle with the 3–5 sets of almost-to-failure work is also worth trying. The logic being that the change in approach and the variety given is good, and the medium volume work (still keeping the number of exercises well cut back) can encourage the body to bring muscular development up on a par with the new level of strength.

If you opt to experiment with almost–to–failure training, be very wary of increasing the volume of exercises in your routine. Increasing to 3–5 sets per exercise for only 3–4 exercises per workout is one thing. Increasing to 3–5 sets per exercise for 8–12 exercises per workout is another thing – the antithesis of what typical people need. Keep workouts short and simple, and don't do them too often. *Stay out of the gym if you still feel beat from the previous workout.*

Fine–tuning your exercise selection

Just because one person raves over a certain exercise, this doesn't mean you should do the exercise if it just doesn't feel right for you. Personally, I think the stiff–legged deadlift standing on a bench or platform is one of the greatest exercises. However, not everyone's back can prosper on it. Some of you will need to modify it so that it's productive for you. To reduce the range of motion, perhaps you prefer stiff–legged deadlifts from the floor, or bent–legged deadlifts with a wide grip, again from the floor rather than a platform.

Perhaps I rave over the bench press and gain size from it. Perhaps the exercise does little for you but parallel bar dips pack on the beef. Perhaps you can benefit from both exercises, choosing to alternate the two from cycle to cycle, or workout to workout.

Perhaps you can progress in the pullup while I can't. Some people gain from wide–grip pulldowns or pullups while others get nothing from the wide–grip versions. Some people can't get "into" pulley exercises. Some bodybuilders "must" do bent–over rows to train their lats and upper back.

Preparing yourself for gaining

Some people need to structure their training so they have periods that make *no* attempt to increase size and strength. The periods are put together so that the body actually gets "softened up." This involves some loss of size and strength in order to make the body receptive to the growth stimulating training to follow. For these people – more of you than you might think – training flat–out for long spells, or even in just part of *every* cycle, is simply too much. High intensity training has to be used much more prudently.

A three month training block could start with a week of rest followed by three weeks of moderate aerobic work plus calisthenics. Follow with three weeks on a basic program of 4–6 barbell exercises twice a week. Take it easy to begin with and build up so that the workouts become *almost* hard at the end of the third week. No rushing it. This initial seven week preparation period has you eating moderately, so as either to maintain bodyweight or just lose a little, but *not* to gain.

Following the seven weeks of preparation come 4–6 weeks of high intensity work. Continue with the same basic routine but now drive yourself to failure in each "work" set and considerably increase your nutritional intake. You must ensure there's absolutely no under–recovery and no shortage of nutrients. Take however many days between workouts as you need – perhaps training the deadlift once a week and everything else three times every two weeks. Use a brief total body routine or an even briefer program on a modified split routine schedule as suggested later in this book. Sleep and rest as much as you can. Be fastidious about getting a generous and very nutritious diet. Let bodybuilding dominate you for these 4–6 weeks.

Do your best to time the stages of the three month training block so your outside–of–the–gym stressful times fall away from the growth stage. This is the gaining period that you have spent seven weeks preparing for. Make the absolute most of it – pour in everything you've got, and then find more effort to pour in. A ten day layoff is then taken and another three month block commenced. You must end the new block with higher poundages than did the previous one in order to have made progress.

This training approach places great importance upon the timing of the heavy and very hard training. It comes in short doses only after you have been prepared for it.

You've probably neither tried nor even read of this approach. If you feel that the regular ways of training aren't delivering the goods for you, even when using the cycling approaches described in Chapter 7, then try this alternative type of training. It's very radical but might just be what you need. The duration of each stage isn't written in stone. You may need to adjust the stages to suit you. Learn from experience of course, refining things each time you use this approach.

Comprehensive but not exhaustive

There are so many interpretations of basic, brief, abbreviated and down–to–earth training. Enough to accommodate all individual needs and circumstances. This book comprehensively, but not exhaustively, covers these interpretations. Before you think I've missed out something of particular importance, wait until you've thoroughly read *every* paragraph of *every* page.

You'll need to read the book more than once to understand the full message – there's so much content in this single book. Each time you read the book you'll see things you missed, understand things you previously didn't, and likely have to reconsider things you previously took for granted. The better your current understanding, the further you can take later understanding.

Understanding of the ins and outs of bodybuilding isn't something you can exhaust. There's always something else to learn and something to improve on.

Bodybuilding is a learning process. There are so many potentially productive interpretations to try. The process can be very time consuming, especially if you don't "listen" carefully enough to your body. Don't battle through difficult times rather than adapt your training to suit changing circumstances.

It doesn't matter if you make mistakes. Mistake making is desirable, so long as you learn from the mistakes. *Someone who makes no mistakes is unlikely to make anything.* Keep at it. Persist, at all times.

To gain the full benefit from this book it's _imperative_ that you study _every_ sentence of _every_ paragraph.

You'll benefit from this book in direct proportion to how seriously you study it, how thoroughly you understand the contents, how well you make the understanding one with you, and how resolutely you apply it.

If you're having trouble getting bigger and stronger using abbreviated routines of basic exercises, you'll make a difficult task into an impossible one if you change to longer and more frequent routines infested by lots of little exercises. Focus on getting a full understanding of how to make the basic formula work – don't change philosophies!

58

6: Effort and Dedication

To deliver progressive poundages performed in good exercise style, and persisted with for a long time, effort and dedication must be in abundance. There's no getting away from it, successful bodybuilding – the realization of genetic potential – demands very hard work and extraordinary dedication.

Be in no doubt that astonishing transformations have been achieved by bodybuilders of average genetic potential who have trained by themselves in garages using just a bench, squat stands and a barbell set. All of this together with ordinary food and no supplements, and done before the razzmatazz and hype that's so influential in today's world. Never lose sight of priorities. Successful bodybuilding is basically very simple – darned hard work on appropriate routines while cycling training intensity, and in combination with sound rest and dietary habits. Effort and dedication (correctly applied) rule the day.

The joy of effort

How true it is that we really appreciate something only once we no longer have it. The opportunity and ability to train hard, to be really able to pour in the effort to work your body to its limit, is a joy, a blessing and a privilege. Think it through. To have a body in sufficient condition for it to be able to be pushed to its limit, time after time, and to keep coming back for more, is a wonder.

Make the most of it. Revel in it. Wallow in it. It won't last forever, though it can last a darned sight longer than many would have you believe. Don't believe the myth that getting old means the cessation of hard training. A modification of training, yes, but the continued putting in of effort and dedication until you expire.

When studying about the why, wherefore and method of getting bigger and stronger, let's never forget the most coveted of all considerations. To be able to train hard, lifelong, necessitates a sound body with a potential for robust health. How easily we forget this as we strive for more and more gains. Inferior, average or superior genetic potential – it's not the priority. Good health is way above in importance.

Health and a top title–winning physique aren't synonymous. The conditions that these "winners" go through are antithetical to health – the extreme diets, the drugs, the overtraining, the injuries. While they may tolerate this over the short–term, giving the semblance of health, the long–term consideration is another matter. "Real" bodybuilders are into training for life, so robust health is a necessity for us.

Training should be a joy, even hard training. Discomforting, yes, but satisfying. It's a privilege to be able to train hard and seriously as advocated in this book. We must always remember that we train for our personal satisfaction. It's a lifetime's activity, not merely a young person's narcissistic fad. Maintain hard and dedicated training for the duration of your life, though you may never exceed 16" arms and a 300 pound bench press. You'll then go a long way to ensuring a long and healthy life. Of course, effort and dedication in the gym have to be married with perhaps the most important exercise – the exercise of discretion at the dining table.

Temporary injuries and sickness are reminders of the importance of dynamic well–being. Only when we're unable to train as we want to, do we appreciate the value of sound health.

When we're sick, be it merely a cold, everything becomes tiresome and we wish away the time until we're our normal selves. Health comes first. Only then does impressive brawn come into the picture. Look after yourselves. Avoid habits and environments that will reduce your potential to be energetic and healthy beyond youth. While doing this you should try your utmost to realize whatever genetic potential you've been endowed with.

To discover just what potential you possess, you have to realize it. To do this necessitates training hard, intelligently and consistently for many years. To be able to do this you need to be healthy and to enjoy the satisfaction that each workout brings. And do this even if you never get within a thousand miles of greatness, or, even if you live by yourself with a set of weights on a desert island devoid of a mirror.

Pouring forth

The name of the game is *EFFORT*. It demands enormous dedication and determination to keep pushing yourself to the limit, time after time. No supplement, no routine, no diet, no training partner, no training supervisor, no trainer, no course, no magazine, no drug, no book, no seminar, no video and no training camp exists to get you to drive yourself to the limit in the gym. The buck stops with you. Only you can push yourself through the pain and discomfort – again and again.

The shortage of the will to work *really* hard is the single factor most responsible for the lack of gains that most trainees experience. Few bodybuilders really train hard. Of the average bodybuilders that do train hard, few take enough rest between workouts to permit themselves to grow. So, effort *and* recovery time is the combination to get in order – the effort must be correctly applied.

When aiming to train with 100% effort you must, while you're in the gym, regard your training as the most important part of your life. Visualize the effort you're going to give forth. Pour everything you have into each rep of each maximum effort set you do. Regard each of these sets as the last one you'll ever do. Give your all.

Each maximum–rep set is a step nearer to bigger muscles and more strength. Never, ever, waste one of these opportunities.

> *A cautionary note here* – maximum–rep sets can't be productively used for week after week and month after month, at least not for drug–free typical bodybuilders. There has to be some cycling of training intensity – detail on this is given in the next chapter. Also, some ultra–hard gainers may not respond well to absolute–effort training until they have already built initial size through almost–maximum–rep training using only a handful of the best exercises.

> The neophyte needs to train hard and seriously, but not in the style of, "I'll finish this set when I collapse, not a rep before." The training till utter failure, nigh–on–collapse style has its uses so long as it's not abused. If you do it too much, not only might you kill your desire to train, and exhaust your recovery ability for a while, but you may make your body resistant to any training other than that which is *even* more intense. Don't neglect training variation and cycling of intensity.

As the reps become hard, take a few seconds rest between reps. Become aggressive. Heighten your resolve. Rise to the challenge. See your muscles becoming larger. Visualize greater size with one more rep, then another and another. Become the set.

Use any idea to help you grind out more reps. Use promises of rewards and deprivations to ensure that you get the reps out.

Many people think they train hard when in fact they cut every set short. Grimaces and grunts alone aren't enough. It's grimaces and grunts through utter muscular failure that mark out high intensity training.

When the correct degree of effort is delivered in the gym, the quantity and frequency are automatically curtailed. When training on long routines, effort has to be diluted so as to spread it more thinly. Training frequency can become excessive if motivation is extraordinarily high. Don't get back into the gym until you know you're *fully* recovered. Kidding yourself that you're recovered, when in fact you aren't, is the route to stagnation through training too frequently for the intensity being given. See Chapter 8 for detail on training frequency.

Get obsessive about delivering true high intensity effort in the gym, then most gaining problems will be solved so long as enough food and rest are had. It's very easy to get caught up in the fine and marginal details of workout and meal planning, while neglecting the omnipotent factor – darned hard work.

When you train, "become" your training. Forget about chit chat and socializing during a workout. Refuse to reply to anyone who talks while you're doing a set.

It's not enough to think you can remember the important points for correct performance of every maximum effort set you do. You need a written note of them. You need to review this check list prior to every hard set you do (unless you're supervised in your training). Something like this is needed for when in the *full–bore* stage of a training cycle:

1. Strict exercise style.
2. Mind–muscle link. Think BIG.
3. Make the most of every "work" set – each is another never–to–be–had–again chance to progress.
4. Annihilate your previous workout's record.
5. The name of the game is *EFFORT*.

Contemplation of such a list before each full–bore effort set you do will help to fire you up with the motivation you need to make each set another step forward. Make the sets count.

As the mind quickly becomes familiar with the same visual appearance, keep changing the presentation of the list. Make several of the lists using different designs, words, typefaces, letter sizes, et cetera. Use a different one each workout, rotating the set of versions.

Training supervision

It's almost impossible to find an individual who's able to push himself consistently to a 100% effort. Sure we can all get ourselves together to push to the limit in two or three exercises in a single workout, especially the easier to do small exercises. But to do it in every exercise in every workout for the duration of the hard stretch of a training cycle?

Very few people push themselves to the limit, especially in the most demanding exercises such as the squat and deadlift. Many people make a lot of fuss in their workouts, suggesting that they are the limit, but very few really are.

Those who train extremely hard are massively motivated and, often, supervised. A training supervisor is nearly always needed to ensure that training is carried out as it should be.

It takes a supervisor to push, urge, implore, motivate and even bully you to do every rep of a set, and to do all but the final non-recorded reps of a set in a *strict* style. As very few of us have our own private training supervisor we have to obtain the next best thing.

You're all urged to keep a training log/diary, and always to train with a partner if possible. Keep a record of every workout so you always know exactly what you need to do to make the next workout a progressive one. Don't leave it to memory. "Did I dip with 55 pounds for nine strict reps then did one loose rep and three negatives? Or was it eight strict reps, two loose ones and two negatives?" Take all the memory and guesswork out of your training. Keep meticulous records.

Training with a serious partner is a wonderful thing. This person should be dedicated to ensuring that you get absolutely *everything* out of all your planned maximum rep sets. While it's not imperative that you're of similar strength, and are training on identical or very similar routines, it's preferred. Better that your partner is a little stronger than you. This will bring out the competitive streak in you, to your benefit. Both of you should be training on the same type of cycle so you both train with the same intensity at each workout. Plan your workouts and cycles, and stick to them. *Don't* let your enthusiasm get the better of your reason thus short-circuiting a cycle.

Whatever pain and discomfort your training partner/torturer inflicts upon you, you give it back when it's your turn to supervise.

With a good training partner, and accurate records, you should know what intensity is about. You may be surprised just how comfortably you were taking your workouts previously. You'll then get an idea of what renowned gym "torturers" would put you through if you expressed seriousness about training hard.

If you're serious about making maximum gains, you'll do your utmost to obtain the finest "torturer" you possibly can. Some of you may not be able to find a training partner. This will probably reduce your progress somewhat, but of course won't halt it.

While it's possible to gain well without a training partner, a motivated and serious training partner can make an enormous difference. Get one if at all possible.

After each workout, go through what you did, preferably with your training partner, and evaluate everything. Did you really go to the limit in the squat? Wasn't there another rep in you? What about the one-legged dumbbell calf raise. Couldn't you have put up with the pain of growth stimulation for another three reps?

I'm writing here of the full–bore stage of a training cycle. Of course, as drug–free and typical bodybuilders, you don't drop straight into high intensity training. You work up to it over the initial part of a cycle, to ensure you develop the gaining momentum and conditioning needed to benefit from it. There are many ways of doing this – a lot of detail on intensity cycling is given in the next chapter.

Following the post–workout evaluation, resolve to make the following workout an even better one. Discover what could be improved, and then do it.

This is a hard and unrelenting demand. Muscular size and strength don't come easily to the hard gainer. They have to be earned. Few people are willing to give this sort of effort. That's why so many people get distracted and confused by the mountain of other considerations that are ubiquitously promoted with great vigor and hype.

How many interpretations of basic training?

There are countless interpretations of basic and simple training, using myriad interpretations of intensity cycling, routine structures, frequency approaches, and so on. Enough of them to last you your entire training life and there will *still* be some you haven't tried. Don't *ever* think that basic and simple training is only for training neophytes.

Only when you've exhausted all the interpretations you know (including advanced ones), having fine–tuned each of them and having satisfied all the out–of–the–gym factors, can you consider that enough is enough. Then, while maintaining your achievements (or slowing down their diminishment as you go beyond middle age) you can set other goals and then set about realizing them. Perhaps goals in the endurance and flexibility domains, or, in an area of skill endeavor. If you're starting bodybuilding while middle–aged, you can expect to increase your size and strength for more than a few years before you experience age–induced diminishment of size and strength.

A final reiteration

Success in the gym stems from effort, *correctly applied effort*, in combination with full satisfaction of all the other factors that contribute to gains. Effort must be combined with the dedication not to have a single factor out of order. The dedication that combines absolute determination with the *individual fine–tuning a routine always needs,* plus adequate nutrition and rest. No off–days, no exceptions.

One of the most troubling sights in the gym is a hard gainer using a routine utterly inappropriate for him. Failure is guaranteed. Alongside this sight is perhaps an even more troubling one: The sight of the hard gainer giving his all to a generally sound routine, while not satisfying all the other considerations. It's not unusual to have skinny and rampant hard gainers trying to build physiques on diets barely adequate for nonathletic people. Neither is it unusual to have a diligent bodybuilder inadequately disciplined in rest and sleep habits.

Dedicate yourself to getting the whole bodybuilding package in perfect order. Not tomorrow, and not later on. Now. Once you've got it in order, keep it there. Always.

The steady and regular building back of the poundages in the early part of the cycle creates the impetus to go beyond the previous best.

One of the biggest mistakes you can make in bodybuilding and strength training is to be impatient. Forget about progressing for a while. Instead, work at creating the "reserve" and momentum needed for gaining.

Most people are in such a hurry to get to their top poundages that they never create much *if any* gaining momentum. They slog away using the same poundages for year after year, and look the same for year after year. Don't imitate them!

7: Intensity Variation

The correct application of effort is the essence of intensity variation – the cycling of training intensity. Intensity cycling is at the root of long-term and successful training.

Very hard training is an irreplaceable component for building greater size and strength, but not if it's done every workout of every week of every month of every year. It must be interspersed between periods of less stressful workouts. This is particularly so for drug–free and genetically typical bodybuilders.

We can't progress in absolute size and strength in a long–term linear fashion. We need to plan to take two steps back in order to take three steps forward. Even the genetically gifted use intensity cycling to some degree. The difference between them and us is that we need to take longer steps backward and, when we do take our forward steps, they are smaller than for the easy gainer.

Intensity cycling refers to the regular varying of training intensity through changes in poundages used and the effort level given forth, together with variations in other aspects of the training program. It's an amalgam – intentional or accidental – of the concepts of variation and Dr. Hans Selye's General Adaptation Syndrome. G.A.S. has three phases of alarm, resistance and exhaustion and is also called the "Stress Theory." Training is designed to prevent adaptation to a constant training load and to reduce and change the load to avoid the exhaustion phase of G.A.S.

Putting all this together means the removal of persistent sticking points. Other variables can be involved in cycling too – numbers of sets, super high intensity techniques, training frequency and selection of exercises. Some people vary the volume of the training load considerably. Though moderate variation of the total training load may be useful, routines for the typical hard gainer should always be of low volume, or, at most (and only sporadically) medium volume. High volume training is for other creatures – drug–using and genetically blessed creatures. Or, hard gainers who have already built *considerable* size and strength and want to experiment, sporadically, with high volume loads. For more on advanced training, see Chapter 10.

The body of the typical hard gainer doesn't respond well to consistent full-bore, maximum effort battering in the gym. Even drug-using genetic mega-superiors can't grow indefinitely on it. We simply can't bully our bodies to grow big muscles. We have to firmly coax them. This is where cycling comes in. Cycling has many interpretations.

The neophyte need not be concerned much if at all with intensity cycling. The novice can productively stick to a simple, basic and not-too-frequent routine, training hard under his own steam – no forced reps, drop sets, negatives, et cetera. The novice can productively maintain this for a year or more. All that's needed is having a week off followed by a break-in week or two every 10-12 weeks and perhaps making a couple of exercise changes for variety's sake. Once gains dry up, it's time to start taking advantage of cycling.

The most impressive gains should occur in the initial stages of training, providing that all the contributing variables are in good order. However, once you're beyond the beginners' stage this isn't necessarily the end of very rapid gains. If you've been in the training doldrums for a long time; if you've never seriously tried a size and strength abbreviated routine with a heavy and quality eating schedule; if you've never trained extremely hard; if you've never been truly generous with rest between workouts; if you've never experienced the benefits of having a highly motivated training partner; if you've never really "gotten into" your training with massive desire to improve, then rapid gains – almost all of it muscle – of 10-20 pounds over a few months of training are a possibility. Some people have gained more than 10-20 pounds of muscle during such a short period.

This very rapid rate of progress can't be maintained, but it *is* possible if you get all the conditions right and you're a *long* way from your maximum size and strength. What others have done, you can do too, so long as you have the will and follow the appropriate program.

Training flat-out all the time always ends up in overtraining. Once you're overtrained, you can't bully your way out of it. Don't waste years trying to prove to the contrary.

As well as the body rebelling against consistent full-bore effort, so does the mind. To strive to do more reps and/or more poundage than you've ever done before, every workout, and every week, becomes a tremendous mental burden. Always to have to do more, when you're already at the zenith of your current capacity, is too much. There *have* to be slack periods. There have to be workouts in which you purposely avoid pushing yourself to the limit. This is very difficult to accept if you've been locked into the "hard all of the time" philosophy.

Beyond the initial gains of the properly trained neophyte, the near linear progress ceases. From this point on, progress is irregular – full of plateaus, valleys and peaks. Cycling is an organized and planned effort to arrange the irregular progress into a regular progression of ups and downs, with each new "up" or "down" being a little higher than the previous one. Cycling is about taking steps backward to prepare for enough forward steps to go beyond previous best achievements.

Beyond the introduction period to weight training, think of seeing absolute progress every three months or so. Consider where you are now. Look at 10–20 pounds on your bench press every three months, 15–30 to your squat and stiff–legged deadlift, 3–5 pounds of muscle on your body. Maintain this progress for a year and a half – six cycles of three months each – and what will you get? Assuming the minimum gain, that comes to sixty pounds on your bench, ninety on your squat and stiff–legged deadlift, and eighteen pounds on your body. Then do it again over the next year and a half. Hardly the sort of progress that someone genetically blessed can make, if not yet at his full potential, but terrific progress for hard gainers.

Successful bodybuilding and strength training are long–term activities. Be patient.

A modified powerlifting cycle

Many powerlifters have been into cycling for a long time, accumulating steady gains every year. Cycles are fixed with contests in mind, and timed so that the "peak" week is contest week. Cycling is much less popular among bodybuilders.

One type of powerlifting cycle lasts 12–15 weeks, with the goal of a 10–25 pounds increase on each powerlift. The first week starts with 80% or less of the previous cycle's maximum poundages for whatever reps you're using. Successive weeks steadily build up the poundage. After 8–11 weeks, the previous best is once more achieved, with room for improvement. The final weeks of the cycle see personal best achievements in successive workouts.

A modification of this type of cycle, for pure bodybuilding purposes, runs something akin to the following. Note that reps get no lower than five, whereas in a pure powerlifting cycle they would go lower. Also, the more intense the stage of the cycle becomes, the less work that's done. Both volume of work, and its frequency, are reduced as the cycle progresses.

Taking the squat as an example, suppose that before reading this book you could just manage to squat 260 for six reps. To start this program, select 200 (about 75%) and do two sets of ten reps (2x10) even though you could do a lot more reps without much struggle. Remember, cycling is about taking it easy to begin with, building up the intensity over a few weeks, then going full-bore for a while, then having a layoff, and then repeating the cycle though not necessarily the same interpretation. The initial training frequency, because the intensity isn't high, is twice a week. Later it reduces to three times every two weeks. If this frequency is too much for you (you can't recover between workouts) then start with squatting three times every two weeks and reduce to once a week after week 6.

Week 1: Mon. 200 2x10   Fri. 205 2x10
Week 2: Mon. 210 2x10   Fri. 215 2x10
Week 3: Mon. 220 2x10   Fri. 225 2x10
Week 4: Mon. 230 2x10   Fri. 235 1x10 1x8
The sets are getting hard now.
Week 5: Mon. 240 1x10   Fri. 245 1x10
The second top set has been dropped.
Week 6: Mon. 250 1x10   Fri. 255 1x10
Frequency now reduced to 3 times every 2 weeks.
Week 7: Wed. 260 1x10
Week 8: Mon. 265 1x9   Fri. 270 1x9
Week 9: Wed. 275 1x9
Week 10: Mon. 280 1x8   Fri. 285 1x8
Week 11: Wed. 290 1x7
Frequency reduced to once a week.
Week 12: Wed. 295 1x6
Week 13: Wed. 300 1x6
Week 14: Wed. 305 1x5
End of the cycle, terrific progress.

Bear in mind what was written in Chapter 4 on the importance of making small poundage increments to avoid premature stagnation. The increments above could be reduced to only 2½ pounds a week after, say, week ten when the workouts are becoming very hard. It's fine to have bigger increments when the cycle is in its easy stage so long as you don't "short-circuit" the cycle.

While doing this routine you will have done some progressive warmup sets before the top "work" sets. Do two or three warmup sets for the squat. Good strict style and no cutting the depth as the cycle progresses, not even cutting the depth a single millimeter.

By backing off at the beginning of each cycle, and taking it quite easy for a few weeks, the body and mind are given a break from the battering of constant flat-out training. The steady and regular building back of the poundages in the early part of the cycle creates the impetus to go beyond the previous best. Had there been no cutting back of poundages and intensity, the same personal best achievements (perhaps less) would likely still be being struggled with, together with all the stagnation and frustration that accompany a persistent sticking point.

An "off" workout

If you have an "off" workout, no matter what interpretation of cycling you're using, don't force yourself through it using the scheduled poundages. If you felt "off" before training, it would have been better to have delayed training a day or two. If you didn't feel "off" until actually into your workout, drop your poundages 50% and rep out to a few reps short of the maximum number you could do. This will prevent you suffering any physical injury and damage to confidence of failing with the scheduled poundages. Next workout, do what was scheduled for the "off" workout and resume the cycle. This will help ensure that the gaining momentum is sustained and the cycle isn't "killed."

Poundage miscalculation

If you misjudge the cycle's starting poundage in one or more lifts, correct matters at the next workout. For example, the squat may feel "heavy" relative to the other exercises. Cut back the squat poundage by 5–10% next time and get all exercises feeling "heavy" (or "light") to the same degree.

The mini-cycle

Cycles need not be as long as the previous example. A short but successful mini-cycle lasts for 6–8 workouts and runs as follows:

A sticking point is the stimulus for a new cycle, accompanied by a few days longer than usual between workouts – say an *extra* four days or more. Get yourself fully rested. Cut back all training poundages to 85% of what they were at the sticking point.

Warmup sets aside, the workouts will run as follows. The first two workouts – the 85% and 90% ones – will be comfortable. You do just your usual number of repetitions – *don't* rep out to the limit with the reduced poundages. The next workout – the 95% one – will be demanding but a good success. Then comes the 97½% workout followed by the (100%) one that you ended your previous cycle on. This workout will be very testing but, so long as you've eaten and rested adequately between workouts – that's a big "so long as" – it will be successful and you'll get your full target of reps.

Next comes the 102½% (or 101¼%) workout, the new personal best for whatever reps you're doing. You must be successful (full completion of rep targets) at this workout, or at the next, or else the cycle won't be a gaining one. With 102½% (or 101¼%) successfully done, try another 1¼ or 2½% at the next workout, perhaps taking an extra day or two of rest between workouts. Be *very* wary of the danger of pushing yourself too much and burning yourself out. Be conservative so you can gain again next cycle. Being stuck at the same poundage and reps for two successive workouts is enough.

As an example of a mini-cycle, say you're stuck at 240 pounds for ten reps in the stiff-legged deadlift. Take ten days off training this lift and resume as follows, training the lift only once each week. Other exercises – bent-legged deadlift excluded – can benefit from a training frequency more often than once a week, whether that be once every five days, four days, six days or three days. *You* have to decide what is optimum for you.

Different body parts recover quicker than do others. How quickly you recover will vary according to factors of age, the intensity you train with, how much you do each session, the stresses and strains of life outside the gym, the quality and quantity of your sleep, quantity and quality of your food intake, and other factors. More on this is given in the next chapter.

Workout #		
1	204x10	(85% of 240)
2	216x10	(90% of 240)
3	228x10	(95% of 240)
4	234x10	(97½% of 240)
5	240x10	(100% of 240)
6	246x10	(102½% of 240)
7	252x10	(105% of 240)
8	258x8	(107½% of 240)

(Round these poundages up or down a little
depending on the plates you have.)

For this example, warmup sets have been excluded. Only the final single heaviest set has been noted for each workout. Warmup thoroughly. One set of five slow reps with 135, a few minutes later another five reps with 180 will be enough for most of you for the first three weeks. For the fourth week onward, add a third warmup set of 220 for two reps. Use good safe form – see Chapter 11.

Eight weeks is a long time for a mini-cycle, but bear in mind that the once weekly training frequency for the stiff-legged deadlift extends the time duration of the eight workouts. Had the example been for the barbell press, trained every fourth day, then the duration of the mini–cycle's 6–8 workouts would be 3½–4½ weeks.

Refinements and additional considerations

This variation of intensity cycling is subtle and effective. Some bullying is recommended, but only in the second half of the cycle. Not only is some bullying recommended, but it's an absolute must. There must be periods in which you drive yourself to your limit, as the previous chapter made clear. Effort *is* the name of the game, but it must be correctly applied effort.

It's during the second half of a cycle – whether a mini–cycle or a longer cycle – that *prudent* use of forced reps, negative reps, rest pause and descending sets can be productive. Choose one of the ultra–intense techniques and use it in the final set for each exercise, once a week at most. Over–using these techniques will "kill" a gaining cycle for sure. Be conservative.

Make sure you complete a set properly before adding a couple of forced reps or doing a drop set. Don't add the ultra–intense technique onto a poor set in the hope of making it into a good set. (See page 132.)

These intensity heightening approaches are generally safe and recommended (if not abused) but they aren't equally suited to all exercises. For example, I wouldn't recommend you do forced reps with squats unless you have *very* proficient spotters, and I would urge doing neither forced nor negative reps in the deadlift. Rest pause reps and descending set style reps are safer and more controlled choices for squats and deadlifts.

The very advanced trainee who is very close to the limit of his potential may "burn out" if using the "bullying" techniques. This man may be better off just concentrating on the balance between volume and "regular" effort within the context of cycling. If he gets too enthusiastic, and adds the beyond–failure techniques, he may find he's "flattened" at the next workout and has "killed" the gaining progression.

The previous examples of cycles are theoretical. Each successive cycle of the same construction won't be equally successful. After a few cycles of the same type you'll need to be more subtle and innovative to keep progressing. Don't let your body get into a training rut.

Though the recommendation for the mini–cycle was to cut back to 85% at the start, this isn't sacrosanct. For a longer build–up period, and a probable longer period of gain, cut back a bit more.

As a general rule, the longer the build–up period, the longer the gain period. Invest more time and patience and you should profit more.

Alternating-intensity cycle

A cycle need *not* show progression every workout. One cycling method follows a hard workout with a not-quite-hard workout. Each hard workout is harder than the previous hard workout. Each not-quite-hard workout remains constant (80%x2x6 in the example below) and will "feel" lighter as the cycle progresses. This provides "built-in" recuperation and variety as the cycle goes along.

An example of this comes from Professor Alexei Medvedev, a Soviet weightlifting coach. It's an eighteen-workout cycle aimed to deliver a 5% higher maximum single. (It was designed for elite and probably drug-assisted lifters, but with modification *may* be useful for typical hard gainers.) While 5% may not sound much, 5% of say 280 pounds is 14 pounds. Good for a single cycle. A little at a time, remember.

If you follow this cycle three times a week (too much for drug-free, typical trainees), the cycle will last six weeks. If you follow it twice a week, the cycle will last nine weeks. If you follow it three times every two weeks, the cycle will last twelve weeks. The frequency you choose will be determined by factors stressed so much in this book. As the progressively harder workouts are alternated with less-than-hard workouts, you may be able to recuperate well enough training twice each week, assuming you're using brief workouts. If you need more rest between workouts, take it and thus extend the cycle.

The cycle is based on percentages of a maximum single. 70x2 means two reps with 70% of what you could do for a single repetition immediately before the cycle. 70x2x6 means 70% for six sets of two repetitions (constant poundage). As the cycle progresses, the hard workouts get increasingly more demanding. The first two sets for each day are warmup sets. If you need more warmup work than suggested, do it. You're the judge. Do enough but don't overdo it and tire yourself out. (I would recommend 90x2 as the third warmup set for workouts 16 and 18.) Rest just enough between sets to be able to get out the prescribed repetitions. *Don't* do more reps or sets than prescribed.

The cycle is designed for the powerlifts, overhead barbell pressing and the Olympic lifts, not for the small basic lifts such as barbell curls.

Workout #	
1	70x2, 75x2, 80x2x6
2	70x2, 75x2, 80x3x6
3	70x2, 75x2, 80x2x6
4	70x2, 75x2, 80x4x6
5	70x2, 75x2, 80x2x6
6	70x2, 75x2, 80x5x6

7	70x2, 75x2, 80x2x6
8	70x2, 75x2, 80x6x6
9	70x2, 75x2, 80x2x6
10	70x2, 75x2, 85x5x5
11	70x2, 75x2, 80x2x6
12	70x2, 75x2, 90x4x4
13	70x2, 75x2, 80x2x6
14	70x2, 75x2, 95x3x3
15	70x2, 75x2, 80x2x6
16	70x2, 75x2, 100x2x2
17	70x2, 75x2, 80x2x6
18	70x2, 75x2, 105x1x2

For advanced men, a 5% gain may be unlikely – better to reduce workouts 16 and 18 to 97½% and 102½% respectively. For *anyone*, if the increments listed are too big, reduce them and extend the cycle.

A variation of this approach is to have several weeks in which every workout shows progression and then have a week or two in which you drop back to where you were a few weeks earlier. Return to progressive workouts for another few weeks before cutting back for another week or two and then pick up the intensity for the final stretch.

Periodization

This is another interpretation of intensity cycling, and comes in different shapes though the same form. A basic format is a twelve–week cycle divided into three four–week periods, each using a different repetition target. Each four–week period starts light (relatively speaking) and builds up. In the final week of each four–week period a new personal best is achieved in each exercise for that period's repetition target. There could be twelve reps in the first period, for example. Then starts the second period with lower repetitions, nine, and poundages that are comfortable for the new repetition target. They are built up over the first three weeks so that in the final week of the second period new personal bests are achieved for the new repetition target. Then immediately comes the final four–week period in which low repetitions (six or less) are used and again the poundage is built up so that in the final week personal bests are achieved for the low repetition target.

The design of this method of cycling has you training flat–out only in the final week of each four–week period. So, over the whole twelve weeks you only train full–bore for three weeks at the most. Progress hinges on what you do in the final week of each period.

As the twelve–week cycles go by, each period should start, and finish, with a few more pounds on the bar than in the previous twelve–week cycle. Progress is slow but sure. Having so few weeks to go full–bore in keeps your mind fresh and avoids overtraining. This sets you up to make new personal bests each final week of each period. It works, but needs patience and faith, and careful planning in writing. *All* sound cycles need patience because you must not train full–bore until the predetermined time. If you jump ahead, all you'll likely get is stagnation – haste makes waste, remember.

The l–o–n–g cycle

As mentioned earlier, the longer the build–up stage of a cycle, the longer the period of gain should be. If you use very small discs (or even a collection of washers) to register your poundage increments, your body can adapt with strength increases time after time after time after time. How about a cycle for a minimum of a year, without a break, in a single exercise? Try the following:

Let's use the stiff–legged deadlift (again) as the example. Assume that your current best is ten reps with 250 pounds. To create a long cycle, cut the starting poundage back to 75% – 187½ pounds. Start with this poundage for ten reps, 2–3 sets with the same poundage. *Every* workout, you increase the poundage by five pounds until you're up to 90% of your previous ten–rep best – 225 pounds. Now, reduce the every–workout increment to 2½ pounds.

Concerning training frequency, because the intensity is low at present, train the deadlift three times every two weeks. Assuming having trained at this frequency, it will take you eight workouts or nearly six weeks to get to 90% of your pre–cycle 250 poundage for ten reps. Now, switch to training once a week and only two top sets of stiff–legged deadlifts. You'll need ten more workouts (about seven weeks) to get you to your former best of 250 pounds for ten repetitions. As you're doing two top sets, you'll have progressed in volume with the same poundage that you could previously only do one set of ten with.

Now that you're at 250x10 for two sets, you're in a very different position to when you were at that poundage before. You've built a good gaining momentum because you built–up the poundage over about sixteen weeks. To make the most of this gaining momentum, reduce the poundage increments to the smallest discs you've got, and only put on the increment every second or third deadlift workout.

Doing just *one* top set now, with such a slow poundage increment of an average of a mere *one pound* a week, you can keep this going for *months*. This assumes you're doing everything correctly as stressed throughout this book. Don't ruin things by training too much on other exercises, by not sleeping enough, by not eating enough, or by getting impatient. One pound a week average increment *at the most*. Sixteen weeks to get to your original working poundage has built the "reserve" for perhaps forty weeks or more of gaining. Forty weeks means 40 pounds, fifty weeks means 50 pounds, sixty weeks means 60 pounds. It has been done before. It can be done again. Do it!

One of the biggest mistakes you can make in bodybuilding and strength training is to be impatient. Forget about progressing for a while. Instead, work at creating the "reserve" and momentum needed for gaining. Then you can progress for longer than you probably thought you could. Using this l-o-n-g cycle as the example, can you train for sixteen weeks before reaching your previous best? Most people are in such a hurry to get to their top poundages that they never create much if any gaining momentum. They slog away using the same poundages for year after year, and look the same for year after year.

Fallibility of cycling

Cycling isn't infallible. It depends on many variables. No method of cycling will work if you simply do too much work, train too frequently and rep-out to your maximum too early on in the cycle. Throughout your training life you'll need to experiment. Trial and error is a vital part of the activity. Learn from your mistakes.

Cycling is all about upping the poundages a little over the short and medium-term. In between, you'll have regular cut-back periods in which you give the impression of having gotten weaker. This is part and parcel of cycling. No longer can you continue to batter yourself with your top poundages for week after week, and month after month.

You now know that cut-back periods, and comfortable weeks, provide the stepping stones to new personal best achievements within a few weeks or few months. What others in the gym might think, seeing you having a run of less than full-bore workouts, isn't important. You can't be at your absolute best all the time. Don't wear yourself out by persistently battling with a sticking point so as to show yourself constantly working with your top poundages. This is stagnation.

> *Three big misuses of cycling:*
> a. Don't overdo the easy workouts and neglect to push yourself very hard in the second half of each cycle.
> b. Don't reduce the number of easy workouts to get almost immediately back into the very hard sessions.
> c. Don't rep out to the limit with the reduced

poundages that commence each cycle. If you do rep
out to the limit with reduced poundages, where is the
cycling of training intensity?

Getting the balance right is where individual understanding,
experimentation, fine–tuning and experience come in. A 50:50 split
between comfortable and hard workouts is a sound *starting* place. As
with all instruction, you must apply it to yourself.

During the early workouts of a cycle, if you do rep–out – albeit with
reduced poundages – then you'll be training flat–out right from the
start. Where is the building up of intensity and the development of a
gaining momentum? Training full–bore too early is a big mistake when
using intensity cycling. Be watchful.

Preparing yourself for gaining

A different interpretation of cycling was outlined in Chapter 5,
where an exaggerated "softening–up" period precedes the period of flat–
out effort using the big basic exercises. This is another potentially
productive interpretation of cycling to add to your armory. Try it.

Dealing with sickness

When you get a minor sickness, such as a cold, you can keep your
current cycle going by inserting a mini–cycle. Once back in the gym,
following a short layoff, use the exact 85–90–95–97½–100% format of
the mini–cycle described earlier in this chapter. Take the 100% workout
as the one you were at just before you got sick. It will take you three
weeks or so to get back to where you were before you got sick.
However, you'll get back there with momentum to spare, enabling you
to forge ahead over the completion of the original cycle.

If you try to jump straight back into the original cycle, you'll likely
"kill" the gaining momentum and be eventually forced into starting the
whole cycle again. Much better to insert the mini–cycle. It can save you
much frustration and many wasted workouts.

If you get a serious sickness, you'll have to start with very light
poundages following the layoff. Anticipate needing a progressive cycle
of ten or more weeks before getting back to where you were before the
sickness – be patient. If you rush it, you risk injuring yourself, getting
overtrained, exhausting your enthusiasm, and even getting sick again.

An oversupply of cycling methods?

The purpose of this book isn't to give you a single "do it like this"
approach to training. The purpose is to give you a thorough (but not

exhaustive) coverage of the variety of ways that typical bodybuilders can train productively. There are many ways.

While all these ways won't suit all people all the time, many of them (with individual fine–tuning) will suit most of you for a lot of the time. A variety of approaches to select from, as the years go by, is what you need to maintain motivation and progress.

How you train in general and, how you cycle your workouts, will depend, among other considerations, on your goals, current development, time available, enthusiasm, and current rest and sleep habits. Sometimes you'll prefer to have short cycles, sometimes you'll want to use longer cycles.

Several short cycles add up to a long cycle and total gains from each approach, over the same period, may be similar. On the other hand, they might not be. It depends on how you implement the different approaches and how appropriate your selection is relative to your current circumstances.

What worked for you in summer 1991 might not work in autumn 1992. What didn't work for you last year when you were rather rundown might deliver great results later this year when you fine–tune it and get out–of–the–gym factors in 100% good order. What worked for you when you were single and twenty-five may not work for you when you're thirty–two, married, and with two young children.

Now that you understand what intensity cycling is, you can add it to the list of vital factors to consider when you're devising, adopting or modifying training programs. Cycling is one of the most useful tools you have available to you. Take full advantage of it.

The appalling irony of modern bodybuilding is that the training methods appropriate to only a small minority of bodybuilders are given massive promotion, while the training methods most appropriate to the masses are largely hidden from the very people who need them the most.

Do everything you can to ensure you sleep generously. If in doubt, get more sleep. Arrange things so you always wake *of your own accord*. Cut back on evening television, increase your sleep and increase your gains.

8: Rest and Recovery

Popular bodybuilding programs have their adherents clocking up many hours in the gym each week. Three days a week is the rock bottom minimum, with routines of four, five or more workouts a week being the rule. Split routines of two days on and one day off, three days on and one day off, five days on and two days off, six days on and one day off. Twice a day workouts in some cases. Eight, ten, twelve, fifteen or more sets per body part, and two, three or even more exercises per body part.

This very frequent and high volume type of training is what the top bodybuilders use. That this genetically gifted and (probably) drug–using minority has progressed on this type of approach, and can continue to do so, is irrelevant to us hard gainers. However, it's important to remember that the routines that built the initial size of top bodybuilders are usually shorter, less frequent and a lot heavier than the routines done to refine their already large physiques. Even these routines that are simpler and less frequent than those that get heavy publicity in today's bodybuilding literature are still inappropriate for typical hard gainers.

Promoting programs comprising as many as eight exercises done twice a week – a sound starting point for many hard gainers – is heresy for bodybuilders used to reading the popular literature. To promote programs of five, four, three or even two exercises, to be sometimes done no more than twice a week, may seem lunacy to the uninitiated.

Extreme abbreviated routines are often the only routines that extremely hard gainers will grow on. To end up spending less than three hours a week total training time will strike most bodybuilders as a joke. The mass consumption approach to bodybuilding is to have workouts of ninety minutes to two hours at least 3–4 times a week, making six hours a week a minimum in the minds of the many. Plus, such a minimum is seen as only short–term for neophytes getting ready to jump into something "more serious."

If the popular methods delivered the goods – for drug–free and genetically typical bodybuilders – there would be no need to discuss alternatives. The sad reality is that the popular training methods have an appalling failure rate.

This is emphatically confirmed by personal training experience, observation, communication with countless other bodybuilders, and publishing HARDGAINER. The need for the promotion of simple and infrequent training routines is huge. No, it's colossal. No, it's *enormously astronomical.*

> The need for such simple workouts is *not* isolated to neophytes. Simple workouts are needed by the great mass of bodybuilders *throughout* their training lives. Not the same interpretation of "simple" all the time, but simple and basic nevertheless. Very few bodybuilders develop to the point where they can productively use "finishing" routines or even very advanced hard-gainer type routines.

> For those of you new to the promotion of radical training approaches, please understand that training a hard gainer necessitates strategies that may, at first sight, appear absurd.

> No training and no dietary schedule will deliver substantial gains in muscle size unless there's adequate rest and recovery. Even if you train on an abbreviated routine, doing only two hard sets per exercise, you won't grow if you train too frequently.

Three-times-a-week training

The recommendation of training the whole body three times a week is still common today. This training frequency is too much for archetypal hard gainers *if each workout is to be an all-out effort.* This frequency – commonly the Monday–Wednesday–Friday training days – has been a standard recommendation for decades. I "swallowed" it too, years ago, until I read articles in Peary Rader's Iron Man that advised experimenting with less frequent training. By getting away from the mind-set of training three times every week I was on the road to gains.

As I became more experienced, and developed the ability to train harder, even twice a week – when training hard – was too much, especially for the deadlift and squat. For many hard gainers, not just me, training each exercise twice a week can be too frequent, even when using abbreviated routines of four exercises or less. Some hard gainers can't gain on anything much more than four exercises each done only once every five, six or even seven days.

Rather than the twice a week training frequency (for the same exercises) becoming a norm for hard gainers, three times every *two* weeks may be a better standard. For some hard gainers, training a major basic exercise only *once* a week can be more productive. You don't read much about this in the popular literature. I know of many bodybuilders who belong in this category. You may be one of them. Experiment with very infrequent training if the regular routines aren't working.

Making three-times-a-week training work

If pushing hard each workout – within the confines of intensity cycling – then training the *whole* body three times a week will usually be fruitless for typical hard gainers. If the intensity of effort is *varied* over the three weekly training days, then the strategy has a *chance* of working. If the three weekly workouts (say, Monday, Wednesday and Friday) are heavy, light and medium, then only one workout per week is an all-out effort.

Words like "heavy," "medium" and "light" are relative words and need to be defined. To illustrate why, suppose John can squat 380 pounds for ten reps, and George can squat 250 for ten reps. For John, 300 pounds in the squat is no trouble and he will consider it quite light. For George, 300 pounds in the squat will be very heavy.

To define heavy, medium and light, take the heavy all-out day poundages as the 100% mark. If you squat 350 for six reps in Monday's workout, and you're at or near to your limit (according to the stage of the cycle you're in) then 350x6 is 100% for the squat. Wednesday's "light" day uses 80% of Monday's poundages for the same reps – 280x6. Friday's "medium" workout uses 90% of Monday's poundages – 315x6. (The 100–80–90% schedule is modified by some to twice a week total-body training using a 100% main day and a 80–90% second day.)

Some people spread the all-out effort sets over the week, not having all the "heavy" sets on the same day. The whole body is still trained three days a week but, each workout, something is pushed to the limit. This means your body is getting no days of "working rest" and may be more likely to be overtrained than on the strict heavy, light and medium division of days.

Training three times a week can be very productive when you do a different workout each session and each lift is trained either once a week or three times every two weeks. This is very different to training the whole body three times a week.

For the typical hard gainer who is pushed for time as well as for recovery ability, I don't believe a three-times-a-week *total-body* routine is the best way to go.

Personal example

As made clear in earlier chapters, though effort is vital, it must be applied appropriately. Cycling of intensity is part of this, as is training frequency.

In my late teens and early twenties I was strongly influenced by the writings of Arthur Jones and Mike Mentzer. From what I read of their work they believed that it's impossible to train too hard. (I read a lot of their writings but, to be fair to them, I haven't read all they wrote. Perhaps I didn't get the whole story.) Concerning training frequency, the popular recommendation was that rest between workouts shouldn't exceed ninety six hours, though Mentzer did advise a three–times–a–week split routine that worked each body part three times in a two week period. This was a step in the right direction, at least for me.

During a two year period, when I was around twenty, I lived the belief that it's impossible to train too hard. I made the belief my existence, and crucified myself in the gym. Training the whole body each workout, I only used two sets at most, and of each of only eight exercises, twice a week; but what workouts they were.

I wasn't training hard in spurts, and neither was I cycling the training intensity. It was full–bore effort for months at a time, until a point where my body rebelled. Sickness or injury would force me to rest a short while. I would then further study up on the need for brief high intensity workouts, and then get back into the twice a week training with renewed vengeance. I did this for about two years. This was before I was married with children – at a time when I had long and undisturbed nights of sleep, when recuperation needs could be met much more easily than at any time since, and when I was very young.

I would take every non–warmup set to positive failure under my own effort – until I couldn't get another rep out, even with cheating. I would then have my training partner assist me in eking out three or four forced reps. To finish off the set – as if I hadn't already done more than enough – I would then do a few negative resistance reps. Helpers would lift the weights up and I would lower them as slowly as I could.

This style of training would exhaust me and render me sore after every session. This was training insanity. How I could keep it up for so long, I don't know, especially when I made no gains in size and strength the whole time. Incredible that I could put in so much effort for so little return. Despite being a long way from my full physical potential, I gained nothing from this battering. Getting sick or injured forced me to stop training for a couple of weeks or so. I'd lose strength and then manage to build back to where I was before, but nothing further. This happened again and again.

My explanation for the lack of results was always the same – I wasn't training hard enough. I would resolve to train even harder. Madness.

Seeing the light

Rest and recovery are about having the most appropriate training schedule – not just workout frequency per se, but also the frequency of using full–bore effort training. The latter was covered in detail in the previous chapter on cycling. Workout frequency is the main topic here.

Looking back on my "training insanity" days, here's what I should have done: The workout outlined above should have been done just once every third or fourth week, with the other workouts being taken to positive failure only. Intensity should have been cycled along the lines of the previous chapter's recommendations. Squats and deadlifts should have been trained once a week, on different days, and the other exercises trained once every fourth or fifth day. Each workout should have had a maximum of six exercises and pre–set days of training shouldn't have been adhered to.

Thus, I should have trained according to how well I had recovered, not according to an arbitrary training frequency determined by an author in a magazine or book.

No matter how intense your gym sessions are, how well you eat or how well you sleep, if you visit the gym too often you aren't going to progress much if at all.

Optimum training frequency can't be fixed for universal application. It varies according to individual physical capacity, tolerance of exercise, age, lifestyle, training intensity, diet, quality of rest and sleep, among other factors. Discovering *your* ideal training frequency – for the moment – involves experimentation and objective analysis.

Components of recovery

Muscles grow only if, first, they are stimulated to grow by adequate training intensity and, second, if sufficient time is provided between training sessions to permit the body to recover and grow. There are two components of this recovery.

The first component is the recovery from systemic fatigue – the feeling of being "wiped out" that follows a demanding workout. The localized fatigue of individual muscle groups is only a fraction of this overall fatigue. The emphasis upon the major exercises – squats, deadlifts, bench presses, et cetera – delivers a lot more systemic fatigue than an equal number of small movements such as leg extensions, hyper–extensions and cable crossovers.

After a workout, the body's priority is to get over the systemic fatigue. Only after it has recovered from this fatigue will it be able to concern itself with the second component of recovery – producing growth and strength increase, the "overcompensation."

During my period of "training insanity" I was piling up massive systemic fatigue. Even before I was recovered from the systemic fatigue I was back in the gym. Not only had I not fully recovered from the immediate effects of training, my body never got close to being able to do anything about growing even a scrap of extra muscle.

No wonder my body would eventually cave in with either sickness or injury. How else could it get me to keep out of the gym? How else could it get around to getting fully recovered from the state of exhaustion I was in? My body wasn't interested in building size and strength – it just wanted to survive.

Few people actually drive themselves into a state of long–term systemic fatigue by training too hard. Most people do it by simply training too much, and too often, albeit at a lower intensity. Long workouts and popular split routines will drive you to exhaustion. That you won't have stimulated growth and strength increase is irrelevant. You'll never get over the systemic fatigue to be able to get around to any growing. This is the lot of the mass of bodybuilders that fills gym membership rolls.

Never visit the gym unless you feel completely recovered and rested from the previous visit. Never pile on more fatigue when you already have a stock of fatigue inside you. Get rested!

Just how many days you need between workouts is an individual matter. If you're feeling very vigorous, are sleeping well, have a stress–free life and are twenty years old, you may be able to fully recover from a very hard full–body workout (even including squats *and* deadlifts) every third or fourth day.

On the other hand, if you're a parent of young children, have regularly disturbed nights, are working at two jobs, dealing with stress from all sides of life, and are over thirty, don't expect to be able to recover from a hard full–body workout every third or fourth day. Every sixth or seventh day may be a more likely frequency for each exercise, with more time in between deadlift sessions. Or, the set of six exercises could be divided into two sections and the two routines alternated at an appropriate frequency.

If rest and recovery are in extremely poor order, and stress is piled high, then forget about training hard. Just concern yourself, temporarily, with hanging onto as much size and strength as you can until circumstances pick up and you can train properly again.

Exceptional genetics and/or drug use greatly enhance the body's tolerance of exercise, and its ease of growing muscle. Another set of instructions can apply here. Though of course these easy gainers must still recover between workouts, they can train more frequently and with a greater volume of exercise than we can, and still grow.

All this is written not to foster a negative attitude but to remind you to follow the advice of people who are very similar to you. Don't imitate those who have advantages and assistance you don't have.

There *are* hard gainers who train quite soundly in the gym – not too many exercise or sets, properly cycled intensity, and plenty of motivation and planning. However, they visit the gym too often, therefore undoing all the good of having the other vital factors in such sound order. As the cycle progresses, fatigue slowly builds up, the gaining momentum doesn't appear, training zest slips and gains don't happen. When can their bodies get the chance to deliver some growth? Think this through. It's at the very foundation of bodybuilding success.

If every bodybuilder in the world was to add an extra two days of rest between workouts, there would be a lot more muscle in the world within a few weeks.

Split routines

Split routines reduce training time per workout but increase the number of gym visits. Split routines encourage the adding of extra sets and exercises because the individual workouts may appear too short. Increased gym visits mean more frequent demands upon the systemic system. If the body is in a state of near constant systemic fatigue, how is it going to be able grow and get stronger?

This isn't to say that even modified and hard–gainer–type split routines are ineffective. There are some interpretations that may be *very* helpful, but they are *nothing* like traditional split routines. For example, some hard gainers successfully train three times a week, but only work each main exercise *once* a week. A week's work could run like this: squats and T-bar rowing on Monday; bench presses, curls and dips on Wednesday; deadlifts and presses on Friday. Calf, abdominal and neck work could be done on two of the three days.

Two less radical split routines, though *perhaps* effective if each workout is kept short and you're resting, sleeping and eating extremely well, are the three–days–a–week split routine and the alternate–day split routine.

Suppose you currently do ten exercises to cover the whole body, and do the workout twice a week except for deadlifts that are done once a week. (Nine or ten exercises each workout is a *lot* of work for a typical bodybuilder – probably too much.) Supposing you think you can gain on this amount, and can ensure adequate rest and nutrition, then divide your workout into two equally stressful parts. *Don't* add exercises to the shortened routines or else you'll undo all the good of dividing your basic routine into two simpler parts.

Train the first routine on Monday, the second on Wednesday and the first on Friday. With the three–days–a–week split routine, the second routine opens the next week, on Monday. With the alternate–day split routine, you train alternate days regardless of the day of the week, and alternate the routine used at each workout. The second interpretation gets you in the gym more often and so is more demanding. Over a four week period the three–days–a–week split routine will have you in the gym twelve times. Over the same period, the alternate–day split routine will have you in the gym fourteen times.

While training regularity is vital, don't be so locked into pre–fixed training days that you ignore signs of inadequate recovery. Don't drive yourself to train before you've really recovered. Take an extra day of rest if you feel you need it. You're the judge.

If you feel you can benefit from it, try the three–days–a–week split routine, but use only 3–5 exercises each workout.

With few exceptions, I don't advise hard gainers to train more than three times a week, *no matter how they divide the work*. I *don't* advise training every exercise three times a week. (Short specialization periods for single body parts is another matter though.) You need more rest days than training days.

Many of you will be better off sticking to twice a week training *at the most*, and even then not training every exercise at each session. Many of you will need to modify the above split routines. Try the first routine one day, rest *two* days, second routine, rest *two* days, first routine again, rest *two* days, and so on. This is training each exercise once every sixth day. More suggestions for split routines are given in Chapter 10.

If in doubt, train less often rather than more often.

Too much rest?

There are people who have gotten bigger and stronger by training each exercise – on a regular basis – only once a week, and even less frequently on the deadlift. Don't be dissuaded from experimenting with infrequent training by those who would have you believe that if you don't train at least once every ninety six hours your muscles will atrophy. Avoid fixing yourself into pre–set schedules. Take whatever rest you need between workouts to ensure that you're fully ready for your next workout, be it seventy two hours, ninety six, a hundred and twenty, a hundred and forty four, or even more. What matters is progress, not slotting into a fixed schedule.

During the initial part of a training cycle – when intensity is being built up – you can train more frequently than when in the full–bore stage of the cycle. An indicator to use when determining training frequency, in *addition* to systemic fatigue, is local muscular fatigue. If your back and/or legs are still sore, be it just a little, then wait another day or two, or even more, before training either again, or even before training *anything* again. Have *at least* one day clear of any soreness before training again. Soreness from the major basic movements will always accompany systemic fatigue. Can you imagine having deep soreness in your thighs, buttocks and lower back – from the squat – and not being systemically *very* fatigued as well?

If you build up the intensity, over the course of the first stage of a training cycle, you should never experience debilitating soreness. Instead, you'll have "regular" soreness that usually clears within 2–4 days. If you're conditioned to your training – you don't just drop into full–bore training with no break–in period – you can clear the local fatigue and yet still feel systemically fatigued. Don't think that just because you feel no soreness you're guaranteed to be recovered and have the okay to train again. Recover both locally *and* systemically before training again. Otherwise, you'll be on the slippery slope of frustration and despair.

> The speed of your progress is, at least in a big part, a reflection of how many growth producing workouts you can put in. If you can train each body part every other day, and recover in between, you'll quickly accumulate the many productive workouts needed to build impressive muscular size. If you can only train each body part hard once every 5–7 days (and perhaps even less frequently for the deadlift), it will take you far longer to accumulate the same number of productive workouts. Be that as it is – you can't hasten your progress by getting in the gym before you've recovered from the previous workout.

> The more less–than–100% intensity workouts you have in your training cycles, the less growth producing workouts you'll get into a single cycle. Be that as it is – you won't hasten your progress by skipping on the necessary less–than–100% intensity

workouts. You must adhere strictly to avoiding overtraining and burning yourself out. Don't try to do things that don't help you in the cause of adding more muscle. Follow your own body and its responses, not the bodies and responses of others.

Never again must you short–change yourself between workouts. Always avoid training unless you feel fully rested and raring to go. If in doubt, take extra rest, not less.

Some people have taken this farther than you've probably ever heard of. (Don't start being ridiculous and visualize training once every six months.) How about dividing three exercises so that each exercise is worked by itself once every five days? How about training each main lift once every 8–10 days? How about deadlifting once every 2–3 weeks only? Such training frequency hasn't been arrived at out of laziness but out of necessity by the practitioners because they couldn't gain satisfactorily on more frequent schedules. You may not need to train this infrequently to gain well, but the examples make the point that the standard training frequency recommendations leave a lot to be desired.

The power of sleep

The poorer the quality and quantity of sleep – relative to what your body needs – the more your training will suffer. While you might not think you're suffering by cutting out an hour or two of sleep most nights, you'll feel it in the gym, eventually. If you get into an almost permanent sleep deficit, you can forget about progressing in the gym.

If you ensure not being woken up by artificial means, or being woken by someone, and keep this going for week after week, and month after month, the difference to your progress will probably amaze you. To have a fully rested body, *each* day, is a big step to having wonderful progress in the gym. High intensity workouts can be maintained for longer stretches, cycles can be lengthened and there's far less waning of energy and effort during a workout.

How much sleep you need is an individual matter. Err on the side of too much, if you want to grow a lot of muscle. While there are people who need very little sleep, they are few and far between. The most striking example I know from this minority is Dr. Ken E. Leistner. In the fourteenth issue of HARDGAINER, page 9, Dr. Leistner wrote, "I sleep on the average of five nights per week, and usually three hours per night. Everyone who knows me thinks it's unusual but, because it's normal for me, it's normal." He's been doing this since he was sixteen, including the years when he gained over sixty pounds of muscle and a *lot* of strength.

Do everything you can to ensure you sleep generously. If in doubt, get more sleep. Go to bed early whenever possible, ideally being consistent about it so your internal "clock" gets adjusted. Sleep late whenever possible. Avoid being woken up whenever possible. Arrange things so you wake of your own accord. Cut back on evening television, increase your sleep and increase your gains.

I know all about having stressful working conditions and having children that cause consistently disturbed nights, at least during the early stage of their lives. There are times when it's impossible to get sleeping habits in good order. Tolerate these times and when things improve, as they will, then pile on the sleep. You'll be rewarded with gains piling on a lot easier.

Becoming a great sleeper will go a long way to making you less of a hard gainer. This is especially so when in the second half of a training cycle. When the intensity reaches its peak, do your utmost to get an extra hour of two hour of sleep each night.

Don't train late. Don't use stimulants, take a warm bath before retiring, investigate meditation and relaxation techniques to relax you, and – if you take mineral supplements – take them before bedtime as they naturally relax you.

Abbreviated workouts

Abbreviated training cuts back training to the absolute basics, to the skeleton shorn of all secondary and superfluous work. It focuses on the most basic and demanding exercises. Such routines go as low as four, three or even two exercises, and, in the extreme, just one exercise in a workout. Take this seriously. This is the way to gains for many hard gainers who can't gain on other routines for hard gainers.

Such an abbreviated training procedure is usually used as a last resort, after their users have unsuccessfully used all other routines. Don't see abbreviated training as a last resort. It should be the first resort for hard gainers, especially extreme hard gainers.

Abbreviated routines can provide the quickest way to unabbreviated gains in size and strength, even for those of you who can gain on longer routines. The less you train, the more you can gain is undoubtedly true in the case of the typical drug–free hard gainer. Try it for yourself, with commitment and determination.

The abbreviated routine has two primary advantages. First, because the volume of exercise is so low, the intensity of effort can be very high because there's so little work over which to spread your effort and application. The second advantage is that the demands upon your recovery ability are reduced relative to conventional routines.

Demanding less from your recovery capacity means you're far less likely to overtrain. Being more likely to recover quicker between workouts you'll get in more productive workouts within a given period.

You'll recover more quickly than usual, be less tired during your off days, and be more enthusiastic for your next workout. By being able to put more effort into less work, and being able to tolerate more of such workouts, you *will* grow more. A magic formula.

Another big advantage of abbreviated routines is the spending of less time in the gym. This is important for those who have very congested lifestyles. So, for drug-free and genetically typical bodybuilders, not only are abbreviated workouts convenient, they are far more *effective* than long and excessively frequent workouts.

Spending a few cycles on abbreviated routines, or longer in some cases, gives you the foundation for responding to a moderately expanded routine later on. Praise the abbreviated workout.

The abbreviated routine is the only way forward for the extreme hard gainer who has physically demanding employment. Even for some hard gainers that have comfortable and non-tiring jobs, the abbreviated routine is the only way to pack on the mass, at least in the early part of their training lives.

Confusion, but hope

Occasionally, in the mainstream bodybuilding literature and gym-lore, attempts are made to produce a basic, somewhat abbreviated routine, as a "mass and power" routine. While the number and selection of exercises show hope and a big step in the right direction, the second step wasn't taken. It's not just the number and selection of exercises that matters, but how those exercises are scheduled.

A routine of 4-6 "power" exercises may be recommended, to be trained full-bore three days a week. Which drug-free, typical bodybuilders can squat, bench press and deadlift hard three days a week? Sometimes, a split routine of basic exercises is designed so that squats are done twice a week and deadlifts are done on another two days a week. Pounding the lower back four days a week? Forget it.

This sort of interpretation gives basic, abbreviated training a bad name. If you abuse training in this confused way, then of course you're going to stagnate and get injured. Those who are so poorly guided then think the squat and deadlift are dangerous exercises. Of course they are, if you abuse them. Don't abuse them! Follow the advice in this book and reap the rewards of the most productive exercises.

So often, the actual list of exercises may be sound, but the way those exercises are scheduled is a disaster.

Do abbreviated routines neglect body parts?

Very abbreviated routines do lack something in terms of balance. Their purpose isn't to attend to the finer points of balance and "finishing." Bodybuilders who are in the greatest need of abbreviated routines shouldn't be concerned about aspects of balance.

Concern with complete balance and attention to the little details comes *after* you've developed considerable size in the first place. Trying to do everything at the same time – substance *and* detail – is, at least for typical hard gainers, a recipe for stagnation and the development of neither substance *nor* detail.

It's the very fact that training has been cut back to its absolute skeleton that abbreviated routines can be so effective – there are no distractions, no marginal concerns, no syphoning off of energy and effort, no excessive demands upon recovery capacity.

Abbreviated routines don't provide specific arm and shoulder work. However, these areas get a good working over from the indirect work they get from the very hard work you're able to put into bench presses or dips, and the back work, alongside the other exercises. Don't think that your arm and shoulder muscles will atrophy because you won't be doing specific isolation work for them.

The irony is that many hard gainers gain little or nothing on arm specialization work. However, on an abbreviated routine, effort is poured in and you can add substantial poundage to the few exercises used. Then your arms will grow. Stick with an abbreviated routine for enough cycles to add 100 pounds to your squat and stiff–legged deadlift, for plenty of reps, and 75 pounds to your bench press. How then can your arms and shoulders not grow?

This book, together with HARDGAINER, has a different message to promote than has the mainstream bodybuilding literature. The appalling irony of modern bodybuilding is that the training methods appropriate to only the minority of bodybuilders are given massive promotion, while the training methods appropriate to the masses are hidden from the very people who need them the most.

Believe in the message of this book and HARDGAINER, adjust it to your individual circumstances, "sweat blood" on it, and you'll get results that will make even the most doubting of doubting Gym Thomases sit up and take notice.

Body part specialization

Chapter 12 delves into this subject. Suffice for the moment to note that the interpretations of training frequency covered in this chapter refer to training where progress is desired throughout the body. When specializing upon a single body part, short–term periods of interpretations of training frequency different to those given in this chapter can be productively used. More on this later.

Recreational activities

Be careful with your choice of recreational activities outside of bodybuilding. If you're playing a lot of basketball, football or any other physically demanding activity, you'll be making major inroads into your recovery ability. If you're having trouble gaining in the gym, the last thing you want is to have your recovery ability largely used up by other activities. Cut back demanding activities – just concentrate on the skill aspects for a while. Or, consider changing your recreational activities.

Coping with excessively demanding employment

Long hours of hard manual labor, especially in high temperatures, can take a heavy toll on the body's capacity to respond normally to a typical hard gainer's routine. It usually makes a hard gainer into an extremely hard gainer. As with almost everything though, there are exceptions. A striking one is the sixteen year old Randall J. Strossen who, back in the late sixties, gained his "30 pounds of muscle in 6 weeks" on a 20–rep squat program during a hot summer vacation from school and while working as a construction laborer. At the end of the program, Strossen reported, "I feel that I am in about as hard a condition now as I was at the beginning of the program." This was reported in the January 1969 issue of Iron Man. (Who knows, he may have gained 40 pounds had he been lounging around at home between workouts.)

It's not just manual labor that can be a hindrance. Anyone who works long and difficult hours, be those hours at a desk or in the home, may have additional obstacles in the way of progress in the gym. Anyone who even has physically non–demanding employment can suddenly feel the difference upon the arrival of offspring.

While there are times that circumstances are so temporarily trying that progress in the gym has to be forgotten for a while, a solution must be found for dealing with long–term "regular" difficult circumstances.

The solution is to reduce the demands upon the body from every single source. Train less often, do less training at each workout, sleep more whenever you can, rest whenever possible and consume more calories to compensate for the increased energy output from all the work and late hours. Just how you do this is up to you. Experiment. Whatever you need to do, do it. Never mind what anyone in less trying circumstances has to say about your strategy.

If you've had a particularly tiring day (or night), avoid training the same day or even the following day. You can't adhere to a pre-set schedule of training days. Try to pick your training days when you're least tired. Do your best to ensure that the night before a workout you have a good night's sleep. One good day and night of rest can correct a run of "deficit" days and nights.

Sleep and rest as much as you can. Even if sound sleep is unattainable, rest in the best way you can. Avoid, whenever possible, all energy leaks. To paraphrase Peary Rader – quoted in Super Squats, page 76 – don't run when you can walk, don't walk when you can sit, don't sit when you can lie down, don't merely lie down when you can sleep, and don't get up when you can lie in.

All of this may seem excessive in the minds of people who have been spared the enormous demands of constant over-work, disturbed nights and lack of rest. For those of you who are familiar with the extreme situation I'm writing about, you'll know that what I'm recommending is a method of trying to cope with what would otherwise be an unbearable situation.

Try working at a full-time and tiring job followed by looking after young children for a couple of their pre-sleep difficult hours, followed by working at a part-time job until midnight or later, followed by being woken up at 3.30 a.m., followed by getting up at 5 a.m., followed – in theory – by a visit to the gym the following afternoon, followed by a similar chain of events for the days before the next workout.

Now try to follow the routine of a top title-winner. Don't even try to follow the routine of a typical hard gainer. Forget it. Cut back, cut back, and cut back again.

Another problem arising from working very long hours is that meal timing can be upset. Try to stick rigidly to your meals. If you skip some, you'll reduce your energy intake and further exacerbate the obstacles in the way of mere maintenance training, let alone progress-orientated training. If solid meals are made impossible at times, rely more on liquid meals. Get more use out of milk concoctions and the use of a blender.

Even with all of this in mind it's still possible to be side-tracked if you're not thoroughly resolved to stay on the sane but radical course. Getting too interested in the training of genetically superior and drug-using bodybuilders who can devote themselves to training, rest and eating – with few distractions – will lead you astray. Avoid being "seduced" into having anything to do with the irrational.

Remember, do less training, not more – cut back, cut back and cut back again.

The criticism that the squat sometimes receives usually arises from two points. First, most gym members (and instructors) simply don't know how to squat. Second, of those who try to learn, most don't invest enough time and patience to learn to squat properly. They are then unable to maintain good style when building up the poundage.

While the technique of the regular squat and the bent-legged deadlift are different, they share similarities in their effects and productiveness. Some people are better suited to squatting, others are better suited to deadlifting. While neglecting neither, in the early stage of your development you should consider focusing more on the movement you're better suited to.

9: The Squat

The regular squat – with bar held on the trapezius – is one of the most productive of exercises *for all who can safely perform it.* (The trapezius is a large, flat muscle that covers much of the upper back region. It's responsible for rotating the scapula and providing the natural padding for the squat bar.)

Variations of the regular squat are given later in this chapter, some of them being excellent alternatives. It's not a case of either regular squats or no squats.

While great praise is rightly given to the classic 20–rep squat routine, the 20–rep deadlift routine is definitely worth experimenting with. Though the focus of this chapter is upon the squat, don't belittle the value – for some people – of using the bent–legged deadlift as the linchpin in some training cycles.

The squat, together with variations of the deadlift, are *the* most productive exercises that can be done to stimulate muscular growth and strength gains. For so little (but hard) work, these two exercises can produce mounds of muscle and get the body into a more responsive condition for bodybuilding. It's because these exercises demand such hard work, and affect a large mass of muscle, that they are so productive.

Hard work on the squat and deadlift provides a mysterious growth effect by improving the metabolism and internal efficiency. This improved metabolism makes you less of a hard gainer.

Testosterone production

Testosterone is the hormone produced in the testes. This hormone has anabolic and androgenic effects. The former are related to the development of muscle tissue and the latter are related to the male sex characteristics. Anabolic steroids are synthetic forms of testosterone that provide their users with more of this hormone than can naturally exist in their systems.

The body was designed to respond to very demanding work with the secretion of testosterone. While the unnaturally high levels that users of steroids have can't be imitated, we can temporarily raise our testosterone levels by "triggering it" with exercise. Which exercises "trigger" the most testosterone production? The big basic exercises. The ones that use the biggest muscle mass and demand the most from you – the squat and the bent–legged deadlift. Doing the squat and stiff–legged deadlift back–to–back may do just about all that can be done to "trigger" testosterone production. Merely *doing* these exercises isn't enough though. They have to be worked *hard*.

Becoming able to squat

Very few people have the structure of body needed to build up to the enormous poundages of competitive powerlifters. You can't do anything about your length of legs, femur and trunk construction, muscle size potential and tendon attachment points.

Very few people *can't* squat productively as long as they train themselves to squat properly. If your Achilles tendons are inflexible, you're not going to be able to squat down without lifting your heels off the ground and toppling forwards. If your shoulders, hamstrings, hips and back are tight then *of course* you're not going to be able to squat well.

Construct a program that will slowly but progressively improve the flexibility of your Achilles tendons, hamstrings, hips, back and shoulders. Diligently follow this program at least every other day. Stretching *after* your bodybuilding workout is the safest and quickest way to improve your flexibility. Together with the seven stretching exercises given in Chapter 11 you need additional work for your shoulders and Achilles tendons. Add the broomstick circling exercise described under *Positioning the bar* in this chapter and the heel raise exercise described under *Raising the heels*, also in this chapter.

While working on your flexibility, learn how to squat with an empty bar. Develop a good stance, posture and style. All of this takes time – be patient. It takes years to get a body inflexible – don't expect to correct things in just a couple of weeks. Only once you're flexible – and the squatting technique is sound, smooth and consistent – should you *slowly* add poundage while maintaining impeccable style. You'll then be able to squat well enough to benefit from squats. Once you're flexible, keep doing the flexibility program to maintain your flexibility.

For goodness sake don't start piling on the poundage before you've stretched out your body and before you've learned to squat with good style. If you're too impatient then of course you're going to hate the exercise, never be able to progress well with it and maybe injure yourself.

Follow the technique guidelines for the squat given in this book and search out someone in your neighborhood to supervise your learning of squatting technique. The body is designed by Nature to squat. It's neglect of the body's flexibility, and inappropriate training procedures, that cause the problems.

When learning how to squat safely and productively you must start with very light weights, and s–l–o–w–l–y add poundage to the bar. Ignore those who may deride the little weights you're using. Keep making small increments and, a couple of years later, when you're using big poundages and have transformed your physique, you'll have the last laugh.

No matter how difficult, at least initially, you may find it to squat, *don't* automatically abandon the regular squat. Following getting your body prepared for the squat, and then learning how to squat, you must continue to give great attention to technique. Combine this sound technique with rational routines, intensity cycling, avoidance of excessive low rep work, common sense, balanced development, experimentation and a ton of perseverance. *Doing all of this can perform near miracles.*

Some bodybuilders do have back or knee problems that prevent the use of the regular squat. These are usually incurred from contact sports, accidents or unwise training procedures. However, these people belong to a small minority of bodybuilders. As long as you can squat, and almost all of you can, squat on.

An inspiring example

Peary Rader, founder of <u>Iron Man</u>, back in the thirties, has been one of the most forceful and consistent advocates of the squat. He spent decades promoting the value of abbreviated routines and high repetition squatting with maximum poundages. It was this approach that transformed his body after having spent more than ten years fruitlessly trying other systems of exercise.

As described by Randall J. Strossen, Ph.D., (<u>Super Squats</u>, page 34), Peary Rader finally got into the 20–rep squat routine and built his strength and development against the odds. At only 128 pounds, and nearly 6', he started the program very thin and weak. He started the squat using only 35 pounds for ten reps and progressed to using more than 300 pounds for twenty reps (<u>Super Squats</u>, page 46). Inspiring stuff. In a year, he gained some eighty pounds. Another year later, he became a lifting champion. All this without modern dietary supplements.

His transformation wasn't an isolated case and it drove him on to promote the same message to all who were interested. Even in the final issues of <u>Iron Man</u> he continued to promote the undiluted message.

The knock-on effect

The squat not only directly affects the thigh, hip and lower back structure but has a knock-on effect throughout the body. The squat "anabolizes" the metabolism, making the whole body more likely to grow and get stronger. The squat by itself isn't going to pack inches of muscle onto your arms. However, good progress in the squat will make it far easier to push up poundages substantially in rows and bench presses. That will pack size onto your arms.

Without the squat and deadlift providing the "engine" for growth throughout the body, it becomes harder to get the rest of the body moving in size and strength.

With the squat and deadlift (regular style, stiff-legged or snatch grip) as the linchpins of a routine, the scene is set for big results. The drawback is the cost side. Squats, when done with as heavy poundage as possible for maximum reps, are brutally hard, as are deadlifts. With these two exercises you can come close to taking your own life with a barbell.

Cutting through the hype

Today's age is one of sophistication and the belief that if something isn't a new concoction – expensive and glamorized with a mountain of hype – it can't have much going for it. In the world of getting bigger and stronger there's little that's new. Most of what is claimed as new either isn't, or is just a derivation of something that's been around a long time. Watch out for misleading hype.

Squat hard and briefly – no more than twice a week. Combine this with only a handful of other exercises. Drink generously of milk if you need lots of extra calories – skimmed if you prefer. Eat lots of quality food. Rest and sleep as much as you can – get lazy. Do all this and you'll be unable to stop growing.

As old-fashioned and crude as this growth package may appear, it can pack on muscle today just as it did in decades gone by. Squats aren't the whole story, but they are a darned big part of it.

What about the other types of squat?

The squatting movement stressed here is the traditional back squat, not its inferior substitutes such as sissy squats and hack squats. The latter have their uses, for very advanced bodybuilders. However, the traditional back squat is in a *different league* for building substantial size and strength.

The value of a weight training exercise, for building size and strength, can be determined by its degree of discomfort when worked to the limit with *proper form*. (Abusive exercise form will exaggerate the discomfort but this isn't the type of discomfort that will make training more effective.) Sure, leg extensions when worked hard are tiring, as are the other small exercises, and generate a big ache and pump. This localized fatigue is small stuff compared to the enormous total body *and* localized fatigue that comes from a single set of properly done squats, especially high rep ones. Sissy squats and hack squats can be very tough to do, but still come second to the absolutely devastating effects of high rep regular squats.

Leg presses can get *very* uncomfortable. In the domain of high quality exercise machines, Nautilus and Hammer produce models that can provide masochists (the most determined bodybuilders) with ecstacy. The deadlift can successfully compete with the regular squat for the title of the masochist's favorite exercise.

How many people really pay their dues in the squat rack? Not so many. How many people are really big and impressive? Not so many.

If the squat just stimulated growth in the thighs, all this praise would be hyperbole. The squat directly involves all the main muscular structures of the body together with forcing heavy breathing and involving everything from the neck down to the toes. It's this total impact (when combined with adequate rest and food) that makes the squat a vital component in any program to stimulate big increases in size and strength.

Once you get the main muscular structures of the body growing, the rest of the body comes along far more easily. Once you can squat at least a rep or two with 400 pounds – and deadlift with more than 400 – your arms and shoulders will respond more receptively. Try to get big arms and shoulders while only being able to squat with 200 pounds and you'll be onto a loser.

Development of the leg, hip and back structure is the base for growth throughout the body. By training hard on the squat – whether for low, medium or high reps – you'll automatically experience a knock–on effect elsewhere. As the squat improves, so does the potential for growth everywhere else. If you want big arms and shoulders, your priority is to be sure that your hip, leg and back structure is growing and becoming powerful, closely followed by the upper–body pressing structure.

Developing the buttocks

Don't be put off by the thought of developing your buttocks, or "glutes" to use gym jargon. You need to develop your buttocks just as you need to develop your thighs, back and other body parts.

Flat and undeveloped buttocks look ridiculous on an otherwise well-developed body. If your thigh biceps (rear thighs) are flat and not developed enough, then your buttocks will appear bigger than they should. Develop your thigh biceps and then the development of your buttocks and thighs will be in proportion. If you keep your stiff-legged deadlift poundage near to your squatting poundage, your thigh biceps should be fine.

The snag

The drawback with the squat is that it's brutally hard when worked to its absolute limit, especially for high reps. Knowing this, many bodybuilders shirk the exercise, concocting many pretexts for not doing it. A popular one was the opinion that the exercise is dangerous for the knees. If the exercise is done safely, not only will the squat *not* damage the knees, it will actually do much to prevent knee injury.

The discomfort from full-bore squatting is plain awful. You've got to earn the benefits from squats by pushing yourself harder than you ever thought possible.

There's too much promotion today of comfortable methods of training and the near miracle effects of combinations of food supplements. While some food supplements may help you along a bit, there's no combination that can substitute for what has to be done in the gym. If you want to grow some substantial muscle, you'd better accept the need for some substantial discomfort and true gut-busting effort.

Sustaining motivation

Driving yourself to your limit week after week in the squat, or in any other exercise for that matter, will wear you out both physically and mentally. Too much, even of a good thing, can be detrimental. This is especially so of the key exercises.

Don't drive yourself into the ground with the squat more than twice a week. Many people, not just hard gainers but genetic mega-superiors, find that squatting just once a week is enough. If you work hard, and keep adding poundage, then you're progressing. If you can do this just squatting once a week, fine, it's working.

As has already been made abundantly clear, cycle your training intensity. On top of this, have short periods each year in which you don't use the regular squat. Have a break.

Another approach is to squat in the regular manner one thigh workout and then use a variation at alternate workouts. Some of the variations of the regular squat are more productive than others, with some of them being quality exercises.

Some of the squat variations come way behind in mimicking the bountiful benefits of the regular back squat. They do serve, however, to give the mind and thigh, back and hip structure a stimulating break from the brutal stuff. This prepares you to make the most of the next cycle with the regular squat.

A year's schedule of the squat and its variations could run like this:
1. Eighteen weeks of regular 20–rep squats with a slow poundage progression to ensure a good gain.
2. Eight weeks of front squats.
3. Nine weeks of bent–legged deadlift specialization.
4. Eight weeks of regular squats working up to a maximum single.
5. Five weeks of Gerard trap bar deadlifts/squats.

This totals forty–eight weeks. The outstanding four will be layoff weeks spread over the year. Each of the five cycles will start light for the first part, and work into the "taking your life with a barbell" style. The squatting frequency during each cycle will be determined by you. Just ensure that each cycle ends with the final weeks taking you into poundages you've never used before. While the deadlift is specialized upon in the third cycle, this isn't to say that the deadlift isn't done in the other cycles. In the third cycle the squat *isn't* done so that complete focus can be given to the deadlift.

Getting the most out of the squat

When you have the regular squat in your routine, learn how to minimize the discomfort. Some body structures are much more suited to squatting than are others. If you find it impossible to squat without leaning over a lot, your lower back is likely to be your weak link. This may be so even if you work hard on your deadlift as well.

Doing the good morning exercise in place of the full–range deadlift for a cycle or two may help to strengthen your back so it's better able to tolerate leaning over during the squat. Take the bar on your trapezius as if you're going to squat. Bend your legs a little, keep your back *flat* and slowly lower yourself until your back is parallel to the ground. As you bend forward, bend more at the knees so that when your torso is parallel to the floor your lower rib cage is against your thighs. As you slowly straighten up, lessen the bend at your knees but maintain a slight break.

Do this exercise between safety bars (like when squatting) so if you "lose" the exercise the bar can be caught on the safety bars. This exercise is *very* demanding, especially if you're not an experienced deadlifter or squatter. Start *very light*. Add weight slowly so it takes at least a month before you're working with the heaviest poundage you can, for the reps you're doing. Avoid very low reps here, keep them above six.

Doing partial deadlifts may be a better movement to condition your lower back. With this exercise you can load your back with weights bigger than you're squatting. Using a power rack, or resting the barbell on sturdy boxes, just do the top six inches or so of the deadlift, pulling with your back only – not involving the legs. Keep the back flat and start within your limits. Build up to working "hard," but *not* till failure. No pulling a final 10–15 second partial, no pausing with the weights in the upright position, and no hyperextension – don't abuse your back.

If you're conditioning yourself for low and medium rep squatting, work up to a top weight for about five reps no more than once a week, after the regular full–range deadlift. This might be too severe once you're working with your top poundages – consider reducing the partial deadlift to alternate deadlift workouts only. Build up the poundage over a cycle or two. Your back should then be better able to take the stress coming out of the bottom of a squat and may no longer be the weak link. Overdo it, and your back will be fatigued and you'll be weaker.

If you're conditioning yourself for 20–rep squatting, you might want to try this partial deadlifting with a lighter weight and twenty reps, with pauses between reps (taken in the upright position, but *without* any leaning back) as in the 20–rep squat. You need to experiment.

Positioning the feet

Of course you *have to* lean over when doing the regular back squat. You can only do an upright squat on a machine. Having your feet too close together, and the toes pointed straight forward, encourages excessive leaning over and the production of a modified "good morning" rather than a squat. A wider spacing of the feet, and toes pointed out, should improve squatting style. The longer are your femurs (thighbones), the more you should experiment with pointing your toes out. You also need flexible Achilles tendons, hamstrings and shoulders to adopt a good squatting position. Work on your flexibility if your squatting style is poor.

The starting placement, when learning to squat, is to have your heels 12–14 inches apart. If you're tall, or have wide hips, then more like 16–18 inches may be better, and some people go over 20 inches. As you become more flexible you can experiment more with positioning your feet to establish the most comfortable and efficient position you can.

Footwear

Don't squat in shoes with spongy soles or air in them – these aren't designed for heavy lifting and may cause you to lose your balance. Be sure you're solid and stable in your footwear.

Positioning the bar

Don't have the bar too high up on your neck. Lower it a little and you may find it more comfortable and safer. Experiment with placement until you find the most comfortable and effective position for you.

You may need to increase your shoulder flexibility before you can hold the bar lower down on your shoulders. Hold a broomstick in front of your thighs with a very wide grip, and keep your arms straight. Grip the bar lightly with your thumbs and first fingers. Keeping your arms straight, bring the bar over your head and then behind you as far as you can. Letting your palms face outward during the course of the exercise should make it more comfortable. The wider the grip during these dislocates, the easier the exercise. To progress in flexibility, gradually decrease the distance between your hands. Take your time with this exercise – don't force the exercise and injure yourself.

You may want to use some cushioning between the bar and your shoulders. Avoid using too much or else you'll find that the bar becomes unstable and likely to roll down your back. I've seen bodybuilders use two cushions in addition to the quarter of an inch compressed foam already around the bar. The bar almost ends up tottering around on a tripod on the lifters' backs. All of this with little more than bodyweight on the bar. The compressed foam alone should be adequate so long as you have the bar properly placed on your back. If you have the bar in the right position, and if you have some trapezius development, you may prefer not having any padding around the bar.

Grip the bar some 6–8 inches or so wider than shoulder grip. An extremely narrow grip puts great stress on the elbows; a very wide grip can leave you without much control of the bar. If you wrap your arms around the plates themselves, you can't be squatting with any intensity or even with any seriousness.

When you're setting yourself up under the bar, in the rack or stands, be sure you have the bar centered on your trapezius. Be sure your hands are evenly spaced. If you use padding on the bar, be sure it's centered on the bar before you take it on your shoulders.

When you've taken the bar on your trapezius, back away from the stands just enough so you're not going to hit the stands as you squat. Don't take so many steps back that you tire yourself and mar the set to follow. Also, don't wait so long with the bar on your back that you tire yourself.

Cambered squatting bar

Some people find that a cambered squatting bar makes the squat a great deal less uncomfortable – those who have long femurs, for example. Probably everyone will find it an advantage to some degree. The bend in the center of the bar allows the bar to drape over the shoulders with less discomfort, akin to the old milkmaid's yoke. The cambered squatting bar also makes it harder for the bar to roll up the trapezius if the hips rise too quickly during the recovery in the squat.

While it makes sense to make the squat as least uncomfortable as possible, you can't make muscle–building squats comfortable. If the squat ever becomes easy, it becomes useless for producing size and strength gains.

A cambered squatting bar is a rarity today, though it was common before World War II. The cambered bar you may be visualizing is one that's like a regular bar except that in the middle area the bar has four near right angles in it. This is a bench press cambered bar, designed to permit a very deep bench press. If you use this bar, take great care as it may injure you because of the exaggerated range of movement.

A cambered squatting bar is very different. The dimensions of such a bar are provided by Randall J. Strossen, Ph.D., on page 80 of his first–rate book, <u>Super Squats</u>.

> Chester O. Teegarden used to make the Rolls–Royce of cambered bars: He bent a 7–1/2 foot length of 1–3/4 inch round steel bar in five places to produce a 4–inch arc. One foot on either end of the bar was turned down to 1–1/16 inch, to fit exercise plates; and the ends were bent up to keep the plates on a level bar without requiring collars. The bar was balanced and weighed 50 pounds when finished.

(Quotation used with permission of the publisher of <u>Super Squats</u>, IronMind® Enterprises, Inc.)

Much of the information in this section on the cambered bar comes from <u>Super Squats</u>.

20–rep squatting modification

If you can't get into 20–rep squats because your back continually fails before your legs do, you need to compromise. I'm assuming you're already tried conditioning your back using a couple of cycles of the partial deadlifts mentioned earlier in this chapter. I'm also assuming you've tried a couple of cycles of front squats – see later in this chapter. The problem may not be so much with the back getting tired during the actual squatting, but during the rest pause between reps. To do heavy high rep squats it's necessary to pause for a few breaths between each pair of reps – the rest pause. This enables you to ready yourself for the next rep.

For the first ten reps or so you can probably manage with 2–4 deep breaths between reps. For the final reps of a 20–rep set you may be taking ten or more breaths between reps. It's at this stage that you'll know what really hard work is about. You'll discover just how much control you have over pushing an exhausted and protesting body.

If you use a lighter weight, you can progress through the set while taking shorter pauses between reps. This compromise will almost certainly reduce the overall effectiveness of the movement because the poundage isn't taxing enough.

A better compromise is to add poundage and settle for ten reps a set. You can get a highly productive effect from medium rep squats if you're driving yourself (within the context of cycling) to handle as much poundage as possible for the reps. You only have nine rest pauses in this set, and the duration of the set is shorter than in a 20–rep set, though of course you have more poundage on your back. This should enable you to get through the set without the lower back becoming the single most limiting factor. To compensate for the drop of reps – relative to the 20–rep set – rest a few minutes and do a second full–bore set. Cut the poundage back by about fifty pounds for this second set.

Raising the heels

After you've tried different widths of stance, with the toes pointed outward a little (15–20 degrees, or more for some people – experiment), use a board under your heels *only* if you have trouble with balance and flexibility. Wean yourself off the board by using a thinner piece every few weeks until you can manage with just the heel of your training shoe. Work at increasing the flexibility of your Achilles tendons. Do all–the–way–down one–legged heel raises holding a dumbbell on the same side as the leg being exercised. Progressively, and *carefully*, increase the stretch until you're flexible in the ankles.

Just taking your bodyweight on a fully stretched (all the way down) Achilles tendon will help too. Rock very *gently* in the low position. Do this several times for each tendon three times a week. All of this will eventually help you to squat in good style and without a block, board or something else under your heels.

Some trainees who have always used a thick block of wood under their heels need to make some adjustments to get off the block. They need to increase their flexibility, work into a wider stance and stop having their feet parallel to each other. The benefits of this are that the body mechanics will then be in a more advantageous and "solid" position. This will permit squatting with heavier weights in a safe and productive way. Raising the heels, and squatting with the bar very high on the neck, can put the lower back (and knees) at greater risk of injury.

Depth of squatting

Go down to the point where the tops of the *upper* thighs are at or just below parallel with the ground. At this parallel position that's pretty low. To go much lower puts a great deal more stress on the lower back muscles. This could cause squatting failure through just back exhaustion rather than the combined exhaustion of leg, hip and back muscles. There are better ways of training the lower back muscles than extremely deep squatting with the bar on the traps.

You need to be sure you're squatting to the right depth. Using a very light weight, squat side–on to a mirror and get the feel of where you need to be to have the tops of your thighs parallel to the ground. Then get yourself in your power rack or squat stands and find a way of assessing the depth of your squat without having to look at your thighs. A training partner can help.

Personally, I know I have to squat until the bar (straight bar) is within one inch of touching the safety bars I squat between. A taller person may need to descend until the bar is a couple of inches higher. If you use a cambered bar, the ends of the bar will descend to a lower position than with a straight bar.

When you squat, regardless of what bar you use, ask someone in the gym to keep an eye on you and let you know as soon as you cut a squat even by quarter of an inch.

Bench squats

If you squat over a bench or box, touching it or even sitting on it, you may damage your spine. Each time your buttocks touch the bench, your spine compresses slightly. While a very *light* touch might not cause any problems, a deliberate pause on the bench is another matter. If you "lose" the squat and actually hit the bench instead of lightly touching it, the shock to your spine, let alone your knees, may be severe.

If you sit on the bench for several seconds, setting yourself up for the next ascent, you might regret it. Better to do your squats in a power rack, having set the pins so the bar rests on them in the thighs–parallel–to–the–ground position. You can start your ascent from a dead stop in the power rack without having the potentially dangerous effects of compression when doing dead stop squats from a bench or box.

Lifting belt

Very few people have back conditions that necessitate the use of a belt. Let your body condition itself to squatting and you'll develop your own lifting belt in the form of strong abdominal and lower back muscles. For medium and high repetition squats, as made clear in <u>Super Squats</u>, you'll find that wearing a belt is very uncomfortable. It inhibits breathing, digs into your middle and doesn't prevent back fatigue.

When doing low rep work, and especially *very* low rep work, you may want to use a good lifting belt (not one of the fashionable non-functional ones). It *is* necessary if you're preparing for a powerlifting contest. If you've no intention of competing in powerlifting, and have never used a belt much if at all, you can lift your top weights without needing to consider using a belt.

The modern gym has fostered this notion that you can't squat (or curl, or bench, or even do lateral raises) without wearing a belt. Bodybuilders have become conditioned to believe they will hurt their backs if they don't use a belt. They don't realize that the belts they use, and the way they use them, don't provide much if any protection anyway. It's all in their minds.

If you do plan to compete in powerlifting contests, in addition to a lifting belt you'll need to be familiar with the use of knee wraps, a bench press shirt and a squatting suit near to the date of the contest. Otherwise, you'll be at a disadvantage.

Knees

Keep your knees out as you descend, and keep them out as you rise. The kneecaps should line up on the same plane as the feet. "Buckling in" the knees as you rise out of the squat is a common mistake. While you can still progress well doing it this way, your long–term progress and knee health will be much better if you keep your knees out as you rise.

Cut back the poundage – start a new cycle with moderate poundages – and become obsessed with keeping your knees out. Never let a single rep have you buckling your knees in. If you start off moderately, and slowly build up the poundage, you'll be able to keep the knees where they belong. But you must have your stance wide enough and your toes flared enough to "lock" your knees out. You will need to experiment here to find the best positioning for you.

If you jump up the poundage too quickly you'll drop back into your knees–in style. It takes time to correct this. It's like learning to squat with a flat back. Start light and never let your back round even once as you build back the poundage. Similarly, never let yourself bow your knees in even once while slowly notching up the poundage increments.

Form

The squat is a complex exercise. Learn to do it properly. Invest the time. Develop good technique *before* you start to work with the heaviest poundages you can handle. Unless your style is well-learned and secure, it will collapse once you start to use as much poundage as you can. The criticism that the squat sometimes receives usually arises from two points. First, most gym members (and instructors) simply don't know *how* to squat. Second, of those who try to learn, most don't invest enough time and patience to learn to squat properly. They are unable to maintain good style when building up the poundage.

"Sit" into the squat while sticking your chest out and keeping your shoulders back. Concentrating on these points, during *every* rep, will help you to avoid leaning forward excessively. Keep the stress of the weight travelling through the center of your feet. If the stress travels through your toes you're in danger of toppling forward.

Rise out of the squat faster than you lowered into it. *Don't* collapse so you can bounce out of the low position. While not collapsing, this doesn't mean that you should pause at the parallel position.

Use the tension at the bottom of the descent to help you to drive the bar up. Lower the bar under control, without exaggerated slowness, until you reach the bottom position and *immediately* begin your explosion out of it. Drive yourself up in good form. While rising from the squat, maintain proper body position throughout the movement. Don't keep accelerating to the top position – don't crash into the locked-out position.

Never hold your breath as you drive yourself up. Exhale during a big exertion, always. Between reps, breathe *deeply*, *forcefully* and *noisily*.

The hip and leg muscles are prime movers for the upward movement. Focus on keeping your back flat while driving up with your legs, pushing your hips forward and driving your shoulders up. Trying to drive your shoulders up keeps the bar in place on your shoulders and helps prevent you from toppling over. The thrust from your legs and hips gets you moving up.

As you rise out of the squat, your shoulders need to move at least as quickly as your hips. If your hips get ahead, you'll start to fall forward. You may have the back strength to save the lift, but if you don't you'll lose the squat. This is an effective way of injuring your back if you're not conditioned for this style of squatting. Some powerlifters intentionally have their hips initially rising ahead of their shoulders. They trained for this style of lifting and have the necessary back strength. Forget about this style of performance until you're already moving big poundages and are thinking of lifting competitively.

Relative to the powerlifting competition squat, the bodybuilding style of squatting doesn't have the bar quite as low on the back, uses more leg and less hip strength, and doesn't use a very wide stance.

As you come to the sticking point of the ascent, push up hard on the bar with your arms as if doing a press behind neck, and blast out the air from your lungs. This will help to get you through the sticking point.

It's safest to avoid both rounding and arching the back. In other words, keep the back flat, though of course it will be tilted forward. Avoid throwing your head back as you rise from the low position, though you must drive the shoulders up as you rise.

Looking up as you rise is the traditional advice, aimed at avoiding humping of the back and the squatter losing balance and falling forward. Having your eyes looking up is one thing, vigorously throwing your head back is another. The drawback with not at least looking forward as you rise is that there's a tendency to shift the weight onto the front of the feet, causing the hips to rise too rapidly and the squatter to fall forward.

During the pause between repetitions, *don't* shift or rock the bar. *Don't* sway or rock at the hips. *Don't* take most of the stress on one leg so you can give the other leg a shake. *Don't* round your back between reps – keep "tight" at all times. *Don't* reposition your hands or try to reposition the bar on your trapezius – put it back in the rack or stands, rest, and reposition it before re-starting the set.

It's easy to forget technique pointers as time passes. To prevent this, regularly revise sections of this chapter.

Safety

Never squat to failure without safety devices set just below the point at which your upper thighs are parallel to the ground. The only exception is if you have two strong spotters ready to take the weights off you, if necessary. It's ideal to have both safety devices *and* spotters, to give you the confidence, and encouragement, to really go to failure.

Poundage progression

One of the central points coming out of this book is the need to add poundage slowly. This point is stressed many times. It's so important it's worthy of a book devoted to it. If you add weight to the bar too quickly you can do many things – "kill" the gaining momentum of a training cycle, "kill" good form, "kill" training enthusiasm, and injure yourself. This is especially so in the squat because the exercise is so hard to do with limit poundages for whatever repetition range you're using.

It's *always* better to be conservative and to add less, and to add it less often. This ensures more sustained gaining periods, less sticking points and better adaptation to training. Patience is a virtue in training as in many other things.

I've been guilty in the past of piling on the weight too quickly in a cycle, and of advising others to do the same. All this in the desire to get to the growth producing workouts as quickly as possible. While the enthusiasm is good, its application isn't.

An example of this is the opinion, "Take a weight you can squat ten reps with and force yourself to get twenty." If you do this, your squatting cycle will end almost immediately. You'll be finished off before you've barely started, both physically and psychologically. It should be qualified to something like this: "In the second half of your 20–rep squatting cycle it will appear to an onlooker that you're finished at ten reps, but you continue the set to force out the full twenty."

Start off light, being able to manage comfortably the full twenty repetitions. Add weight slowly, conditioning your body to sustain a long productive cycle. This is miles more productive than "killing" yourself in the first few workouts of a cycle and giving up.

As an example, suppose that with a lot of encouragement and bullying you can eke out twenty repetitions with 220 pounds in the squat. If you start there you might get to 230 or 235 but that's it. You might not get beyond 225. Better to start with 170 and train twice a week, adding five pounds a workout, until you get to 200 pounds. This will take you three weeks. Then change to three times every two weeks and add 2½ pounds every workout. It will take you eight workouts or nearly six more weeks to get to 220x20.

Now, add 2½ (or even 1¼) pounds once a week, perhaps training only once every 5–7 days now. At this rate you should be able to get to 250 or even more before the long cycle "dries up." If you reduce the progression even more, after you get to around the 235 mark, you might be able to build up to an even bigger final poundage.

How many reps to squat?

Some of the bad press that the squat has received (and the deadlift) has been due to these exercises being thought of purely as powerlifts. They are then associated with low reps. Exclusive low rep work will deny you of much of the gains that medium and high rep work can yield. Excessive low rep work will likely leave you far more open to injuries than does medium and high rep work.

When doing very low rep work, the margin for technique error is very small. A slight slip can be injurious. When doing much higher reps it's always possible to "pull in" (as Dr. Ken Leistner has described it) any technique error and not get injured.

This isn't to say that low rep work should never be done. Low rep work is a must for powerlifters, both in the final stages of a peaking cycle and for strength building purposes, and very useful for advanced bodybuilders.

Low rep work, used prudently by those qualified to use it, adds variety to a year's training and will enable you to register your absolute maximum single once or twice a year. Chapter 13 has detail on how to benefit from single–rep (90–95% of maximum) training for a whole cycle. Fastidious attention to flawless technique and perfect safety considerations are paramount during very low rep work.

If it's strength *and* muscular size you're interested in, stick to medium and high reps. Use six as the minimum, and up to twenty or more if your lower back can keep up with it. You can obtain good results from several rep schemes if you give forth of your full effort when it's called for. Remember, how you do the reps is more important than the number of reps. Changing the rep scheme used, from cycle to cycle, is one way of sustaining variety and motivation.

If you can't squat productively

Some people simply can't squat, in the regular fashion, in a safe and productive manner. As long as this is the real situation – not a pretext to avoid the discomfort of regular squatting – it's wise to use modifications, *always*. With a history of orthopedic problems or unusually disadvantageous leverages (very long femurs in proportion to the upper body), the traditional squat may be unproductive.

Knee or lower back injury – sustained through contact sport or accident – can put the regular squat out of reach for some people. Very tall people may not be able to do this movement with the type of poundage that their actual strength levels demand.

The following variations of squatting are given for two reasons:

> i. To provide safe and productive alternatives for those who are physically unable to squat productively with a barbell over their shoulders. This generally means squatting movements that don't have the weight bearing upon the upper back.

> ii. To provide variations for those who can do regular squats productively but who would like to use variations to avoid going stale on the regular squat.

Deadlift

The bent–legged deadlift is an excellent movement that can substitute for the squat, especially for tall and very thin neophytes. These bodybuilders often have an easier time pulling a weight than squatting it. The bent–legged deadlift and squat work similar muscle masses. Some people will be better off working hard (after a break–in period) on the bent–legged deadlift while learning to squat. Spend months perfecting a squatting style and getting yourself flexible enough, while simultaneously building up your deadlift poundage. You'll then have laid the groundwork and development to be able to benefit from hard work on the squat itself. (In Chapter 11 there are detailed instructions on how to perform the bent–legged deadlift.)

The bent–legged deadlift can be worked like the squat is in the 20-rep squat routine. Avoid using a close grip when doing high rep deadlifts so as to reduce the compression from the arms upon the rib cage as the poundage gets heavy. Work the deadlift in a rest–pause manner, working it hard once a week. (You can work it more frequently at the start of the cycle when the intensity isn't high.) If you're an extreme hard gainer, either work the squat hard and the deadlift lightly, or deadlift hard and squat lightly. Working hard on them both may, temporarily, be too much if you're having a very hard time gaining.

Hip belt squat

With a hip belt you can squat without concern for your back caving in. Also, you can squat without the breathing discomfort that accompanies high rep squats with a bar over your shoulders. If you can't make the final rep, just let the plates rest on the floor and crawl away. As with the other variations of squatting, if you work hard at it, and build up to respectable poundages, you'll grow. However, this exercise usually necessitates using a 2" board under the heels – raising the heels while squatting can cause or trigger off knee trouble so be very careful and don't continue with it if you start to get knee trouble.

The Douglass Squat Circle

This device was invented by the late James E. Douglass and has been raved over by some of its users, including J. C. Hise, a pioneer in the use of intense abbreviated programs headed by the heavy breathing squat. Douglass' prototype (the Douglass Harness) consisted of a rectangular frame supported by straps over the shoulders. Weights were loaded on the frame. His later model used a circular frame.

Peary Rader sold this design for many years, through Iron Man, under the name of the Magic Circle. The new name was an indication of how highly Rader rated the invention. It made the squat a more productive exercise for those who couldn't tolerate the pain of a bar digging into the upper back and the crushing effect upon the lower back. A more upright squatting position could be maintained and the back became much less of a weak link. It also altered the mechanics of the squat, making the exercise more efficient for those lacking good leverages.

Of course, the device itself is useless unless coupled with the extraordinary effort and persistence needed to build up to using impressive poundages. Removing the negative discomforting factors of squatting is desirable, but the discomfort from intense squats can't be avoided if you want to gain from the exercise. Savor this discomfort from effort. The more you can stand, the more you're going to gain.

The Douglass Squat Circle has been given another lease of life (as have the cambered bar and hip belt) by IronMind® Enterprises, Inc, P.O. Box 1228, Nevada City, CA 95959, USA. It's being marketed under the name of the Douglass/SUPER SQUATS Circle ".

The sections on the hip belt squat and the Douglass Squat Circle are based on information contained in Dr. Randall J. Strossen's Super Squats and in conversations with Dr. Strossen.

Leg press

This can be a good exercise though the machine used and manner of execution are important. Many leg press machines are not safe. They provide unacceptable shearing forces upon the patella tendon and/or unacceptable compressive forces on the lumbar spine area.

However, if you have access to well designed leg press machines such as those from Hammer and Nautilus, among others, the damaging forces are reduced. Providing the exercise is done through a complete range of movement, and done with the right degree of effort, it will be productive.

Dumbbell squat

By holding the two dumbbells in your hands (with straps) you may find the altered distribution of the training load makes the squat a safer and more productive exercise. There's no longer a bar over the trapezius, and the stress upon the lower back is reduced.

Gerard trap bar squat/deadlift

The trap bar is the brainchild of Al Gerard, designed to make deadlift movements safer and more comfortable when handling heavy weights. It has a rhombus fixed to the plate–loading ends. The gripping sites on the trap bar are parallel to one another and inside the rhombus. This can make holding onto the bar less of a problem than when using a regular bar. (The trap bar can be mimicked by holding dumbbells at the sides of your legs, with hands parallel to each other.) The trap bar decreases the distance between the lifter and weight. This improves balance and leverage, and makes deadlifting more efficient and less stressful on the knees and spine. The bar doesn't tend to move forward as the bar is pulled and it doesn't have to be dragged up the thighs.

You stand inside the bar while doing your squats, deadlifts and shrugs. Your squats will look more like bent–legged deadlifts. You can call the movement simply a trap bar deadlift – the name isn't important. The effect of the exercise is what matters. To increase the range of motion, and give the thighs more work, do the exercise while standing on a block. Experiment with the height, starting with a thin block.

When doing the movement, Gerard's recommendation is not to pull on the handles but to focus on trying to push the feet through the floor. Wrist straps or even hooks may be necessary to be able to hold onto the bar with a heavy weight, especially for high rep work.

Though the bar is no longer above your chest, there will be some pressure on your ribs from the weight pulling on your arms. This may obstruct breathing somewhat during high rep heavy work.

The trap bar is a very useful piece of equipment for exercises other than the deadlift variations, particularly shrugging movements. Also, as pointed out by Paul Kelso, unless you have very wide shoulders you can do overhead presses with it, but not bench presses. It also can be used for a variation of the upright row.

Front squat

Some people find it difficult to control the weight as it sits on the chest or across the shoulders. There's the chance of having the bar fall out of position. The problem here isn't the exercise per se, but that the exercise isn't being done correctly. Some bodybuilders find that the shearing force in the knee area makes it a disagreeable exercise.

Let's look at the other side of the argument. There have been many bodybuilders and lifters who have used this exercise with care, good form and without injuries. They have benefitted greatly from the front squat. Mike Thompson even has his charges periodically focusing on the front squat in order to improve their ability to do the regular squat once they have the latter back in their routines.

The front squat is well suited for squatting all the way down until the thighs fold over the calves. The knees are kept quite wide apart during the course of the exercise. The maintenance of the bar at the front of the shoulders keeps the torso in a more upright position relative to having the bar pushing down on the traps as in the regular squat.

When learning to front squat, the key point is control. Control of holding the bar in position and control over the squatting movement – no bouncing whatsoever at the bottom of the squat. The key to learning the exercise well is to start light and progress slowly and carefully.

A thin block under the heels may make the learning of the exercise easier. As with the regular squat, weaning off the block is a sound idea. There is a bodybuilding tradition of doing the front squat (and other types of squats) with heels on a block to shift more of the stress of the exercise to the lower thighs. As noted under the *Hip belt squat*, raising the heels while squatting can injure the knees – at least in some people – so proceed with great caution unless you have very robust knees.

The elbows must be kept high, cushioning the bar on the front deltoids. Initially, the hands may be crossed over the bar. As the style becomes consolidated, a slightly–wider–than–shoulder–width overhand grip can be used to hold the increasing poundages. As Dr. Strossen told me:

> You don't need a death–grip on the bar as the weight is supported by the shoulder girdle. In fact, many top Olympic lifters front squat with the bar on the very tips of their fingers (to reduce wrist strain) and that's what I recommend for people who find it difficult to clench the bar tightly. Arm strength isn't involved at all in achieving correct position, although flexibility is.

The elbows must still be kept high. This necessitates flexible arms and a strong upper body "holding" structure. This strength and flexibility will come as long as you're patient and persistent, adding weight slowly, always holding perfect form.

Work up to maximum working poundages over months, not weeks, if you're new to the exercise. While working into the front squat, do the regular squat too. Once you're very near to your top working poundages in the front squat – squatting between safety devices of some sort – then drop the regular squat and focus on the front squat. After a cycle or two on this lift, work back into the regular squat (together with maintenance front squatting) over a cycle and you should end the cycle with more iron on your traps than ever before.

Rising from the rock bottom squatting position in the front squat forces the lower back to greater heights of conditioning. That will help you in all "real" leg and back exercises, especially in helping your back to withstand the stress from 20–rep squatting.

A final point, stressed by Dr. Strossen, concerns safety. You absolutely *must* keep your elbows clear of your knees when you front squat. If you don't, and should you have to dump the bar during the exercise, you may hit an elbow on a knee and sustain a serious wrist injury. Develop good safe habits right from the start.

One-legged squat

Stand on your right leg on a *stable* bench or platform. Hold something fixed and secure with your left hand to keep your balance. The left leg is kept out in front or, if you're on a high enough bench or platform, the non-exercising leg can hang loose. Squat with your right leg, only using your supporting hand for help at the end of the set. The procedure will be reversed when working the left leg. Once you're used to the exercise, hold a dumbbell on the same side as the exercising leg.

This exercise may be awkward to do initially. When you've built up to using fair sized dumbbells, you'll find it a very productive exercise. It's a good exercise if you don't have access to a gym for a while and want to get a good thigh workout without formal equipment.

Other variations

If you need to experiment further to find something better suited to your individual structural limitations, try step-ups while holding dumbbells. But avoid crashing your leading foot onto the ground. *Do not*, however, squat in the Smith machine. This machine corrupts the squat because it forces you into an unnatural pathway, and adds shear stress to your knees due to the reaction force from your feet pushing forward on the floor. It can also put your lower back at increased risk.

If you're unable to do the regular squat, you must make *every* effort to find some movement that severely stimulates the thighs and hips. If you don't, your progress - not only in your legs and hips - will be severely hampered.

Poundage comparisons across some squat variations

To get an idea of the poundage comparisons for the regular squat, front squat, hip belt squat, cambered bar squat and the Douglass Squat Circle, I consulted Dr. Strossen:

> Here are some order of magnitude squat weight comparisons. Figure on 50% (or even less) of your barbell back squat weight for hip belt squats, at least when starting off. I can tell you some funny stories about honest 400-500 pound Olympic style back squatters who couldn't do 200 on the hip belt squat to

save their lives. Figure on about 110 or 115% of your back squat weight for the Douglass Squat Circle. Add a couple of percent or so of your back squat for cambered bar squats, and cut your back squat weight about 10 or 15% for front squats. When I say "back squat," I mean an honest, high bar, no wraps, medium stance, below parallel squat. No Mickey Mouse powerlifting stuff.

Rib cage enlargement?

Squats, especially when done with maximum poundage for medium or high reps, produce extremely heavy breathing. There's a strong tradition of doing light, straight–arm pullovers immediately after each of these sets of squats. The traditional opinion is that rib cage size can be increased by this work, and when the rib cage expands so does the future growth potential of the body. The rib cage, according to this traditional view, is one of the growth stimulation areas. The rib cage is what the upper body sits on – with a bigger stage you get a bigger body to set on it.

The combining of pullovers with the squat, to increase the size of the thorax, is regarded as a myth by some. This opinion argues that the only way to increase overall chest measurement is by increasing bodyweight, as for every other body part.

This opinion argues that the full ventilation during pullovers following squats induces a feeling of fullness in the lungs and chest. Despite this feeling of growth and expansion, no change occurs in the bones of the ribs, and the cartilage neither thickens nor lengthens to increase chest measurement.

This argument continues that there's no documented or proven evidence that it was the pullovers themselves that delivered increased bodyweight or chest measurement. Whenever anyone trains hard on the squat, and gains a lot of weight, of course the chest will increase in size. The pullovers, the argument continues, were coincidental, not causative.

As Paul Kelso has written, while it might not be academically proven that the rib cage can be enlarged by exercise, neither is it proven that it can't be. The anecdotal evidence in favor of rib cage enlargement is extensive.

My opinion is that the rib cage *can* be enlarged – I believe mine has been. Rib cage enlargement increases back and chest width, and deepens your chest when viewed from the side. Don't neglect working your rib cage.

Doing the pullover in a safe manner can do you no harm, but it may do you a lot of good. So do it. To be sure the pullover is done safely, the recommendation of Dr. Joseph Horrigan is to lie lengthwise on a bench – not across it. He believes that doing the pullover across a bench, with the hips low, puts damaging stress upon the abdominal wall. Keep the elbows slightly unlocked and the weight no more than 20 pounds. The stress is upon breathing and stretching, not moving a heavy poundage. Be sure to work the abdominals with crunch style exercises to keep those muscles in strong shape.

The Rader chest pull is a famous chest–builder in the tradition of the pullover, building the chest from within – making the rib cage bigger. Many bodybuilders believe it to be a more effective rib cage expander than the pullover.

Peary Rader, in <u>The Rader Master Bodybuilding and Weight Gaining System</u> advised grasping a solid object at slightly above the top of the head, with hands no more than three inches apart. (You can experiment with a slightly lower position.) Stand back from the object. Take a deep breath and, at the same time, pull down and *in* with the arms. Peary Rader stressed the importance of not contracting the abdominal muscles. Keep them relaxed. All this should raise your chest and produce a "pull" in the sternum.

Take it easy the first few workouts. Once you get to grips with it you can feel a tremendous stretching effect in your rib cage. It may take a while to get the exercise right. Persist, even if to begin with it doesn't feel right. This exercise can be done everyday, not just when you're in the gym.

If anything is going to stretch your rib cage, combining the Rader chest pull with heavy breathing squats (and deadlifts) will.

Whatever you do, *squat on*. Savor the discomfort of the squat. There are millions of people in hospital beds that would give almost anything to be able to "suffer" with the squat. The squat is one of the greatest allies you have in your quest for muscle. Exploit it to the full!

That steroids are so widespread today among all levels of bodybuilders — is testimony to the barrenness of popular training methods for building up the genetically great without steroids, these methods just don't work.

Split routines for hard gainers don't spread a high volume of work over the week. They stagger a low to medium volume of work over more workouts. Each multi-joint exercise might by worked only once a week.

When you're already big and strong, you need more force to take you to a new state of strength and development... a power...

That steroids are so widespread today –
among all levels of bodybuilders – is
testimony to the barrenness of popular
training methods for building up the
genetically typical. Without steroids, those
methods just don't work.

Split routines for hard gainers don't spread
a high volume of work over the week. They
stagger a low to medium volume of work
over more workouts. Each multi–joint
exercise might be worked only *once* a week.

When you're *already* big and strong, you
need other tools to take you to new levels
of strength and development. The power
rack is one of these tools.

10: Routines

If you've turned to this chapter first, stop. Turn back to the first page and start at the beginning. You'll get little out of this chapter until you've made the rest of the book an integral part of you – especially the six chapters preceding this one.

The lists of exercises that follow count for nothing unless each is acted upon in the full understanding of everything else written in this book. If your understanding of training has only been in the mainstream of bodybuilding thought, the routines in this chapter may appear too radical. Start at the beginning of the book and get the full story.

Everything written here has to be put into practice in the best way that suits you. It's you that finalizes the precise interpretation of intensity cycling, training frequency and degree of abbreviation of the routine. I can't fix these factors for you. You have to take what I provide as general recommendations and fine–tune them to fit your own individual circumstances, limitations and facilities.

A list of exercises, sets and reps is powerless. You must bring it to life. You must marry the routine – individually tailored – with all the persistence, effort, dedication and intelligence promoted in this book.

The effectiveness of a routine is a result of a whole *package* of considerations. The actual list of exercises is but one consideration. What follows is but a *sample* of potentially productive routines. (Chapters 12 and 13 have more routines.) Once you understand what you're doing, you'll begin to learn what suits you best. You can then go on to compose your own routines according to the circumstances of the time.

Lest you should forget

The message coming from this book is that typical bodybuilders must not imitate the training methods of a gifted minority.

Typical bodybuilders have a lot of trouble – usually an *insurmountable* amount of trouble – when trying to gain on the popular routines. This doesn't mean that easy gainers won't respond to training on simple, basic and infrequent routines. Of course they will, and respond dramatically. Some of the most gifted bodybuilders are learning this lesson and have cut back on their volume and frequency of training.

Equipment

The routines in this chapter have been composed considering that readers at least have access to a free-loading barbell, lots of plates (including the tiny ones), sturdy squat stands and safety devices (or power rack), a strong bench, parallel bars for dips, and an overhead pulley or pullup (chinning) bar. The emphasis is upon strong and practical equipment. Don't even think about using shoddy, flimsy gear.

Even with an absolute minimum of a barbell, a bench, stands and safety devices you can transform yourself. This is adequate for meeting the primary needs to pull, push and squat. All the big basic lifts are either pulling, squatting (lower-body pushing) or upper-body pushing movements – the fundamental exercise planes. As long as you're working hard on these three basic movements, and keeping exercises to the minimum, you're on the right lines.

More equipment, if properly used, can be very helpful. A set of dumbbells (including heavy ones), Hammer and Nautilus equipment (among some others), can provide quality alternative movements. Feel free to make wise substitutions – *not additions* – in the following routines. However, *never let inviting equipment distract you from the progress you must make with the big basic barbell exercises.* So often, the usefulness of a gym is *inversely* proportional to the variety of equipment it has to titillate members with.

How to perform a routine

The easier and most common interpretation is to do warmup work followed by the "work" set(s) for each single movement. For example, take the stiff-legged deadlift: 135x5, ninety seconds rest, 200x4, ninety seconds rest, 250 to one rep short of failure, two minutes rest then 250 to one rep short of absolute failure while trying to get two thirds or more of the reps of the previous set. (Some multiple-set schemes need more than two "work" sets.) Take two minutes rest and then do the warmup set(s) and "work" sets for the next exercise, et cetera.

The length of rest between sets is influenced by the exercise you're doing. You need more rest after a hard set of squats or bent-legged deadlifts than you need after a hard set of calf raises.

The "blood and guts" interpretation of these routines (and the quickest way to get through a routine) gets you warmed up for every exercise in one go. (It also gives you a terrific cardiorespiratory workout.) Do all your warmup work after your abdominal work. Rest ninety seconds or less between sets and then quickly set up all the poundages for the exercises to follow. Then, do all your top effort sets one after the other, almost back-to-back.

If each set is taken to the limit, and you don't rest between exercises any longer than it takes you to crawl to the next exercise, then little can match this training interpretation for severity.

If sets are extended beyond regular failure, using techniques such as drop sets, forced reps and negatives, this is amongst the absolute hardest of hard training. Being so very hard, it has to be used with absolute prudence or else it will overtrain you very quickly. With the back–to–back style of training, if you do any more than a single set to failure for an exercise, just rest a maximum of one minute between those sets, perhaps reducing the poundage for the repeat set.

If you're new to training your top sets back–to–back, consider breaking into it gradually in order to develop the high degree of conditioning that's needed. Start by resting two minutes between sets and cut the rest period by ten seconds each week. By the end of a ten week cycle you'll be training almost in the back–to–back method. For your following cycle, train in the strict back–to–back style.

Both interpretations can deliver impressive results, with each having its merits and demerits. The longer the rest period between sets and exercises, the bigger the poundages you can use. By training, for example, squats and stiff–legged deadlifts back–to–back the latter will suffer in terms of poundage used. This can still build size though, if you use as much poundage as you can for the reps you're doing.

Experiment with different ways of (rationally) interpreting routines, perhaps finally settling on a handful of constructions. Vary which one you use from cycle to cycle, according to the conditions at present.

Suppose you know that over the next few months you're going to be over–worked at your employment together with having many family commitments. Knowing that you're not going to be at your best in the gym, select two or more minutes of rest between sets. This will enable you to maintain high intensity sets though the pace of workout isn't fast.

If you know the next few months are going to provide good recovery and rest, with no over–work outside of the gym, throw yourself into the back–to–back interpretation. Discover what you can do with it. At other times, perhaps train with just one minute between sets and exercises. If you're on a strength peaking cycle you'll rest as much as five minutes between your heavy sets, and even longer sometimes.

Another way to perform a routine is using super slow protocol. This is described in Chapter 13.

Make your plans, and stick to them. If you settle on one minute rests for the next cycle, or training back–to–back, stick to it. If you decide to use heavier poundages, fixing say three minutes between sets, be sure your rest periods are exactly that. If you decide to try super slow, resolve to master the procedure and then give it a fair try.

Being orderly like this will enable you to do justice to your plans and enable you to evaluate, after the cycle is completed, the success or otherwise of whatever you did. Give a single interpretation of training an adequate period before passing judgement. Don't flit from one interpretation to another, never doing justice to a single one of them.

Sets and reps

You determine exactly what to do. As a general recommendation, for your top effort sets, do 1–3 sets of 6–9 reps for each exercise for the upper–body, and higher reps, 10–20, for each exercise for the lower–body. These ranges aren't written in stone, though high reps for lower–body work – especially the squat – belong to the great tradition of programs for stimulating overall growth.

If you want to do sets of 5–7 reps in a cycle for the upper body, or even for the lower body, go ahead. If you want to try sets of 12–14 for the upper body, go ahead. All of this manoeuvre is part of the business of experimentation and trial and error. Find what suits you, at least for the moment. Using the same rep range, for cycle after cycle, will encourage staleness in most bodybuilders. Some variety, from one cycle to the next, is a good idea.

If you're really training *flat out*, I fail to see how you can do more than three (non–warmup) sets per exercise, with often only one or two of such sets being all you can do. However, if you're not doing all your "work" sets full–bore, you could do as many as 5–6 (non–warmup) sets for some exercises so long as you're doing very few exercises. There are times when you may respond to more sets than usual but doing most of them in *almost* full–bore style.

To do the 5x5 format, you do five sets of five reps with the same poundage (following warmup sets). Whenever you can make all five sets of five (25 reps total), increase the poundage by five pounds at the next workout. Once the initial weeks of the cycle are behind you, though the first and second sets won't be very demanding, the final sets will be. Following a weight increase, you probably won't be able to get all five sets of five. Perhaps you make a 5–5–4–3–3 run of reps. Next workout you get 5–5–5–4–4. Next time, 5–5–5–5–4. Next time, all 5x5. Another poundage increase follows at the next workout. Progressively work up to the 5x5 goal. Always remember, bodybuilding is *progressive resistance training*. When you're really having to work hard to get out the 5x5, get your tiny discs out and just add 1–2 pounds to the bar each increment.

As the intensity increases further – following a few more poundage increments – you may find it impossible to build up to doing five reps in all five sets, so drop the last set. After a few more increments, drop another set. Continue until you're down to one set of five reps and one set of three reps. This marks the end of the cycle. Take your time, start with comfortable poundages and add weight in small increments. On this program you can take up to 4 minutes between sets of squats and deadlifts once they become very hard to get out.

Another interpretation of the 5x5 format is to include the warmup sets in the 5x5 scheme. This reduces the number of "work" sets. This is less severe and less time–consuming so may be the best introduction to 5x5 training.

These schemes involve many sets and will only work for typical bodybuilders if very abbreviated routines are used. If you're doing more that 3–4 exercises a workout, the schemes are unlikely to work. Another proviso is that you're already getting close to the goals of Chapter 3. Unless you wait until this stage of development, you'll be using a fairly advanced method before you've earned the right to use it.

In Chapter 13, the subject of sets and reps is delved into further, as are other matters to be considered, including super slow training. The latter has its own requirements as far as sets and reps go, different to the guidelines given above for training with a traditional rep speed. Of course, as with all styles of training, once you're familiar with procedures, and how your body responds, you can modify things to see if you can find a more productive formula.

Neck, calf and grip work

While this work is not written into all the routines, you're urged to include it.

Calf and grip work can be done at full–bore intensity for longer periods than can the bigger structures of the body that need the big basic exercises. Calf and grip work isn't systemically demanding like work on the main structures of the body is and doesn't have to fit tightly into the cycling approach needed for the big exercises. Instead, take it easy the first couple of workouts of a new cycle, pick up the intensity and then get training full–bore in the third or fourth week of each cycle.

Neck work shouldn't be done full–bore, but can be done in a "hard" interpretation for long periods, like calf and grip work.

Calf, grip and neck work can – and perhaps should be – dropped from a cycle in the final stage of the cycle when new territory is being gone into in the big exercises. At this most severe stage of the cycle you need to pour everything into the big and most systemically demanding exercises. Also, you need to spare your recovery "machinery" from having to cope with demands outside of the core exercises.

Total focus upon these few main movements will ensure that, for just a few weeks, there's no siphoning off of training energy and recovery ability. This application of focus can mean the difference between just reaching your previous best poundages or forging ahead into "new ground." Pour everything into the big movements only. (Keep your stretching routine though, just drop everything else outside of the key big exercises.)

For extreme hard gainers, anything and everything outside of 2–4 big basic movements is counterproductive. No calf, grip, neck or cardiorespiratory work, at least not for a few months or even a year or two. This is the sort of focus needed for very abbreviated routines to deliver gains for those people who can progress on nothing else.

Neck work

A well-developed neck is physically very impressive and helps prevent neck injuries from accidents. Neck work can be done in the gym after your regular workout, or at home if you prefer. Traditional bridging exercises, as explained by Dr. Ken Leistner, may cause problems in the vertebrae of the neck later in life. (Bridging used to give me problems with my neck in the days following doing the exercise.) The neck can be developed and strengthened by safer exercises.

If you've access to a four-way neck machine (Nautilus and Hammer make quality units), make use of it. Head straps can be very effective if they are used safely and resistance applied very slowly. Low reps should be avoided.

Be very careful when you start doing neck work. The neck is a delicate structure and is easily strained. Don't work to failure. Just stick to "hard" sets (once you're conditioned for them, that is). The neck can't be pushed like you can push the other body parts. No extremes of movement either, especially to the sides.

Manual resistance is the recommended equipment-free method of training the neck. By yourself, with a short towel or your hands alone, you can apply resistance against each side of the head, and fore and aft. Once you're conditioned to neck work you can apply enough resistance so all but the opening few reps of each set are hard reps.

If you have a competent and sensible training partner, you can have the resistance applied by the partner. You must both work in synchrony to ensure that the resistance is in the right direction and of the right degree. Get it wrong and you could injure yourself.

Calf work

Calf development makes a big impression on your overall development, and calf development receives less "knock-on" work from the big exercises than do other "small" muscles such as the biceps, triceps and forearms. See the next chapter for exercise selection.

Grip work

Grip work can be done out of the gym. Get yourself a heavy duty gripper and really work on it two or three times a week. Over time you'll be able to close the gripper more, and sustain more reps and time with the same extent of closure. This, with the regular work you do in the gym will – in time – greatly add to your gripping strength. Finishing each workout with grip work is a great way to finish.

If you're "wiped out" before getting to the forearm work at the end of the workout, take a breather until you feel ready. Hold plates by their edges or by their hubs (if prominent enough). Pinch–grip smooth plates, keeping your fingers as far down the plates as you can. Do deadlifts without straps, taking the bar from the power rack or sturdy boxes so you only have to pull it up an inch. Use a thick bar if you have one. Hold the bar until it drops, timing yourself to monitor progress. Hold a barbell in your *fingers* or hang from an overhead bar by your fingers. Spend a few minutes working on one or more grip exercises. If available, use purpose–built devices and machines for training the grip.

Don't forget what's perhaps King of grip exercises – one–hand deadlifting, either with a regular bar, cambered bar or thick bar (or handle). If you could only do one grip exercise, do this one. Absolutely no use of straps though – don't even think about them.

Do this exercise on your deadlift day, at the end of your workout. Do full, from–the–floor one–hand deadlifts. Straddle the bar and grip it so you have perfect balance when lifting. Find, and then mark with tape, the center of the bar, and note which of your fingers must be on top of the tape to have the grip centered. Your free hand can balance the bar if it tips a little. You'll need some time to perfect the exercise for your body structure. Add weight whenever you can. On another day each week, do partial one–hand deadlifts from a rack or stands set up so you only have to lift the bar an inch off the supports – exercise your grip while sparing your back. Set a time target for holding the bar – 15, 20 or whatever seconds – before upping the poundage next workout.

Make your own thick bar by sliding plumbers' pipe over a barbell, using it like a sleeve. Have it cut the length between the inside of the collars and keep that bar just for thick bar work. Experiment with different widths of pipe. (Thick bars, as Dr. Ken Leistner has pointed out, can be used with good effect for exercises other than direct grip work, exercises such as the overhead press, close–grip bench press and the barbell curl. Experiment.)

Put together a gripping program – perhaps several of them – and rotate them. Include some finger–tip pushups. You're going to transform your grip after a month or two. After a year or two, few people will be able to touch you, grip–wise. Also, you'll add size to your forearms and greatly add to your presence when wearing a short–sleeved shirt.

If you compete in powerlifting, or plan to, then you need to train yourself to hold as much weight as possible without any gripping aid. Not much point using straps to be able to hang onto a double with 450 pounds in the deadlift if your grip can only hold one rep with 400.

If you've no intention of lifting competitively, then you can use lifting straps without being worried that your leg, hip and back strength is getting ahead of your grip. However, if this strength imbalance bothers you, even you should be wary of using straps too much.

For many people, the trouble with not using straps is that the grip packs up many reps short of what the body can pull. So, the back isn't going to improve any. Not using straps for medium to high rep deadlifts means your attention may be focused on whether or not the bar is going to fall out of your grip rather than on getting the reps out.

Be careful when using wrist straps during deadlifts and shrugs. If you're using a reverse or mixed grip – palms facing in opposite directions – you may cause torque that could injure you. (See page 161 for a possible solution.)

If you intend to compete competitively, or you simply want to deadlift your top poundages without straps, start your next deadlift cycle with a moderate poundage and slowly add poundage, and *don't* use straps even once. If the poundage is added s–l–o–w–l–y, your gripping strength may be able to improve sufficiently to be able to keep pace. Jump the poundage too much and you'll be forced to use straps again and your grip will continue to lag.

Old–time bodybuilders and strength men didn't neglect their grip. They built extraordinary gripping power and forearm development. They didn't do it with wrist curls but with heavy grip work. This tradition needs to be revived. Though you probably won't have inherited long muscle bellies and lots of muscle cells in your forearms, that doesn't mean you can't develop a *very* strong grip

There's a *great deal* of satisfaction to be gotten from working on, and developing, an outstanding grip. Develop one!

Abdominal work

While an abdominal exercise isn't included in each routine, always do one for a couple of hard sets say twice a week. Opening your routine with one – as part of getting you ready for the more demanding work to follow – is a good idea. If you prefer to do it at home sometime, fine. See the next chapter for detail on abdominal work.

General warmup

This activity helps to reduce injury potential in the "proper" workout that follows. Physiologically, it increases muscle temperature, increases blood temperature and flow rate. It also reduces the chance of insufficient blood supply to the heart (cardiac ischemia) and makes the transition to strenuous exercise a gradual one. All this is especially needed when you're cold before starting your workout. In the summer, supposing you live where it gets hot, you don't have to be quite as particular. Avoid training during the hottest part of the day though.

While the physiological basis for a general warmup is convincing, tons of muscle have been built without it. It makes sense for middle-aged and older bodybuilders to be strict about a general warmup, but younger bodybuilders will manage all right with just specific warmup work for each exercise.

Spend ten minutes doing some easy general activity such as peddling a stationary bike, skipping and calisthenics. Your bodybuilding workout's abdominal exercise could be included towards the end of this ten minute preliminary activity. Some gentle stretching *could* end the general warmup. You could do your usual program of stretching exercises here, but don't "push" anything. After your workout, when your body has been "oiled," you'll be much more able to get into your full stretches. You'll need less time and experience less discomfort relative to stretching "cold." (See Chapter 11 for detail on flexibility work.)

Another good time to stretch is during the rest periods between sets, if you're not training back–to–back. Some people argue that stretching between sets (stretching the muscles being trained) can help in the muscle–building process.

Specific warmups for individual exercises

Be sure that you're adequately warmed up before doing an exercise. Either do all the warmup sets at the start of the workout, or do the warmup set(s) for each exercise followed by the top set(s) for that same exercise. The lower the reps (and higher the poundages) you're using for your top effort sets, the more attention you need to give to specific warmup work.

For example, suppose you're doing very heavy (for you) low rep squats for a few weeks, in preparation for a maximum single. Your warmup work could run like this: 135x8, 235x5, and 285x3 as a prelude to 335x5. Suppose you're doing 20–rep squats with as heavy a poundage as possible – say 250 at present. Your warmup work wouldn't be so extensive, say just 135x8 and 200x5.

Generally, the squat, deadlift and bench press need the most care when warming up. The other exercises are adequately provided for with one or at most two progressive warmup sets. Avoid warming up so much – too many sets and too many reps – that you tire yourself out. If in doubt, do the extra set of warmup work, but keep the reps low, as low as just one perfectly done rep.

Exercise performance

Though specific performance instructions for all exercises aren't provided in this book, comprehensive instructions *are* given for many of the key exercises. (See Chapter 9 and Chapter 11.) If you're a novice, you'll need the guidance of an instructor. Or, if you train at home, you'll need to obtain a book that gives a lot of attention to exercise performance. Pictures and photographs will help you to get the technique correct. Be sure to combine this other text and/or instructor's advice with the advice given in this book. Much of the specific instructions given in this book for the performance of exercises *can't be found in another single text.*

Heightening the intensity

Techniques such as forced reps, negatives, drop/breakdown sets, rest pause work, 1½ reps, 1½ rest pause reps, and other methods, take intensity of effort beyond the regular "to–failure" level. Training to failure either means performing reps until another rep can't be performed under your own steam or, in the "old (pure) school" of training to failure, you keep training until you can't budge the bar.

Training isn't done like this during the initial stages of a cycle, but only when you're training full–bore. Training beyond regular failure can be very result producing only if it's used prudently. Don't pile on this degree of intensity every workout, or even more than once every week for a given exercise, or else you'll overtrain for sure.

Be especially watchful that you don't use these techniques to try to "fix" sets that haven't been done properly. You can't make a poor set into a good one by adding a few pseudo forced reps or negatives. Get the basic "to regular failure" sets perfect first.

The squat

As described in Chapter 9, use variations of the squat as you think best fit your circumstances and training motivation.

Shrugging movements

These movements haven't been included in the following routines. If you don't feel you're doing too much already, *and are already gaining on your program*, then add *one* shrug movement once or twice a week. There are some fine shrug movements, not just for the trapezius as in the popular understanding of shrugs. There are even shrugs for the latissimus dorsi and pectoral muscles.

The trap bar is ideal for many shrugs. With or without a trap bar, there are some basic shrugs you can use for the trapezius area. The wide or snatch–grip shrug, done upright, bent forward or lying facedown on an inclined bench. Pull the bar up vertically, pulling the scapula in. The shrug can also be done with the more common shoulder width grip. In either case, no need to rotate or roll your shoulders as you move the bar up. Just up and down is fine.

Between shrugs – when the arms and shoulders are being pulled down – avoid relaxing, especially at the end of a set. If you relax, the resistance you're using will wrench your arms and shoulders down, possibly causing damage. Keep yourself "tight" between reps. If you want a long rest pause between reps at the end of a set, set the barbell down on stands.

For comprehensive tuition on the variety of shrugs, consult the writings of Paul Kelso.

Aerobic work

For the easy gainer, fitting in aerobic work without impeding the ability to recover from the bodybuilding workouts is no problem. For the hard gainer, with less recovery ability to play with, fitting in aerobic work is less easy. For the teenager, or extreme hard–gaining bodybuilder in his early twenties, forget about aerobics. Once you're older than thirty, it's time to fit in aerobic work so that it doesn't mar your bodybuilding progress by "eating" too much into recovery reserve.

Your body adapts best to a stimulus when it only has to adapt to a single stimulus. Give it two or more stimuli and its adaptive ability is being spread more thinly and so adaptation suffers. Better to focus its attention on achieving a single objective. If you want to lift as big poundages as possible, you should focus on that single objective. If you want to get an extraordinarily conditioned cardiorespiratory system, then focus on that. The black and white opinion here says that you either become a Master of one thing or a Jack of many things.

Cardiorespiratory fitness is very important for health reasons, especially once you're older than thirty, and increasingly important as you age beyond there. Cardiorespiratory work needs to have its place.

So, a Jack of all trades is more balanced than the Master of one trade. For the competitive athlete, becoming a Master is the goal. For the typical person who wants to have all-round size, strength, endurance, flexibility and cardiorespiratory efficiency, the Jack of all trades is the position to take.

Also on this side of the argument, good cardiorespiratory conditioning can help you progress with the weights because your body is fitter. If the aerobic work is done shortly after your workout, in addition to stretching, it may aid recovery from the weights.

The problem is getting your cardiorespiratory system in good order without it hindering your progress elsewhere. By good cardiorespiratory fitness I don't mean the conditioning of a middle or long distance runner. If you work up to 20-30 minutes three times a week of age-adjusted heart rate work, at the upper end of the 60-80% range, you'll be *very* well conditioned. The fitter you get, the more resistance you can handle (load on a bike, speed on a treadmill) to elicit the necessary heart rate.

Suppose you're thirty years old. Deduct your age from 220 and you get 190 - 60% of 190 is 114 and 80% of 190 is 152. Monitor your heart rate during exercise, without stopping if possible. If you don't have an automatic device, count your pulse over fifteen seconds and then multiply by four.

Don't jump into 80% work. Start with no more than 60% and then s-l-o-w-l-y work up to the 80% upper limit. If you're very out-of-shape, start with only 50% and *get your physician's approval first*. Be conservative to begin with and progress slowly. Start with no more than ten minutes. Work up to over twenty minutes at the 60% heart rate and then work to increase the heart rate.

If you train your cardiorespiratory system progressively, being patient and persistent without pushing it when training hard with the weights, your body should be able to adjust without slowing or halting your progress with the weights. If you're impatient and try to improve your cardiorespiratory fitness too rapidly, your progress with the weights will dry up and you'll become overtrained. You may then lose interest and motivation in both types of training.

When first bringing aerobic work into your exercise program, cut back a little on your bodybuilding workouts. Do a bit less or do it a little less frequently. Once your cardiorespiratory fitness is good, then you can return to the former format.

As a bodybuilding or strength cycle gets into the full-bore stage, and you're starting to feel tired, consider doing less aerobic work until the cycle is finished. Do the aerobic work only twice a week, and only for 15–20 minutes rather than the full thirty, perhaps dropping to the 70% mark.

In order to keep the dilution of adaptation ability to a minimum, don't mix progressive aerobic work with intense weight training. Focus on aerobic work for a month between weight training cycles, just doing a little weight training to maintain nearly all of what you've built.

After that month, don't strive to increase your cardiorespiratory fitness. Maintain what you had at the end of the month and return to giving your weight training priority. After the new cycle is finished, focus on aerobic training for another month, increasing your conditioning a bit further. Then back to weight training priority and maintenance aerobic work. Once you're in very good cardiorespiratory condition, just maintain it and keep your focus on your weight training.

By doing your aerobic work after your gym workouts, your non-gym days can be devoted to recovery. If you do your aerobic work on the days you don't train with the weights, you may be demanding too much of your recovery ability, always keeping you somewhat drained.

Aerobic training specifically aimed at aiding loss of body fat is a different matter to the aerobic work just described. For detail on this use of aerobic work, see Chapter 14.

The routines

20–rep squat routine
1. Crunch style abdominal exercise
2. 20–rep squat followed by the "breathing" pullover or Rader chest pull
3. Single–leg calf raise holding a dumbbell
4. Stiff–legged deadlift (once a week only)
5. Bench press
6. Parallel grip pulldown
7. Seated press behind neck

An alternative 20–rep squat routine
1. Crunch style abdominal exercise
2. 20–rep squat followed by the "breathing" pullover or Rader chest pull
3. Donkey calf raise
4. Stiff–legged deadlift (once a week only)
5. Parallel bar dip, a dumbbell around your hips
6. Bent–over row
7. Seated press in front

20-rep deadlift routine
1. Crunch style abdominal exercise
2. 20-rep bent-legged deadlift (once a week only) followed by the Rader chest pull
3. Machine standing calf raise
4. 10-rep squat
5. Slight-incline bench press
6. Parallel-grip pulldown or pullup (chin)
7. Seated press in front

A modification of the 20-rep deadlift routine is to use an 11–20 rep range. Start with 11 reps and add 3 reps each weekly workout. After three weeks you'll strike the 20-rep target. Then add twenty pounds, drop back to 11 reps and work up in the same manner as before. Start comfortably, say forty pounds under your 11-rep best. It will take you a few weeks before you're training really hard, after which you try your utmost to keep the progression going for three months, reducing the poundage increment when necessary. This scheme can be used in the squat too, but make the initial poundage jumps less, say 10–15 pounds.

If you find gains extremely hard to make, and are wanting to experiment with focusing on the deadlift, don't go flat-out in the squat. Save your big effort for the deadlift. Vice versa in the 20-rep squat workout if you find gains extremely difficult to make – work hard on the squat but keep something back in the deadlift.

For some of you, even these routines are too much and you'll need abbreviated versions. For example:
1. Crunch style abdominal exercise
2. Alternate these two exercises – one at one workout, the other the next, and so on:
a. 20-rep squat followed by the pullover or Rader chest pull
b. 15-rep stiff-legged deadlift followed by the pullover or Rader chest pull
3. Donkey calf raise
4. Bench press
5. Bent-over row

Some of you won't be able to gain *any* substantial amount of muscle unless you use abbreviated routines and *ultra*-abbreviated routines, and keep using them for *years*. Some hard gainers complain that even two hard sets of each of five exercises is too much work for them. If so, cut back, cut back and cut back again. Abbreviated routines can pack on muscle for even the most extreme of hard gainers. They have before and can again. However, they are less likely to wield their magic now than in years gone by – gyms are now so crammed with non–essentials that all but those who know about "real" training are confused and misled.

Remember, some powerlifters, with more favorable genetics than have typical bodybuilders, do nothing other than the three lifts – pure abbreviated training. They develop loads of strength and muscle. You can do the same.

Abbreviated training will do wonders for you so long as you pour in the effort, don't get in the gym too often, and eat and rest plenty. If you're an extreme hard gainer, don't waste years of your life trying to prove to the contrary.

Try this experiment if you're in doubt as to the value of the abbreviated routine. Whatever is your usual routine, push yourself to your maximum and record the top set for each exercise – poundage and reps for each. Take a week off and get back into the gym. This time, using the same routine as a week before, do the routine in *reverse* order. Use the same inter–set rest periods as in the previous week, and the exact same poundages. Record the reps for the top set of each exercise. Full–bore effort, of course.

Compare your records. You'll almost certainly find that the second workout's initial exercises were done for several reps more than when those exercises were done at the end of the first workout. The final exercises of the second workout would have been done for fewer reps than when they were done first in the first workout.

The lesson? To do maximum justice to each exercise you do, *don't do many exercises at each workout.* This is especially so if your employment and family obligations are taking a lot out of you.

Other abbreviated routines
1. Squat or deadlift (alternating them at successive workouts)
2. Bench press
3. Parallel–grip pulldown
4. Standing calf raise on the calf machine

1. Squat or deadlift (alternating them at successive workouts)
2. Bent–over row
3. Parallel bar dip with resistance
4. Donkey calf raise

1. Bench press
2. Squat (20–rep style)
3. Rader chest pull
4. Bent–over row

This combination, as <u>Super Squats</u> points out, was promoted by Peary Rader for those bodybuilders who couldn't gain from more exercises.

Alternate these two:
Routine A
1. Squat
2. Bench press
3. Pullup

Routine B
1. Seated press
2. Stiff–legged or regular deadlift
3. Parallel bar dip

Ultra–abbreviated routines
1. Squat
2. Bent–over row

1. Bent–legged deadlift
2. Parallel bar dip

1. Squat
2. Pullup

1. Clean and jerk
2. Squat

1. Squat
2. Nothing else

1. Bent–legged deadlift
2. Nothing else

1. Clean and jerk
2. Nothing else

1. Snatch
2. Squat

1. Squat
2. Press (from stands)
3. Nothing else

1. Squat
2. High pull

1. Bent–legged deadlift
2. Bench press

1. Bent–legged deadlift
2. Press (from stands)

The Olympic lifts – snatch and clean and jerk, and assistance exercises such as the high pull – are massively demanding movements that can, when safely performed, yield excellent results. The stress here is upon safety. Olympic lifts demand a lot of use of momentum and explosive lifting. With good coaching this is safe. Without good coaching these lifts may cause injury problems, perhaps serious ones. If you've access to quality coaching, grab the opportunity to learn good Olympic lifting technique and reap the benefits.

The following routines (A and B) are to be alternated, training every third or fourth day. They are very demanding routines that use "beyond failure" training but only *one* all-out set per exercise. This maximum intensity interpretation shouldn't be done every workout. Do it when you feel ready for it, maybe once every two, three or four weeks. With the other workouts you (just!) train to "regular" failure, one or two all-out sets per exercise.

Be warned, these routines are massively demanding. Too demanding for many of you, even within the context of cycling intensity. As soon as you feel you're close to becoming overtrained, back off. For some of you, they will be very productive so long as you get the full package of training and training-related considerations in sound order.

Routine A
1. Full range leg press immediately followed by the squat
2. Dumbbell calf raise – 1–1/3 reps followed by breakdowns
3. Bench press – to failure, forced reps and then floor pushups

4. Pulldown – to failure and immediately followed by negative pullups
5. Seated press – to failure and then continue with the incline press with the same barbell
6. Barbell curl – breakdowns
7. Close–grip (about 15" between thumbs) bench press to failure followed by regular grip bench press with forced reps

Routine B
1. Squat – maximum reps with a fixed poundage, increasing reps every time you use this routine
2. Donkey calf raise – to failure and then rest pause style
3. Stiff–legged deadlift – regular reps and sets
4. Parallel bar dips – breakdowns and negatives
5. Pullups – failure and negatives
6. Press behind neck – to failure and then either rest pause or forced reps
7. Barbell curl – to failure and then rest–pause

Putting the stiff–legged deadlift immediately behind the squat takes training to the outer limits of severity. This is a personal favorite combination of Dr. Ken Leistner, one that has delivered extremely impressive results for both himself and his charges.

Imagine, a set of squats done to absolute failure *immediately* followed by a set of stiff–legged deadlifts to one rep short of utter failure. You'll have already done your warmup work for both exercises before starting on your full–bore set of squats. The bar for the stiff–legged deadlift will be already loaded and ready so that after the squat all you have to do is crawl over to it and get going.

Little or nothing can beat this twosome for wiping you out so quickly, and stimulating a lot of growth. You'll never know how hard it is unless you've been pushed by a training partner or supervisor to ensure that you really go all–out. Try this combination once a week:

1. Squat – use a weight that makes you fail at no less than twelve reps; then immediately get to the next exercise.
2. Stiff–legged deadlift, with a weight that lets you get at least twelve reps. You'll fall to the deck when you're done. Enjoy the rest for ten minutes and then

finish off the rest of the routine.
3. Calf raise
4. Bench press
5. Pullup

This routine is short since the first two exercises will, believe me, wipe you out. At your alternate workout – where you don't deadlift – you can do a couple more exercises if you wish.

Alternate at successive workouts:
   Routine A
   1. Stiff–legged deadlift – 1x15, rest and then 1x10 with same poundage
   2. Overhead press – 1x10, 1x6
   3. Pullup – 1x12, 1x8
   4. Parallel bar dip – 1x10, 1x6
   5. Calf raise – 1x25, 1x20

   Routine B
   1. Squat – 1x15, rest and then 1x10 with the same poundage
   2. Bench press – 1x12, 1x8
   3. Shrug – 1x15, 1x10
   4. Seated dumbbell press – 1x8
   5. Parallel–grip pulldown – 1x10, 1x6
   6. Barbell curl – 1x10, 1x6
   7. Calf raise – 1x30, 1x25

Whether you use the same poundage for each exercise's work sets, or whether you increase the weight a little for the repeat sets depends on how long you rest between sets.

Alternate the next two routines, using a 5x5 scheme, training at the frequency to suit you. Perhaps you start training three times a week – each routine being done three times every two weeks. Later, when the intensity is high, you can reduce training to twice a week – each routine is then done once a week.

   Routine A
   1. Squat
   2. Bench press
   3. High pull or bent–over row or pullup

   Routine B
   1. Stiff–legged deadlift

2. Calf raise (sets of 10–15 reps here)
3. Press (from stands)

Not only are popular split routines unnecessary for gains, but they *prohibit* gains among typical bodybuilders. However, with fundamental overhaul, a split routine *may* be helpful.

Such split routines don't spread a high volume of work over the week, but stagger a low to medium volume of work over more workouts. Each multi-joint exercise may only be worked once a week. This further reduces the length of each workout, thus heightening intensity while keeping inroads into recovery capacity on the low side. Here are some suggestions. Though there are more workouts per week, note carefully the frequency of training each lift. You determine the sets and reps following a thorough reading of the earlier chapters.

#1

Sunday
Regular grip bench press
Seated press
Barbell curl
Close–grip (15" grip) bench press

Tuesday
Deadlift (regular style or stiff–legged)
Pulldown

Thursday – optional
Light bench press
Seated press
Barbell curl

Saturday
Squat

#2

Monday
Squat
Parallel bar dip

Thursday
Stiff–legged deadlift
Press behind neck

Saturday
Bench press
Bent–over row

A typical hard gainer's powerlifting routine will train each powerlift once a week, with a small amount of supplementary work each session. Each powerlift will be done on a different day. Calf, neck and grip work can be fitted in twice a week.

Here's an example:

Monday
Bent–legged deadlift
Barbell curl
Crunch situps

Wednesday
Bench press
Close–grip (15") bench press
Pulldown, row or pullup

Friday
Squat
Press from stands
Crunch situps

Always remember, there's no one way to train. There's a *multitude* of practical and effective routines that can be composed according to the considerations expounded in this book. Different interpretations will be needed according to individual circumstances, experience, level of development and the needs of the moment.

If you pour commitment and resolve into the routines in this chapter, while getting the volume of work and exercise frequency right for you, together with an adequate diet and plenty of rest and sleep, you *will* grow. You'll grow easier than you ever thought you would while trapped in the mire of frustration that goes hand–in–hand with following popular routines.

Sequence of routines

The sequence depends on your immediate needs, long–term needs, time available, season, needs for body part specialization, quantity and quality of sleep, and motivation. These factors can vary over the year and influence both how you can train, and your response to training.

I suggest you sit down and, after thoroughly studying *all* of this book, work out a year of routines. Put them together thoughtfully, bearing in mind events to happen outside the gym during the year.

For example, don't plan to hit the final month of a 20-rep squat routine during a hot summer when you intend having an extra job in the evening and will be short on sleep and energy. Or, don't plan to peak out for singles in the powerlifts during a month when you're going to be out of town on vacation for two weeks.

When drawing up your plans for the year, consider the compatibility of successive routines. After a cycle of single or double set to-failure workouts, your body and mind need a change, perhaps a big change. After an abbreviated, pure power cycle, you'll probably need a contrast. A cycle of more sets, and a few more exercises, done at a slightly reduced intensity may be just what you need to let your mass catch up with your strength.

Set your goals, make your plans, and keep flexible while keeping to the blueprint. Allow for vacations and any periods when you can't get to the gym or can't train properly. Then put the plan into action. When you know where you're going, and know how to get there, you're already well on the way to getting there. Get organized for success.

To keep the faith of the training philosophy, be watchful of being seduced by the irrational, stay clear of negative people, re-read this book, and read HARDGAINER and other sources of practical information.

The power rack

This piece of equipment is so versatile and productive that it deserves a book devoted solely to it. With this device you break the basic lifts into their component parts: start, middle and finish – and other parts of – and train these specific parts.

Used properly, acclimatized to before packing on the poundages, not overused and abused, it is one of the *great* tools of the trade.

Partial lifts enable you to use poundages way above what your body is used to using for full-range movements. These big poundages must be worked up to gradually, in weekly increments and in *perfect* form without holding your breath. If you jump into your maximum power rack poundages, using more than you're used to, albeit in partial movements, you're asking for trouble – perhaps a lot of trouble.

I know of a very experienced and knowledgeable powerlifter who was in a hurry to return to former poundages. He gave himself a hernia while doing partial deadlifts, and heard a loud crack as the tear occurred. Be patient. It's *always* better to make progress slowly and surely rather than be hasty and expose yourself to injury. This is so in all types of weight training, and especially so when you start rack training or are returning to rack work after a long time away from it.

If you've never used the power rack as a mainstay in your training, then you're unlikely to have realized your strength potential. It may help to take you well beyond the strength goals given in Chapter 3.

You're urged to get a power rack if you train at home, or to attend a gym that has one. The only condition is that you're already strong and physically impressive – at or *very close* to the goals given in the Chapter 3. Unless you're at this level of development I don't feel you've got enough from the other training methods. Milk these methods a lot more before applying yourself to the power rack. Then you'll have the strength, development of tissue and tolerance to exercise that you need to get the most from the rack.

When you're already big and strong you need other tools to take you to new levels of strength and development. The power rack is one of these tools.

The injection of a new piece of equipment, after years of training, will open training options that will bolster your training zeal. You need this to fire you onto levels of strength and size that will cause nearly all heads to turn when you're training.

Of course, you can use the power rack before you're already big and strong, and probably benefit from it. However, you would be using an advanced tool before you've made the most of the other tools. There's no need to jump to an advanced technique until you *need* that technique. Don't start to condition yourself to the power rack before you really *need* to use it. Save the rack till later. Once you're big and strong, use the rack as one of the tools to use to make you *very* big and *very* strong.

Using the power rack purely as a safety device, rather than as an advanced strength and mass building tool, is another matter. As a safety tool, it can be used by novices. Even if you're not advanced, still get or use a power rack, but keep its use appropriate to your development – safety initially, safety *and* an advanced training tool later on.

The advanced hard gainer

For the advanced bodybuilder *who has built considerable size* – at least to the goals given in Chapter 3 – are there other ways to train? Yes. Are other training options realistic? Yes. Once you're at the levels of Chapter 3, the options open to you include:

> a. More of what has already worked, together with trying other interpretations of the same approach.

b. Experimentation with advanced mass and strength building programs. Once the body has considerable muscle mass, there's the opportunity to try higher volume and more frequent training routines, for *some* of the time. Routines will still be exclusively or predominantly the big basic exercises, but there will be more sets, with some exercises perhaps being worked more frequently. Very low rep work can be done for long periods without overtraining. The power rack can become a mainstay in training programs. Basic roots won't be forgotten though – 20–rep squatting, for example, will be returned to regularly.

If you feel you've exhausted the other training methods, and still want to get bigger and stronger, you may need to explore adaptation to long–term, hard and heavy training. The change–over will be gradual and progressive, eventually involving more time commitment in the gym.

c. Use of "finishing" routines. If it's pure bodybuilding in the sense of physique perfection – balance, symmetry, detail, fullness of individual muscles, unusual definition – and possible competition, then you'll need to make changes in your routines. This *won't* be for mass building though, be sure of that. If you want to get bigger and stronger, then leave this "finishing" approach alone until you're satisfied with your size. For "finishing" you'll need to use quite a lot of isolation exercises. You'll need to do what can be done – short of surgery – to bring up lagging aspects of muscles, emphasize certain parts of your physique to draw attention away from weak spots, and give attention to the other concerns of competitive bodybuilders.

d. Mixture of a–c, devoting different cycles to each.

There's no shortage of instruction devoted to point c, though most of it advises volume and frequency of training that are excessive for typical drug–free bodybuilders. There's very little devoted to points a and b as applied to drug–free and genetically typical bodybuilders. This book deals comprehensively with point a, and touches upon point b.

Whichever single approach you take, or mixture of approaches, don't think that once you've become big and strong (by drug–free, genetically typical standards) you can rewrite all that has been written in this book. Far from it. While your capacity for work has increased in some areas, and the interpretations of training open to you have widened, you can still overtrain very easily. All that's been written in this book must still be considered when putting together your routines. Otherwise, you'll just stagnate indefinitely.

Another consideration for very advanced trainees is that focus may need to be almost totally on a single lift, to get that lift to progress. When at just about the limits of your development and strength, you need this focus. At this stage, if you try simultaneously to bring up the squat, bench press, deadlift and overhead press you may be onto a loser. Focus on one at a time, bringing each up. After having brought all of them up, spend a cycle aimed at getting all the lifts up to your best lifts when you were applying yourself to each lift with focus. This "compilation" cycle is *not* aimed at going into new poundage territory.

Motivation

To get much bigger and stronger you really have to *want* it. Thinking you want it isn't good enough. Wanting it next year when some other things have settled down in between isn't good enough. Wanting it once you start to attend a better gym isn't good enough. Wanting it when you have more money isn't good enough.

You have to want it *so much* that you're willing to do anything *within the boundaries of reason and safety.*

If you want it badly enough, you're going to get it. You might have to waste years of your life training on useless routines before learning the lessons contained in this book. So long as you're motivated enough, you'll still be training even after tons of frustration and failure.

Program your mind for achieving your (realistic) goals, visualize daily where you're going, think positively, maintain your resolve, don't let negative people have a detrimental influence upon you. Train your mind as well as your body. Get in control, and stay in control.

While muscular might is built over the long–term, you have to get the short–term in good order first. To get the short–term in order, you have to get each day in order.

Your attitude matters, matters a heck of a lot. Explore texts on how to program your mind for success and positive thought. Then unleash it on sound training programs.

The best motivation is success. Once you're training productively, your motivation and ability to train hard increases. Your discipline when out of the gym intensifies too. The reverse is true too. The more failure you have, the more your motivation gets worn away.

> Don't exhaust your motivation by ignoring this book and trying to prove you're an exception to the rules for typical bodybuilders. Of course you may be an exception, but the chances are you aren't.

> Knuckle down in the gym to some darned hard work on the big exercises. Knuckle down at home to some substantial, nutritious eating. Knuckle down at home to getting lots of sleep.

> There's still no other drug–free combination that will help you. The basic requirements for getting big and strong are simple enough. It's marrying productive interpretations with *application, effort* and *discipline* that's tough to do. Make the commitment.

Keep your motivation up by progressing in the gym. Keep re-reading this book, and similar material for reinforcement. Keep on the training "straight and narrow."

Come on now

It's time to put aside the arguments, reasoning, whys and wherefores. Time to put the routines into practice. Time to adhere to the need for progressive poundages (no matter how gradual and slow the increments). Time to be patient and persistent. Time to grow.

Never forget, doing less nearly always results in more. Cut back, cut back and cut back again. Then grow, grow and grow again.

Confirm with your own example what legions of others have proven. Do this now, and put an end to the wasted years.

To paraphrase a Martial Art tenet: "It's better to spend years searching for the right teacher than to spend years studying under the wrong one."

Now that you've found this source of teaching, *make the most of it.*

To benefit from this book it's *imperative* that you study *every* sentence of *every* paragraph of *every* chapter. *Skip nothing.*

11: Getting it Right

To receive the bountiful benefits from the exercises and routines promoted in this book, you must perform them in a safe and productive manner. You can't sustain cycle after cycle of progressive and productive training if you keep getting injured.

The training world is notorious for perpetuating potentially dangerous ways of performing exercises. Rather than just describing how to perform the exercises – concentrating on the "substance" exercises, not the marginal ones – emphasis will be placed upon how *not* to perform them. If you're a training novice, you'll need to *combine* this chapter with either a gym instructor or a text that focuses on how to perform the different exercises.

Concerning injuries, and aches and pains in general, be wary of jumping to the conclusion that certain exercises, and perhaps even bodybuilding as a whole, are not suited to you. If you're abusing training, and/or using incorrect exercise style, you're bound to get aches, pains and injuries. Get your act together – iron out all the flaws and train correctly.

Ensure you're flexible enough before using certain exercises. Warmup correctly and be sure that you're recuperating adequately between workouts. Bodybuilding then becomes the pain–free activity it should be. While some people aren't suited to one or a few exercises, due to previous injury or unusually unfavorable leverages, almost all bodybuilders can benefit from all the most productive exercises so long as they go about it correctly.

Reading Dr. Joseph Horrigan's monthly column in Ironman has been very encouraging. He's iterated some of what I've found to be true over my many years of involvement in bodybuilding. Additionally, he's provided background information that's difficult to come by. By improving my understanding of safe and effective weight training, he's influenced some of what follows.

The abuse of training

Training too much, too often and with poor exercise style ("crashing" when squatting or dipping, "squirming" when benching, "yanking" when deadlifting and rowing) not only fails to deliver size and strength gains, but reeks havoc on your body. Such abuse delivers aches, pains and even serious injury, and all of this in amongst the frustration delivered by stagnation in the gym. The older you get, the more sensitive you'll be to training abuse.

Take the opposite tack now. Consider short, basic and not too frequent workouts, in cycles that vary the intensity of effort, using sound exercise technique. All this not only delivers steady gains in the gym, but delivers them without injury. Once free of the "more is better" mentality, a huge step towards long–term progress and longevity in bodybuilding has been taken.

Of course soreness will be experienced following the scheduled high intensity workouts. Such soreness is good, so long as it's not debilitating. Soreness shouldn't follow every workout – remember, you're cycling the intensity of effort, not training flat–out all the time.

Plain overtraining, even if you're using good exercise style, will wear you down and deliver injuries. The shoulder, lower back and knees are prime examples of this.

The rotator cuff is a group of four small muscles (subscapularis, teres minor, infraspinatus and supraspinatus) that originate on the shoulder blade (scapula) and insert into the upper arm bone (upper humerus). The rotator cuff's function is to keep the head of the humerus stable in the shoulder joint. The head of the humerus is pulled into the socket of the scapula. As explained by Dr. Horrigan, this permits free movement in the shoulder joint without the joint–destroying action of the humerus striking the shoulder joint, and bone hitting bone.

These four small muscles come in for a pounding on any weight training routine, especially on conventional four or more days a week split routines. The rotator cuff is stressed either at or near its limit whenever you do chest, back and shoulder work. The cuff plays a large role when you do arm work and deadlifts. Try designing a conventional split routine that gives the rotator cuff more "off" days than "on" days. All of this will be compounded if you have inflexible shoulders and/or a history of shoulder injuries, even apparently minor ones.

The lower back receives its major stress from squats and deadlifts, but receives a lot of other work when you row, and arch excessively during the bench press and overhead press. (If, on top of the plain overtraining, your squatting and deadlifting style leave something to be desired, then you're ripe for injury, probably a major one.)

At the minimum, such overtraining leads to numerous muscular aches and pains mixed in with tendinitis and bursitis. Then develops a not uncommon situation of bodybuilders (and powerlifters and any other strength athletes) having difficulty doing many everyday activities. Their mighty bodies complain when getting out of bed first thing in the morning, when playing with the children, and when getting in and out of the car. Aches and pains are "trained around" and pain is put up with and battled through, with pain–killers often being used. Training through injury is a dangerous game, don't do it.

Stop overtraining. Put your routines together in a balanced and intelligent way. Cycle your workout intensity. Carefully perform a routine of flexibility exercises at least every other day. Avoid dangerous exercise style when in the gym.

When training full–bore, the local and systemic discomfort has to be savored, but this is a whole different thing to training through the pain of injury and physical abuse. Don't confuse the two.

Overtraining – detection and response

Overtraining means training more than your body can cope with. It may simply be that you're training too much each workout for the training frequency you're using. Or, you're training too frequently for the training load you're using. Do less at each workout, rest more between workouts, or, do less *and* do it less often.

Overtraining can come about as a result of out–of–the–gym factors wearing you down and impairing your body's ability to cope with what was previously a productive training schedule. If your recovery "machinery" goes out of order due to employment, personal or domestic factors, don't expect to continue with your usual training program.

Simply put, when you're "dragging your feet" and training zeal is flagging, you're overtrained. Once you're overtrained, forget about progress.

As well as seemingly constant systemic fatigue, together with excessive local soreness and diminished training zeal, there are other monitors of overtraining. They include stagnant or diminishing poundages (though you may not be at your earlier best working poundages), unintended bodyweight loss, sleeping difficulties, the feeling of being "wiped out" on your non–training days, and low resistance to colds and sickness in general. At a more "clinical" level, your resting heart rate may be raised as may your blood pressure.

While these symptoms are accurate for the typical non–competitive trainee, including those who are advanced, the *very* advanced *and* competitive athlete may exhibit different symptoms of overtraining. The above list is not presented as an exhaustive study.

Local soreness and systemic fatigue are part and parcel of training. However, there's a huge difference between post–workout systemic fatigue that's actually a "high" from training, and the fatigue that's almost debilitating. To train hard, have a shower followed by a meal leaves a great sense of achievement and a "worked" sensation that's a joy. To beat yourself further into the ground, once you're already tired and dragging yourself around, is misery and produces no post–workout "high."

When starting a new cycle, after a short layoff, detraining has been experienced as the prelude to new high levels of achievement later. You *must* take it easy to begin with. If you start back training full–bore, even at lower poundages than at the end of the previous cycle, you'll immediately demand more from your body than it can comfortably deliver. You'll throw yourself into an overtrained state immediately. Local soreness and systemic fatigue will hold you back and mar your training zeal. Persist at this, and you'll have to loosen your training form to keep adding weight. You'll wear your body down and aches and pains will become the norm. You'll "kill" the gaining momentum before you've barely got into the cycle, and with you still yet to be at your previous best poundages.

Start each training cycle comfortably. Let your body adapt to the increasing training poundages gradually, without experiencing debilitating systemic fatigue and local soreness. While avoiding overtraining, you'll be slowly building up the conditioning needed to enable you to forge into new ground of poundages in the final stages of the cycle.

Some people stress the importance of training variety as a means to prevent overtraining. If they mean training variety within the confines of what works for the drug–free genetically typical bodybuilder, fine. If they mean just changing the routine every so often despite the training volume and/or intensity being beyond the ability of the trainee, that's no good.

Appropriate routines and intensity cycling are needed, keeping each cycle going as long as results are being delivered, be that six weeks or even six months or more in the l–o–n–g cycle.

Chest work
Bench press

The bench press, when performed safely, is one of the most productive of exercises, primarily affecting the chest, shoulder and triceps. Exaggerated interpretations of the bench press are usually at the root of problems caused by this exercise. Very wide grip bench pressing, and bench pressing to the neck, are potentially very dangerous. Though there are some bodybuilders who can do these interpretations without apparent harm, they are the exceptions. For sure, if you've any history of shoulder injury, never do these exaggerated interpretations. If you've no shoulder injury history, then doing these two interpretations may quickly get you into the shoulder injury club.

The wider the grip, the more the elbows and shoulders are opened out. The more open the shoulders are, the more vulnerable they are to injury. The widest grip you should take is one that has your forearms parallel to each other when you have the bar on your chest. Once your wrists are wider than are your elbows – when the bar is on your chest – you're asking for trouble. This is especially so if you lower the bar too close to your clavicles. Take a closer grip and lower the bar to the line of the nipples, or lower – "lower" meaning towards the waist. Never mind about getting a "good stretch" by lowering the bar to the clavicles or, worse, to the neck.

Parallel bar dip

The parallel bar dip, safely performed, is one of the best exercises. It's a multi–joint exercise that involves a large mass of musculature.

If the dip causes you discomfort, even when performed slowly and without an exaggerated stretch, you're unlikely to get "used" to it and will need to drop the movement permanently. This is especially so if you've ever had a serious shoulder injury.

If you *can* do the dip, great. Always remember to warmup carefully, doing slow bodyweight dips starting with a partial dip and gradually working into the (exaggeration–free) full–range dip. Never drop or relax into the bottom position. Keep "tight." When adding weight to a dumbbell strapped around your hips, add it progressively, small increments at a time and, when at your limit poundage, don't stay with it for month after month. Cycle the intensity, remember.

The dip works the chest as well as the triceps (and shoulders), as does the bench press. To stress the triceps, the common advice is to keep the body vertical, head up and elbows back. To stress the chest the most, lean forward and keep hunched up, keep your elbows out to the sides somewhat and dip as low as comfortable. Maintain the hunched up position as you push out of the low position. To stress the upper-body more generally, work between these two ranges. Be sure to avoid extreme positions if you want to stay injury–free.

Rather than distorting the exercise to try to focus on one area more than another, it's more natural to dip without unusual positioning. The style that's most comfortable for you will enable you to use the most poundage in good style. That's the bottom line for getting bigger anyway, so build your chest, shoulders and arms simultaneously.

Shoulder work

The mainstays of basic, frill-free shoulder training are the press behind neck and the press in front of the neck - the latter usually just called the press or the military or standing press.

If you do these movements while seated, and with a not-quite-vertical bench against your back (you're leaning back a *little*), your lower back will be kept out of doing much work and the exercise shouldn't cause back problems.

Press behind neck

This is a very risky exercise for many people. The press in front of the neck, and dumbbell pressing, are safer exercises that are still super productive. Substitute either of these exercises for the press behind neck. Injuries, however, are often sown in poor gym habits that have nothing to do with the actual movement that appeared to produce the injury.

If your shoulders don't have the necessary flexibility to be easily able to press a broomstick from a stationary position on your upper back, then you'll likely hurt yourself when you use a barbell. What's likely to happen in this situation is that the "tight" rotator cuff muscles become inflamed and tiny strains occur. This gets worse each time you train.

Never even consider using the press behind neck unless you have the flexibility to do it safely. If you employ the press behind neck, use very light weights until you're sure you can perform the full-range of motion without any ill effects. Use the broomstick shoulder circling exercise described in the section on *Positioning the bar* in Chapter 9.

Upright row

The upright row is an exercise that's often recommended. It always hurt my shoulders and, until recently, I used to think it was a problem unique to me and just a few others. The more the elbows are encouraged to lead the bar, the more exaggerated is the discomfort from the exercise, at least for some bodybuilders.

Dr. Horrigan is insistent that the upright row can be a dangerous exercise. He advises eliminating the exercise from training programs.

If you're sure the exercise doesn't cause problems, and you want to continue with it, still take great care. Don't get carried away with working into large poundages, and, don't cheat and heave the weights up with momentum. Your shoulders will eventually prevent you from doing this if common sense doesn't. The deterrent will be pain.

Not only will shoulder pain limit you, but so may lower back pain. A relaxed performance style may give you lower back problems - from incubation, exacerbation or creation.

Lateral raise

The lateral raise doesn't come into the category of the "substance" exercises that are multi–jointed, involve a large amount of muscle mass and produce great systemic fatigue. Leave the lateral raise until you're big enough to have lots of passers–by in the street gape at you.

However, as a "footnote," bear in mind that doing the lateral raise with the thumbs pointing down – the "pouring out of water" position – can cause shoulder discomfort. (That's why it was so uncomfortable when I used to waste my time doing this exercise.) For many people it *sounds* and *feels* bad, especially the higher the arms are raised. Goodness knows how this style of performance became so popular.

The lateral raise is much safer when done with the hands kept parallel to the floor and the wrists not bent down. To place more stress from the movement upon the side or lateral head of the deltoid, just do the movement while face–down on an inclined bench set at about seventy five degrees.

Partial press

To work the side head of the deltoids specifically, while using a big basic lift, use the top 3–4 inches of the overhead press – "lockouts." I was taught this movement by Richard G. Abbott.

Set up a power rack – or Smith machine if there's no power rack – so the bar rests 3–4 inches from your lockout position. Space your feet wider than shoulder width and your hands about shoulder width. Dip at the knees and lock your arms. Keeping the legs locked, press the bar up and down over these few inches, without resting in either the lockout or low position.

Slide the bar up the back two uprights of the power rack. (The exercise can be done seated as well.) Keep the bar going until you can't budge it. As you go into the lockout position, your head should be well forward of the bar, akin to the lockout position of the press behind neck. Your shoulders must be flexible here. If they aren't, leave this exercise until they are. Work on the broomstick shoulder rotations.

This partial exercise can take a much bigger poundage than the full–range press. Warmup well, take at least a couple of weeks before you're blasting full–bore, build up the poundage a lot, and your shoulders will grow. You should like the soreness the exercise produces in your shoulders.

Back work

Doing high intensity bent–legged or stiff–legged deadlifts no more than once a week is a big step towards making big gains from these movements, and a big step to injury–free training. On top of training frequency and intensity cycling, safe performance of deadlift movements must be studied in depth if you're to avoid back injuries.

The deadlift variations are some of the most productive exercises you can do, so long as they are treated, almost all the time, as exercises rather than as strength demonstrations. With the deadlift being one of the competitive powerlifts, together with the squat and bench press, it's too often treated solely as a very low rep exercise.

To get the most from the deadlift, do it for medium or higher reps. Avoid very high reps though – twenty is high enough, while 6–12 is more typical for general use. Refer to *How many reps to squat?* in Chapter 9 – the information there applies to the deadlift as well as the squat.

Stiff–legged deadlift

This is a magnificent exercise, one that works you from top to bottom. It's unusual in that it's an exercise that you shouldn't work to absolute failure. Working to failure pushes the back structure too far and could cause injury. Stop this exercise one rep short of failure. Such a point, if really gotten to, is still many reps further into the set than the vast majority of bodybuilders take it to. The deadlift variations, like the squat, are "beast" exercises.

With the stiff–legged deadlift being such a major movement, it needs a thorough description. While it's one of the finest exercises, when properly performed, it's one of the most dangerous exercises when incorrectly done. Take care:

a. If you've had a serious back injury, don't do this exercise without the clearance of a sports–orientated chiropractor. If you've had any minor back injuries, still get a chiropractor's clearance.

b. Don't do the full–range movement unless you've the flexibility to touch your knuckles to your toes while keeping your knees *locked*. The wider your grip on the bar, the more flexible you need to be. Avoid using a wide grip if you're doing the full–range movement – it may expose the back to excessive stress if you're using your top working poundages. A hip–width spacing of your hands is fine.

c. To increase your flexibility, follow the program given later in this chapter, especially the first listed stretch (page 175).

d. Until you have the necessary flexibility, do stiff–legged deadlifts while standing on the floor using 45 or 35-pound plates on the bar. This will prevent you from overstretching.

e. During the exercise, keep the bar smoothly moving right next to your legs. Don't allow the bar to fall out and away from you.

f. Once you have the flexibility, do the stiff-legged deadlift while standing on a sturdy bench or platform or, better, stand on a sturdy block that's just the right height so that the loaded bar can be taken off your instep.

g. If taking the bar from a bench, take the bar off the bench using a regular bent-leg deadlift style, and immediately assume the stretched stiff-legged position. The stretched position is *not* where your fingers touch the bench in front of your feet. It's where the bar touches the laces nearest to your shins. You *must* keep the bar next to your legs for safety, always.

h. From the stretched position, you smoothly and steadily lift the bar. No jerking, no twisting, no bouncing, no rapid acceleration. Smoothly up, very short pause at the top and lower smoothly.

i. Don't try to keep your lower back rigid or flat as in the bent-legged deadlift. Keep your head up as you pull the bar and you'll avoid excessive rounding of your back.

j. Avoid a backward lean at the top. Hyperextension in the top position of *all* variations of the deadlift invites damage to the vertebrae because the stress is moved *away* from the load-bearing body of each vertebra and onto weaker structures.

k. My general recommendation is always to keep the knees *slightly* unlocked throughout the exercise. However, if you have no back or knee problems, you may do the exercise with legs completely straight. Work into the latter style carefully, without using your limit poundages for whatever rep range you're using. Build up to your limit working poundages over several weeks. If you experience any problems, return to the slightly unlocked-knees style.

l. If you're new to the exercise, start with half bodyweight, and add poundage slowly – at most ten pounds each week to begin with. Build up the intensity slowly. Later, as the sets become hard, reduce the size of the increments.

m. When getting acclimatized to the exercise, train it twice a week. Once you're training hard on it, once a week is enough. Perhaps once every ten days may be better.

n. Use lifting chalk. If you can't hold onto the bar long enough to work your back, rear thighs and hips to one rep short of failure, you need to work more on building your gripping strength.

o. If after pursuing all of the above you're unable to do the full-range movement safely, avoid this interpretation. Do not take any chances! I now (1996 edition) no longer even recommend the full-range stiff-legged deadlift. To minimize the risk of injury, always do the stiff-legged deadlift from the floor, not an elevated surface. You may even need to raise the bar an inch or two in order that you can keep a flat back throughout the exercise.

There are variations of the deadlift - other than the regular bent-legged deadlift - that can substitute for the stiff-legged version. These include the wide or snatch-grip deadlift, using a flat back and less leg action than a regular bent-legged deadlift needs.

Gripping the bar
When doing medium and high reps - don't do *very* low reps (singles, doubles and triples) in the stiff-legged deadlift - the grip is so often the weak link. Use a grip that has both palms facing you. This will keep stress evenly balanced. Use lifting chalk, but don't neglect to work your grip elsewhere or else it will fall behind your back strength.

The reverse or mixed grip - one palm facing your body, the other turned away - is used for a stronger grip. This is often a necessity for shrugs and low rep bent-legged deadlifts.

No matter which variation of a straight bar deadlift you're doing, holding onto the bar can be a problem. The stress of the lifting is symmetrically distributed if you use a pronated (palms to the rear) grip. The stronger mixed or alternating grip has one hand supinated (palm to the front) and the other hand pronated. The wrists should be directly over the bar. Check that this is the case before your first pull.

Using a mixed grip results in torque imbalances. To balance these out, to reduce injury potential, alternate from workout to workout which way round you have the mixed grip. Even if you find one way round gives you a stronger pull, still work it the other way round.

To offset the dangerous torque (from a mixed grip) that can turn your body to the side somewhat as you pull a very heavy bent–legged deadlift, pay attention to the spacing of your hands. This is a suggestion of Roger Benjamin from <u>Powerlifting USA</u> magazine (reported in <u>Raw Muscle</u> by Robert Kennedy and Dennis B. Weis). Experiment with having the supinated hand 1–2 inches nearer the center of the bar than is the pronated hand. Start experimenting with this from the beginning of a deadlift cycle and find the best grip for you as the weeks go by. By the time you reach the final weeks of the cycle you should have the hands perfectly spaced *for you.*

Bent–legged deadlift
    While the regular competition–style deadlift doesn't work the rear thigh, hip and lower back structure as specifically as the stiff–legged version, it combines great stress in this structure with colossal demands throughout the body. It's a marvelous "growth" exercise. Pulling a maximum poundage for low rep work, or pulling the final reps of a medium or high rep set, is what effort is all about. Be very prudent though with very low rep work. Such work should be used more sparingly with the deadlift than with the other key lifts.
    Properly done, the bent–legged deadlift is safe and super productive. Use poor form, abuse low reps, try to pull a lift you don't have the strength to, and you're going to hurt yourself. Do the exercise properly or not at all. Like with the squat, learn to deadlift properly before you concern yourself with poundage, and add weight slowly while maintaining perfect form. Performance pointers:
    Keep the heels a little closer than the toes – the toes should be pointed out a little. The feet should be close enough so that the grip lines up with the hands on the outside of the ankles, or a *little* wider so the hands don't get in the way of the tops of the legs when in the final position. The arms should hang in a straight and vertical line. This ensures that the pull is upward. The arms should remain straight throughout the lift and not actively pull so they bend at the elbow. The arms just link the torso to the bar.
    You must neither be standing too far from the bar nor too close to it. If you pull the bar into the shins, or into the quadriceps, you're too close to the bar. If you're too far from the bar, it will travel too far from the legs and you'll place too much strain on the lower spine, risk losing the lift and, perhaps, injure yourself.
    Don't wear shoes with an obvious heel or else you'll be at a leverage disadvantage – the heels will cause you to tip forward a little. Wear shoes with little or no heel and with a non–slip surface.

Before the pull, the knees should be well bent, with the hips much lower than the shoulders. The back should be flat and the head looking forward. The lift is done by the legs and back *together*. Don't try to pull it with the legs or back alone.

When you pull, make it a smooth pull, even on the slow side for the first few inches. *Squeeze* it off the floor. The strain of the exercise should be felt through the middle to rear of the feet, not the toes. You should be able to wiggle your toes as you begin the lift. If the weight is felt to be on the toes, the bar is going to travel forward and, if not dropped, will place undue stress on the lower back, causing it to bend excessively – very dangerous.

Don't snatch at the bar. If you do, you'll throw yourself forward and likely lose the lift. If at your absolute limit poundage, you'll rip your back into the bargain.

Drive your head and shoulders back right from the first slow pull on the bar. This will encourage the shoulders to move to the rear, and the back not to round excessively. (Don't whip your head back though.) It also helps to prevent the hips rising too quickly so avoiding throwing the weight forward. The bar needs to travel right close to your legs. If it drifts even an inch out of the groove you'll be in trouble, at least in low rep work. In medium and high rep work, there's room for small deviations from the groove without causing any trouble.

When you complete the deadlift, *don't thrust the hips forward or exaggerate pulling the shoulders back*. Doing these moves will cause hyperextension in the lower back and invite serious damage (see point k of the stiff–legged deadlift). Stand upright at the top of all deadlift movements. Upright does *not* mean leaning back.

The bent–legged deadlift just described is the conventional style. The sumo style (wide stance and with hands holding the bar between the legs) is a powerlifter's maximum–poundage–for–single–rep competition style. If you're interested in competitive powerlifting, you'll need to experiment with the sumo style as you may be able to lift more with it. However, for bodybuilders and non–competitive powerlifters, you're recommended to stick with the conventional style.

While training very hard on the bent–legged deadlift, just as in the stiff–legged version, you shouldn't train till utter failure. (Don't do forced reps and negative reps either – see page 73.) Always keep the I'll–make–this–even–if–it–kills–me final rep in you. If you go so near the limit that it takes you 10 seconds or more just to get the final 3–4 inches of the lift, especially when doing very low reps, the stress upon your lower back is colossal – colossally colossal if you hump your back too. This type of lifting will cause *very* serious injuries. Don't do it!

Take care

The back takes a heavy pounding in regular squatting and all types of deadlifts. Hyperextension of the lower back, even a little when deadlifting, sets you up for trouble because the squat also stresses your back and, if you excessively arch your back when bench pressing and overhead pressing, your back is being asked to do too much. Lower back pain will follow. If so, pay more attention to avoiding hyperextension of the lower back when deadlifting, and to maintaining good form in the squat and pressing movements.

More rest between heavy lower back work may be needed too. If you squat and deadlift on different days each week, that means your back is getting two heavy workouts each week. Experiment with squatting and deadlifting once a week on the *same* day. You then get seven days of rest before heavily training the lower back again. You could also experiment with training the deadlift less often than the squat - only once every 10-14 days.

Don't take any chances with your back. If you have *any* ache or discomfort in your back, delay a squat or deadlift workout until your lower back is fully recovered. Bear in mind that a day gardening or doing some other manual work can fatigue your back sufficiently so you need an extra day or few of rest before giving your back a hard workout in the gym. Either time your manual work to fit in with your workouts, or vice versa.

If when training you feel *any* twinge in the lower back, stop the lower back work *immediately*. Rest, and come back with a 100% sound back a week or so later. Even slight discomfort in the lower back can cause a slight change in deadlifting or squatting form that could be just what's needed to give you a serious injury. If any discomfort is persistent, get it investigated professionally, and without delay.

Strong and correctly trained abdominal muscles are important in keeping your body conditioned for squatting and deadlifting. Study the section *Abdominal work* later in this chapter.

Straps and hooks

Other than wrist straps, there are other straps and hooks that reduce or even eliminate dependency upon the natural grip. They usually enable you immediately to pull more poundage, whether on a barbell, dumbbell, pulley or machine. But this hinders improvement in gripping strength, and may even lead to a decrease in gripping strength.

Be careful if you use these straps and hooks. Don't put them on for the first time and immediately increase your pulldown poundage by 25 pounds, or your deadlift poundage by 40 pounds. If you do, you may injure yourself because your shoulder and elbow connective tissue haven't been conditioned to the poundage increases. This is especially so if you're yanking the bar instead of pulling it. Increase the poundage in small increments over a few weeks, and don't relax your form. But rather than use grip supports, be more patient and build your gripping strength using specific thick-bar work. Then you will be able to hold whatever you can lift or pull.

Bent-over rowing

The traditional bent-over row with a barbell, if performed with good technique, can be a fine exercise. But in practice it is a very risky exercise because good form is so difficult to implement. Good technique means keeping the knees bent and the abdomen "sitting" on the upper thighs. The upper-body should be at an angle of about twenty degrees to the ground. Keep the head up and grip the bar at about shoulder width. The initial pull is done by moving the arms, not by swinging up with the back. If you yank at the bar, you're inviting trouble.

Once the bar is well on its way to touching your abdomen, or lower chest, then there's some synchronized movement of upper-body with the arms - a smooth motion. Experiment with different width grips and pulling a little higher or a little lower. The grip can either be palms down (pronated grip) or palms up (supinated grip). Form can be kept strict by keeping the forehead placed on a comfortable waist-high bench. This is a good way to learn to do the exercise without yanking the bar and putting your lower back at risk.

But because the regular bent-over row using a barbell is very dangerous if not done with perfect form, or if you have a "dodgy" back, make it safe by modifying it. Get a high bench, sufficiently high so that when you're face down on it, holding a loaded bar with arms stretched, the plates just touch the floor. Arrange this by raising the bench or reducing the diameter of the plates used. Do the bent-over row while face down on the bench and then you can't heave the bar up using loose form - your back is then no longer put at risk.

Alternatively, place a padded bench across the support bars or poles in a power rack. Arrange the height to suit your arm length and diameter of the plates. Fix it so that you can only just grip the bar when it rests on the floor.

For both of these prone rows, dumbbells permit the more natural wrist positioning that has your hands parallel or near-parallel to each other. With a barbell your hands can only be pronated or supinated.

The T-bar row is also a very risky exercise. To play safe with the bent-over row, avoid the free-style barbell version and the T-bar row. Instead, stick with one of the prone styles described above, or the one-arm dumbbell row with the non-exercising arm braced against a bench.

Pullups and pulley work

When doing pullups (chins), neither drop in the bottom position nor relax and stretch while you're hanging so that your head goes forward and your shoulder blades rotate out and up. Keep your head vertical or your eyes looking up slightly, and your shoulders "tight." The same things apply in the pulldown when your arms are at full stretch. Keep your eyes looking up, and your head tilted back. Don't let your head fall forward, don't let your shoulders and arms relax, and don't let the weight stack yank your arms and shoulders up and back.

Incorrect performance of some pulley exercises for the back can be injurious for the shoulders. While a full–range exercise is generally the recommended thing to do, it's only recommended when the joint(s) are not put at risk.

For example, take the seated pulley row that has the cable running parallel to the ground. The absolute full–range movement has the arms and shoulders relax, to permit a full stretch between reps. Doing this puts great stress upon the rotator cuff muscles and sets up an injury. If you use this exercise, keep the shoulders "tight" and the head up when in the stretched position at the end of each rep. Don't drop the head and let the weight stack yank on the relaxed arms and shoulders.

There are many variations of pulley exercises for the back. Choose those that put you in a strong pulling position. Use a medium or close-grip rather than a dangerous very wide–grip spacing. Use a parallel-grip or curl–grip (depending on the exercise) as this puts you in a stronger and safer position than in a regular palms–forward grip. Avoid bars so designed that they have you pulling in a way that not only feels bad but is plain dangerous. No extremes – safe form, please.

Using a very wide grip in pullup and pulldown exercises also sets you up for injury. This isn't to say that everyone who does these will get injured, just that the injury risk is raised considerably. Play safe – use a medium to narrow grip in your pulley exercises.

Leg work

Calf work

Calf work is straight-forward enough. How often do you hear of people injuring themselves doing calf work? It's possible though, if you're doing standing calf raises with sloppy, partial reps, and with way too much poundage. You could injure your back due to the stress upon your spine. In all calf exercises, use a full–range of movement and smooth reps – medium or high numbers. Big poundages in standing calf machine work shouldn't cause problems as long as your back is strong from deadlifting.

One-legged calf raises are recommended, as are donkey calf raises. In these standing calf raises, keep the knees locked other than for doing reps beyond regular failure. Bent-legged calf work should be reserved for seated calf raises where the stress of the exercise is primarily aimed at the soleus muscle, rather than the gastrocnemius which is best worked when the knees are kept locked.

Regarding seated calf work as against other calf work, my personal findings have been that seated calf work hasn't contributed a single eighth of an inch to my calf growth. Nearly all, if not *all* my calf development has been due to one-legged calf raises holding a dumbbell on the same side as the working leg. The other exercises that may have contributed have been donkey calf raises and standing calf machine work. The seated calf work can't even get close to the direct, excruciating and growth-producing ache and pain that the stiff-legged calf raises can.

To add variety and a change of stimulus, try calf raises with a barbell over your shoulders. Do them on a block for full-range of motion. The free-moving barbell will force you to maintain balance by yourself. This may help to stimulate your calves in a different way to the other exercises you've used. For safety, do this exercise in the power rack so if you lose your balance the safety bars/pins will catch the barbell.

If your Achilles tendons are tight, then slowly and progressively work into deepening the stretching part of calf exercises. Don't bounce.

Squat

"Real" leg work rests in the squat and its variations. Hip belt squats, trap bar squats and other-device squats present less performance troubles and dangers than does the regular back squat. When done with *care and correct style*, the traditional squat is safe for all who have neither extraordinarily poor leverages, nor history of serious injury. That means it's safe for nearly all of us.

For a comprehensive description of how to squat safely and effectively, see Chapter 9.

Abdominal work

Traditional methods of training the abdominal muscles can cause back problems. Leg raises, straight and bent-legged situps, Roman-chair situps, hanging leg raises and other "abdominal" exercises are still traditional in many gyms. These exercises can either create a back problem or exacerbate an existing one. (The modified hanging leg raise where the knees are kept bent and pulled into the chest can be a terrific abdominal exercise *if* the focus is upon tilting the pelvis upward – the short–range motion of moving the hips towards the chest.)

The problems that these exercises cause or exacerbate arise from the confusion between spinal flexion and hip flexion. Spinal flexion is the curling of the spine brought about by the rectus abdominis and the obliques – the abdominal muscles you see on a well–defined physique. They are fixed from the sternum and ribs down to the pubic bone and sides of the pelvis. Strengthening these muscles keeps the curve of the lower back in healthy order by reducing inward lumbar curvature.

Hip flexion is another matter. This occurs when the trunk or lower–body is bent at the hips and when the knees are brought to the chest. Hip flexion exercises include the leg raise, Roman–chair situp, hanging leg raise and standard situp variations. These movements involve the abdominal muscles isometrically, giving the impression of their primary involvement. However, the actual action of these exercises is performed by the hip flexors.

The hip flexors are the iliopsoas – buried in the body and not visible unless you're cut open – and the rectus femoris, part of the quadriceps (thigh). Unusually developed hip flexors can lead to an exaggerated curve or arch of the lower back, and back pain. This is a point stressed by Dr. Horrigan. Very strong hip flexors are not visible and provide no advantage for bodybuilders. Those sports that do need them, such as gymnastics, may cause back problems as a result.

Not only do some of the most traditional "abdominal" exercises fail to train the abdominal muscles in the most effective way, they can actually cause back problems. They do cause discomfort and ache in the abdominal region of the body. However, the ache and "burn" you feel is a result of the combination of fatigue of the hip flexors plus the fatigue from the abdominal muscles that are isometrically contracted while the hip flexors are working. This combined effect provides the illusion that the abdominal muscles are being thoroughly trained.

If you're going to train the abdominal muscles, choose exercises that train the spinal flexors, not the hip flexors. Choose exercises that curl the spine rather than have the upper or lower–body moving at the hips. Spare your back and train the abdominal muscles.

Your abdominals are important in providing mid–section stability for squatting and deadlifting. When strong, they provide a natural training belt that protects your spine. Train your abdominals hard and seriously. If you train them immediately before you squat or deadlift, you may reduce the mid–section stability you need for those exercises. Better to have a pause long enough so your abdominal strength doesn't suffer, or do the abdominal work another time.

Twists

Twists – as in a bar or stick across the shoulders, legs astride a bench, and doing numerous twists to each side – are ineffective for reducing fat. They *are* effective at providing unnecessary shearing force upon the fibrous covering of the lumbar discs. The spine isn't well suited to rotation, but to extension and flexion movements like deadlifting. While incubating lower back injuries, all the twists in the world won't reduce a waist that has too much fat on it. Fat reduction is achieved through other means. Forget the twists and concentrate on useful exercises.

Crunch–style situp

When performing an abdominal exercise, remember to concentrate on moving the shoulders towards the hips; forget about moving the knees to the chest. The key is to curl the hips to the chest or to curl the shoulders towards the hips. This takes some getting used to because so many bodybuilders are used to banging out predominantly hip flexion exercises.

For example, take the crunch–style situp. The old style situp has you rotating at the hips and touching the elbows to the knees. The crunch–style movement has no rotation at the hips.

Lie on the floor with your knees bent at a right angle, with your calves resting on a bench. Simply curl the shoulders off the ground. You can't get your head very far off the ground without bending at the hips and making it into a hip flexion exercise. The crunch is a short–range exercise. The lower half of your spine always retains contact with the ground – no more lifting it off the ground to touch the elbows to the knees. Really "crunch" your abdominal muscles.

Overhead pulley crunch

The crunch using an overhead pulley can be a terrific movement. Ensure that the lower back stays fixed throughout the exercise. All that moves is the upper trunk (and arms holding the pulley handle) so the head (and therefore the shoulders) are curled down. Use a curling or supinated grip rather than an overhand grip, to reduce stress upon the elbows.

Try this exercise alongside a mirror and watch out for the whole upper–body moving at the hips. Avoid piling on the resistance so that you just yank the cable while flexing at the hips and using your arm and upper back muscles. Do the exercise properly – no flexion at the hips. Just curl yourself up and "crunch" – flex the spine, not the hips.

This exercise can be dangerous if, after the "crunch," you let the pulley's resistance pull you up, causing hyperextension in your lower back. Do the exercise smoothly and under control. Avoid sudden hyperextension, especially hyperextension under great pressure.

Machine work

If you use an abdominal machine for crunch–style situps, be sure you use it correctly. The aim isn't to pile on as much weight as possible and heave your whole torso forward so as to get your chin near your knees. How some people abuse equipment. While not training the target muscles, they *are* setting themselves up for injury.

Neck work

There are factors of safety other than those mentioned in the previous chapter.

Neck injury can occur in the course of exercising body parts other than the neck itself. Avoid performing your exercises in a dramatic way, with legs and head moving around during upper–body work. Keep the body in firm control. Keep your head facing forward while doing everything other than lateral neck movements. If you're getting towards the end of a hard set, and you sharply turn your head to the side, you invite trouble. Keep the stress of an exercise symmetrically distributed.

If you're holding onto something fixed, such as the sides of a leg press machine, and aren't conditioned for it, a big effort for a final rep can cause a tremendous isometric shrug which could injure you. Avoid surprising your neck with something it hasn't been progressively trained to become accustomed to.

Don't throw your head back when grinding out a final rep. It's one thing to move your head back slowly, another to rip it back. Neither should you force your head onto your chest. Such an action is likely to overstretch the neck.

Arm work

If you're neither overtraining your arms nor using uncomfortable hand placements, but are using basic movements rather than isolation ones, and in good style, arm injuries are likely to be unusual. Watch out for anything that doesn't feel "right."

For example, take the close–grip bench press. If you do the exercise with a very close grip, it feels very uncomfortable both for the wrists and elbows. Use a grip of about fifteen inches between the thumbs instead of a very close grip.

Stick to basic arm exercises such as close–grip bench presses, parallel bar dips and standard barbell curls – rather than lying tricep extensions, pushdowns and preacher curls. You'll then train the muscles safely and more productively, at least for the typical bodybuilder needing size and strength.

Don't join the masses who are "blasting" their 11–16 inch arms with pushdowns, lying extensions and concentration curls. Leave this sort of movement until you're already big and strong from having paid your dues on the big basic movements.

Jerking, dropping and yanking the weights invite trouble, whether in specific arm work or in exercises that involve the arms as accessories such as pulldowns, deadlifts and rows. Train with good form.

What about all the isolation exercises?

While mention has been made of a few isolation exercises, the emphasis has been upon the big basic lifts, because these are the ones that matter the most.

I could write reams on the safe way to do cable cross–overs, flyes, bent–over tricep kickbacks, pec dec flyes, cable laterals, leg extensions, and many other detail exercises. Heaven knows I've wasted enough time on these little isolation movements under the pretext of training each muscle "from all angles for full and complete development." While I don't doubt that I trained my muscles from many angles, these isolation exercises didn't contribute a smidgeon of size or strength.

All the most perfect leg extensions in the world won't give you big and powerful thighs. All the A1–perfect one–arm cable cross–overs you can do during the rest of your life won't give you a big and powerful chest. Hours of tricep kickbacks won't give you big and powerful triceps. Set after set of one–arm preacher curls with a dumbbell won't build big biceps.

> When you have a job to do, choose the appropriate
> tools. When you're digging a deep hole in the garden,
> you don't use a toothpick. When you're *building* your
> body, don't use detail exercises.
>
> Detail and "chiseling" are different matters, but how
> many of you are so big you can primarily concern
> yourself with the "finishing" details?

Breathing

The usual tendency, especially when training hard, is to hold the breath during the hard stage of each repetition – the big push or pull. This can cause blackouts – very dangerous if you're pressing or squatting. Also, breath holding can increase blood pressure to potentially dangerous levels, at least for some people. This increases the chance of a stroke, at least for older people not used to hard training.

Stop holding your breath when you're driving through the sticking point of any exercise – exhale instead. Even when you're not in the gym, whenever you have to make a big effort, don't hold your breath – exhale during the effort.

Start now, and develop a life–long habit of not holding your breath during a big exertion. It may add years to your life, literally.

General points of safety

Properly done, weight training is a safe activity. In relation to many contact sports it's very safe. Incorrectly done, it can be very dangerous. Unwise and reckless performance has caused some terrible injuries, especially in combination with anabolic steroids as these can disturb the strength balance between muscle and supporting structures.

Impatience and showing off are often responsible for using sloppy exercise style. Muscle and strength increase slowly. They can't be hurried by using poor exercise style. Cheating – using loose exercise style – only has its place when used in a very selective way in some exercises to get out a rep or two beyond regular failure. Other than this limited use, it's a recipe for stagnation and injury. While exposing you to injury that either prevents or inhibits training, it simply prevents the proper stimulation the muscles need in order to grow and get stronger.

If you train by yourself, use equipment that has sturdy safety bars or supports to catch the barbell if you can't make the rep. If you train with others, you may have reliable spotters to watch you while you bench and squat. However, even supposedly reliable spotters can be caught off–guard. Ideally, have spotters *and* safety bars.

Keep a close eye on what others are doing about you. Respect your limitations. Always warmup adequately. Develop and maintain suppleness. Don't train when injured. Then welcome an enjoyable and injury–free training life – training longevity.

Especially for the teenager

The teenager is usually excessive in enthusiasm and energy, but immensely deficient in effective instruction. Being so young, impressionable and gullible makes teenagers perhaps the most easily exploited among bodybuilders.

Those teenagers who have read the popular literature will likely find it impossible to believe that progress in the gym isn't a result of long and frequent workouts, wondrous sounding food supplements, use of machines, sophisticated restoration procedures and dedication to the point of fanaticism.

Regardless of whether or not the individual is gifted for bodybuilding, precautions must be taken in order to keep training safe.

Youngsters shouldn't be rushed into weight training. Due to great variations in structural maturity, there can be no standard starting age. It's possible that normal growth may be disturbed if excessive loads are placed upon the immature bones. Other than for especially immature individuals, most teenagers of fourteen should be up to benefiting from a safely constructed bodybuilding program. A program nothing like that of someone in the late teens though.

All interested youngsters will benefit from safe and practical training, especially those involved in competitive sport. By strengthening muscles, joints and ligaments the youngsters will be provided with much resistance against injury. Very young teenagers can't pack on size and strength like older teenagers can, but they can still benefit greatly.

Explosive lifting, and exercises that compress the spine and apply shearing forces, shouldn't be used by youngsters. Once physically more mature – sixteen and older for many teenagers – some of these stressful exercises can be carefully brought into training. Potentially dangerous movements for the early and mid–teenager include squats with a bar over the trapezius, conventional (vertical) leg presses, deadlifts and plyometrics. There are plenty of productive alternative exercises.

The very early teenager – both pre–adolescent and adolescent – can derive abundant benefit out of exercises that use the bodyweight as resistance. Pushups, dips, chins, crunch situps, and hyperextensions without any hyperextension. These exercises will thoroughly work the upper–body. High repetition step–ups holding dumbbells, or high repetition trap bar squats, together with regular running activities can round out the program.

Low repetition work is out for a long while yet. Maximum singles *don't even come into consideration* and neither do forced reps, negatives and the like. If competition is wanted, have it for high repetitions – "Who can do twelve chins with the most weight?"

Once in the later teens – sixteen and older for most – comes the time for more serious training. As long as low repetitions are avoided, and exercise execution is safe, exercises such as regular squats and deadlifts can be safe and productive. Olympic style movements can be used too, even at younger ages, as long as expert coaching is available and poundages are kept moderate.

Rather than trying to determine physical maturity by chronological age, it's better to determine it according to actual maturity as indicated by secondary sexual characteristics. While some boys can grow a beard before they are fourteen, and some girls have large breasts and hips at eleven (and have started menstruating), others have to wait a few years yet. The chronologically young but sexually mature can benefit from training procedures suitable for adults while older but less sexually mature teenagers can't.

Consider the fifteen year old boy who still looks like a ten year old. Compare him with a classmate who is visibly as physically mature as a typical man. Though the same age, one is a boy and one is a man. The "boy" can't possibly benefit from the hard and heavy training that the "man" can, but he *can* damage himself by using adult training methods.

Unless the teenagers are unusually blessed genetically, are extraordinarily mature physically for their age, or are fooling around with steroids, they can't build substantial size and strength until in their late teens. Expectations have to be kept realistic.

The very skinny teenager who "eats like a horse" isn't unusual. Adding a lot of size and strength demands determination and application at all times. For the hard-gaining teenager, the usual "formula" needs to be followed, but followed with extraordinary conscientiousness. More (nutritious) calories need to be consumed, an abbreviated routine followed, physically demanding activities outside the gym severely curtailed or (temporarily) eliminated, late nights avoided, and a "clean" lifestyle followed.

Supervised workouts are a must with teenagers, to keep them on the given program and prevent unsafe training. Regular reassurance concerning the appropriateness of the program needs to be provided. The temptation to follow irrational and potentially dangerous programs must be countered.

Whatever you do, you have to spill some hard earned sweat in the gym, and do so for a long and sustained period. The poundages you use must slowly inch their way up. Progressive poundages in good strict form are the name of the game – never lose sight of this.

Flexibility

While it's not necessary to become a contortionist, or to develop the flexibility of an Olympic gymnast, a moderate program of flexibility exercises, performed regularly, will help prevent injuries and help you to train more safely and productively. In saying this, understand that getting into a stretching program with excessive fervor will injure you. As with weight training, be careful.

The most troublesome injury I've had from the gym was from doing pressups (or pushups) using raised bars whereby I could go 5–6 inches farther down than in a floor pressup. I did the exercise slowly but didn't work into it by going a little deeper each session over a week or two. I hurt my left shoulder and needed more than six months before I was free of discomfort. Be careful.

Rather than following a long routine of flexibility exercises, to be performed daily, adopt a moderate program of stretches to be done alternate days, without fail. Such a plan is likely to have the best chance of being maintained. Maintained it must be, to reap the rewards.

As well as it being beneficial to you in the gym, stretching is enjoyable and valuable from the point of view of health, fitness and practicality.

Avoid performing the flexibility program when you're "cold." Much better to do it when you're warmed up. If you're "cold" you're more likely to hurt yourself if you don't work into the exercises very carefully. Also, when "cold" you take longer to get into your stretches.

Doing the program *after* you've trained with the weights is strongly recommended. By then you're "oiled" from the weights and you'll develop more flexibility more quickly, and with less of the discomfort from stretching. Also, stretching after a workout helps to reduce soreness from the workout.

If you stretch before you train, get yourself warmed up first with ten minutes on an exercise bike or the like. I recommend you don't try to get into your full stretches before your workout. Just go as far as you can without discomfort; save the full stretches until immediately after the workout.

If or when you stretch at home, do it in a warm room and later in the day rather than earlier. You'll be more "pliable" then.

Hold each stretch for at least ten seconds, relaxing as much as possible while holding the stretch. You should only feel *slight* discomfort in the areas being stretched. Let the tension in the stretch go for 5–10 seconds and then repeat. Three holds for each stretch.

Don't get into each stretch quickly. Take whatever time you need before reaching your fully stretched position. Then start the count of ten or more seconds. You'll probably need a few progressive stretches, or "holds," before you're at your full flexibility for each move. When you're at your full position of stretch, then do your three holds before moving onto the next exercise.

Never bounce while stretching. Don't place your joints in positions that are plain uncomfortable and might harm the integrity of your body. No extremes.

Here's a set of stretches that will give your body a good going over without taking a long time:

1. Rest your right foot on a bench or back of a chair, depending on your flexibility. Keep both legs straight. Without rounding your back to give the illusion of flexibility, lean forward as much as you can. Hold. Repeat for the left leg. Start with a low bench and add to the height as you make progress. This is an excellent stretch for the hamstrings and lower back.

2. Keeping your torso erect and vertical, lunge forward with your right leg, keeping your left as straight as possible. While keeping the torso vertical – not bending forward – "sit" so the left knee touches the floor, or at least moves towards it. Hold. Repeat with the other leg. This is an excellent stretch for the hips and legs. By increasing the distance between your feet, you increase the severity of the exercise.

3. Lie on your back and, with your right leg bent, pull it onto your chest and over to the left, using your arms. Hold. Repeat with the other leg. With both knees on your chest, roll backwards so your knees are touching your face. Eventually, with patience and a few weeks, you'll be able to place your knees on or very near to the floor at the sides of your head. Don't rush though or else you'll hurt your neck. These stretches work your hip flexors and spine.

4. Stand, holding the back of a chair or desk with your right hand. Lift your left foot behind you, bending your leg at the knee only. With your left hand, grab your left ankle and pull straight up. Hold. Repeat on the other side. This stretches your quadriceps.

5. Stand, keeping your forearms flat against the sides of a doorway. The palms face forward and the upper arm is kept parallel to the ground. The elbow joint is maintained at an obtuse angle. *Very* gently and slowly, lean forward, feeling the stretch in your shoulders and pectorals. Great care here – don't overstretch and hurt yourself. Don't try to pull your shoulder forward. Rather, as your torso leans forward your shoulders will be pulled forward too. To progress in flexibility, step back a little from the doorway (maintaining the arm placement) so there's more tension in the shoulders when you lean forward. Do this very carefully, finding your way into the "groove" of the exercise. Don't be in a hurry.

6. Sit on a chair. Keeping your feet planted on the ground, and your backside on the seat, rotate your torso and grab the back of

the chair with both hands. Turn as much as you comfortably can and then hold. Now turn to the other side. This is a fine stretch for the spine, back and neck muscles and shoulders. Don't attack the exercise though. Work into it slowly and carefully.

7. Rotate your ankles, wrists and then neck in a series of *slow* motions, back, forth and circular.

This set of stretches, three holds in the fully stretched position for each exercise, can be completed inside twenty minutes. Don't see it as another burden on your time. See it for what it is – an injury–proofing and enjoyable supplement to your training program. Done alternate days it makes little demands upon your time and it's not physically stressful. Enjoy it.

Finish off your stretching routine with a favor for your eyes. Sit comfortably and move your eyes in a variety of directions. Up and down, side to side, clockwise rotation, counterclockwise rotation. No forceful movements though. Do several repetitions of each movement, starting very conservatively – your eyes will quickly get tired to begin with. Over a few weeks, slowly build up the repetitions and range of movement. This only takes a few minutes and will help to keep your eye muscles in good shape.

This stretching program should be considered as the *minimum*. You may want to do more, investigating the subject in depth. The first additional movement I'd recommend is the broomstick circling exercise (dislocates) described in Chapter 9 under *Positioning the bar*. However, don't get so keen that you try to do too much and end up, after a few weeks, exhausting your enthusiasm for any flexibility work.

An additional component in flexibility, and gaining better control over your body, is learning muscle control. While popular much earlier in the century, it's fallen out of favor now. If you have the time, consider pursuing this art. It's fun as well as beneficial.

Chiropractic

Get to know a chiropractor with a training background. Have the chiropractor be familiar with you *before* you get injured, then consult him whenever you have an injury problem. Ask for advice specific for you on how to use the RICE process (rest, ice, compression and elevation) to rehabilitate minor injuries quickly, and the correct use of heat treatments and exercise.

Don't treat yourself based on hearsay and myths. Find out which symptoms, for you, should direct you *immediately* to the chiropractor's office.

Don't train through injuries. (However, when properly supervised by an *expert*, appropriate exercising of some types of injuries can hasten recovery.) Learn what caused the problem, make the necessary corrections when you're back in the gym, and learn the lessons well.

A chiropractor, or other practitioner specializing in structural injuries, who isn't experienced in weight training is unlikely to be able to give you the service and results you want. Choose the most appropriate professional you can find.

This is a *very* important chapter. Heed its advice. What you do in the gym will make a major contribution to how you feel in years to come. *Don't abuse your body now and pay the price later.* The positive aspect of all this care over exercise performance is that it's not only a prerequisite for longevity in the gym and an injury–free training life – it's a necessity for gains in the present. There's no advantage, even in the short run, for unsafe exercise style. Train safely.

To try to stimulate substantial increase in size in a single body part, without first having got the main structures of the body in pretty impressive condition, is to have turned bodybuilding upside down, inside out and back to front.

12: Specialization

One of the biggest mistakes that typical bodybuilders make is to use specialization routines before they have earned the right to use them.

It constantly amazes me just how many neophytes, near neophytes and other insufficiently developed bodybuilders plunge into single body part specialization programs. The most commonly chosen body part is the upper arm. For a typical bodybuilder who is miles away from squatting for twenty reps with one and a half times bodyweight, an arm specialization program is utterly inappropriate and useless. The development needed to squat well *over* one and a half times bodyweight for twenty reps is better proof of having built .the foundation needed to have a chance of productively using body part specialization routines.

All gyms I've been in have teenaged boys blasting away on routines dominated by arm exercises without their physiques having even the faintest of resemblance to those of bodybuilders. Thin arms, connected to narrow shoulders, fixed to shallow chests, joined to frail backs and skinny legs don't need body part specialization programs. Let's not have skewed priorities. Let's not try to put icing on the cake before the cake has been baked.

Priorities

To try to stimulate a substantial increase in size in a single body part, without first having the main structures of the body in pretty impressive condition, is to have turned bodybuilding upside down, inside out and back to front.

The typical bodybuilder simply isn't going to get much meat on his arms, calves, shoulders, pectorals and neck unless first a considerable amount of muscle around the thighs, hips and back has been developed. It simply isn't possible – for the drug–free typical bodybuilder, that is – to add much if any size to the small areas unless the big areas are already becoming substantial.

There's a knock–on effect from the effort to add substantial size to the thigh, hip and back structure (closely followed by the upper–body pushing structure). The little areas come along in size (so long as you don't totally neglect them) pretty much in proportion to the increase in size of the big areas. It's not a case of getting big and strong thighs, hips, back and upper–body pushing structure with everything else staying put. Far from it. As the thigh, hip, back and upper–body pushing structure grows, so does everything else. Work hard on squats and deadlifts, in addition to bench presses, an overhead press and some row or pulldown, and add a little isolation work – curls, calf raises and neck work (not all of this at every workout).

The "driver"

The key point is that the "engine" that drives the gains in the small areas is the progress being made in the big areas. If you take it easy on the thigh and back work you will, generally speaking, have trouble making big gains in the other exercises, no matter how hard you work the latter.

All this isn't to say just do squats, deadlifts and upper back work, quite closely followed by some upper–body pressing work. While such a limited program will deliver good gains on these few exercises, with some knock–on effect throughout the body, it's not a year after year program. Very abbreviated routines are great for getting gains moving, and for building a foundation for *moderately* expanded routines. They are fine to keep returning to on a regular basis. The other training periods should include more than four exercises in them – not necessarily all in the same workout but spread over the week. This will maintain balance throughout the body and capitalize upon the progress made in the thigh, hip and back structure.

Just remember that the thigh, hip and back structure comes first and is the "driver" (closely followed by the upper–body pushing structure) for the other exercises. These other exercises, though important in their own right, are passengers relative to the driving team.

Big arms

To get big arms, get yourself on a basic program that focuses on the leg, hip and back structure without neglecting the arms themselves. As you improve your squatting ability, for reps and by say 100 pounds, your curling poundage should readily come up by 30 pounds or so if you work hard enough on your curls. This will add size to your biceps. While adding 100 pounds to your squat, you should be able to add 50–70 pounds to your bench press, for reps. This assumes you've put together a sound program and have worked hard on the bench. That will add size to your triceps.

If you're desperate to add a couple of inches to your upper arms you'll need to add thirty pounds or more over your body, unless your arms are way behind the rest of you. Don't start thinking about 17" arms, or even 16" arms, so long as your bodyweight is 130, 140, 150, 160 or even 170 pounds. Few people can get big arms without having a big body. You're unlikely to be one of the exceptions.

Fifteen sets of arm flexor exercises, and fifteen sets of isolation tricep exercises – with a few squats, deadlifts and bench presses thrown in as an afterthought – *will* give you a great pump and attack the arms from "all angles." However, it won't make your arms grow much if at all unless you're already squatting and benching big poundages, or are drug–assisted or genetically gifted.

As your main structures come along in size and strength (thigh, hip and back structure, and the pressing structure), the directly involved smaller body parts are brought along in size too. How can you bench press or dip impressive poundages without adding a lot of size to your triceps? How can you deadlift the house and row big weights without having the arm flexors – not to mention shoulders and upper back – to go with those lifts? How can you squat close to twice bodyweight, for plenty of reps, without having a lot of muscle all over your body?

The greater the development and strength of the main muscular structures of the body, the greater the size and strength potential of the small areas of the body. Think it through. Suppose you can only squat and deadlift with 200 pounds, and your arms measure about 13". You're unlikely to add any more than half an inch or so on them no matter *how much* arm specialization you put in.

However, put some real effort into the squat and deadlift, together with the bench press and a few other major basic movements. Build up the poundages by 50% or more, to the point where you can squat 300 pounds for over ten reps, and pack on thirty pounds of muscle. Then, unless you have an unusual arm structure, you should be able to get your arms to around 16". If you want 17" arms, reckon on having to squat more than a few reps with around twice bodyweight, and on adding many more pounds of muscle throughout your body (unless you have a better–than–average growth potential in your upper arms).

All of this arm development would have been achieved without a single concentration curl, without a single pushdown and without a single preacher curl. A lesson in priorities.

Proportions

Of course body proportions can become out of balance if you use unbalanced routines indefinitely. (Short and medium–term use of very abbreviate routines is highly desirable though, and a long–term necessity for some extremely hard gainers.) You're not recommended to use unbalanced routines for year after year. Pile most of your energy and determination into the basic exercises that stimulate the thigh, hip, back and upper–body pushing structure. Put the remaining energy (at least in some cycles, though not necessarily all of them) into a few exercises to cover the small areas. You'll then grow pretty much in balance throughout the body.

The balance may not be "perfect," but it's good enough to last you until you're really big and strong. Once you're big and strong – by the standards of successful typical bodybuilders, not the professionals – then you'll have the foundation to prudently use specialization programs to bring up any lagging body parts.

Equal attention?

> Why not just give *every* body part equal attention right
> from day one in the gym, so no body part ever gets
> behind another?

The amount of work you'd need to do, to do this, will exceed the recovery capabilities of the typical person. Also, the quantity of work involved will necessitate training intensity being spread so thinly that little or no growth will be stimulated.

So, you'll either get growth stimulation that can't be responded to because you don't have enough recovery capacity. Or, you'll never be able to stimulate growth in the first place.

If you've no intention in engaging in competitive bodybuilding – as indeed most bodybuilders don't – why be concerned if the rear head of the deltoid is 10% less developed than the other heads? Similarly, why be concerned if the serratus isn't 100% up to scratch? Why be concerned if the inner head of the triceps is a smidgeon behind the lateral head? Glaring imbalances matter, of course, but not the small things that only judges of top level contests will notice. Let's keep things in perspective.

Get everything growing, while avoiding glaring imbalances. Leave concern for whether or not every single aspect of every muscle area is 100% up to scratch until after you're so big that your main concern is refinement. You can then devote yourself to bringing up very slightly lagging areas and "polishing" your physique, while forget about building more size. How many bodybuilders get to this stage?

Of course, different variations of the same basic movement may emphasize one head or aspect of the involved musculature more than the others do. However, this small variation is of little importance compared to the total effect of the movements on the involved musculature.

It's growth of the whole involved musculature that should concern you, not little bits of the area. Big gains in the squat mean big gains in the thighs. Big gains in the deadlift – whether regular style, stiff–legged or wide–grip – mean big gains in the back musculature. Big gains in the bench press or dip mean big gains in the chest, shoulder and triceps.

If you never do calf work, neck work and overhead presses you're going to develop some major lagging body parts. Don't totally neglect anything, just keep things in the right order of priority.

Generally speaking, I don't recommend specialization programs other than those that focus on the thigh, hip and back structure while also working hard on the upper–body pushing structure. In effect, nearly all of the routines in this book concentrate on the thigh, hip and back structures, with the bench press or dip in close attendance. In this way, all the routines are specialization programs. This approach is the best way for the *typical* bodybuilder to get big and strong throughout the body, including building the small and "showy" muscles into impressive condition.

Look of power

Suppose that you could get big arms, shoulders and pectorals without building up the main structures. What a wimp and a sham of a body it would be. A body with fully developed legs, hips and back (especially the traps and lower back) has an aura and semblance of power and impressiveness that make a mockery of size concentrated on the front of the body. This is what is meant by the *look of power*.

What about the notion that undeveloped buttocks are desirable so as to create the "illusion" that the rest of the body is larger than it really is? That notion is as attractive to me as is the belief that an undeveloped neck and undeveloped trapezius are assets because they make the shoulders appear wider than they are.

A well–developed pair of legs, and a strong and impressive back, look out of place – ludicrous, even – if not accompanied by correspondingly well–developed buttocks. Of course big buttocks with thin legs and back look even more unattractive. You need to be big and strong throughout your body. A large neck not only looks very impressive but is desirable for doing your best to make your neck "injury–proof."

If you've been conditioned to believe you should keep the buttocks as small as possible, you'll have an aversion to the basic squat and deadlift. This will make your body averse to developing mounds of muscle – not only in your leg, hip and back structure – but throughout the rest of the body as well. A loser from all points of view.

Specialization techniques

Let's suppose you've developed enough of a foundation to benefit from a specialization program aimed at bringing up a lagging body part. How should you go about it?

> First off, be sure that you really do have a sufficient foundation. Squatting for twenty reps with 150% or so of your bodyweight is a minimum. That means about 240 pounds if you're 160 pounds, about 270 if you're 180, and so on; for twenty down–to–parallel reps, with a few breaths between reps (not continuous reps). For bent–legged deadlifts, ten reps with 175–200% bodyweight, again with a few breaths between reps.

Perhaps you'll benefit from a specialization program at this stage, but maybe it's still premature. Only actual practice will let you know. Perhaps you're such a rule unto yourself that the conditions I have given don't apply to you, or at least you don't think they do.

Don't think I'm anti–specialization. I'm *for* specialization, so long as it's justified, but I want it to be effective. Hence the stress upon building a foundation first.

A different reason for specializing on a single body part is training variety. Perhaps you feel the need for a few weeks of focusing on a single area and giving heavy training on the most demanding exercises a rest. Perhaps you need something to slot into a period of only a few weeks before being unable to get in the gym for a while. How well you respond to the specialization will be largely if not wholly a reflection of what I've written in this chapter.

Precisely how you specialize can be the factor determining the effectiveness. If you do too much, and/or do it too often, you'll still get nowhere even if you have the base of size and strength. When specializing, you need to find a productive volume and intensity of work. Merely doubling, trebling or even quadrupling the volume of work for a given body part isn't the line to take. While not building you up, this approach will wear you down and make you ripe for illness.

Target area

Specialize on a single area – don't try to specialize on two, three or even more body parts. Some bodybuilders' specialization routines end up as total body specialization routines. Take one body part only – upper arms, shoulders, calves, pectorals, upper back, or wherever else – and increase your attention there while decreasing your attention elsewhere. If you increase the demands upon your body in one location, you must compensate by reducing the demands elsewhere.

Length of specialization

A specialization program is a short–term thing. "Milk" *it* dry without it "milking" *you* dry. Get the most out of it but don't battle on with it beyond how long it can yield results for you. Just how long this is, will vary according to the individual, the program used and how well the recovery factors are satisfied.

Perhaps four weeks are all you'll be able to gain for, perhaps six weeks, perhaps even eight weeks or more. As soon as you feel about to get stale, stop it. Take a week or so off and return to a non-specialization routine for a cycle. Return to another specialization routine if you feel the need.

Individual fine–tuning

As with all the routines given in this book, you must tailor each one to fit you. This isn't a "cop–out" on my behalf, but an acknowledgement of the role individual variation plays. Not just individual variation in genetically determined factors, but variations in lifestyle, quality of rest and sleep, training facilities, and other factors.

Getting started

A good starting place is to train the chosen body part twice a week and the rest of the body once a week. The body parts not to be specialized upon should be worked hard enough to prevent atrophy, but no more. After a warmup set or two, do two sets of "hard" work. Hard, as in not–quite–to–failure. If you drive yourself into the deck in the non–specialization work, how can your body devote its attention to a single body part?

What an irony it would be if the area being specialized upon failed to grow while the low volume and "just hard" work for the rest of the body actually delivered gains.

A specialization program for the upper arms:

> *Monday and Friday*
> Barbell curl
> Parallel bar dip using a comfortable style which allows you to use the most resistance
> Reverse barbell curl, using an EZ curling bar if a straight bar is uncomfortable
> Close–grip bench press (15" between thumbs)

Wednesday
Crunch style abdominal exercise
Squat
One-legged dumbbell calf raise
Stiff-legged deadlift or bent-over row
Bench press
Press behind neck

On this program the specialization work is done on different days to that for the rest of the body. This is good in the sense that you've no distraction on your specialization days. However, you have to come into the gym three days a week and your arms get worked three times a week, albeit indirectly on Wednesdays. This may be too much work for the arms. It may be better to combine the work for the rest of the body with the arm specialization work on either Monday or Friday, doing the arm work first.

The arm work could be followed by the work for the rest of the body on Monday. This gives you four days rest before an arms-only workout on Friday. This gives five rest days and two training days each week, as against four and three respectively in the other interpretation. Such a difference can make a big difference for typical bodybuilders.

Pursuing a different course, perhaps during a *short* period of specialization you could gain from training a single body part three times a week. For this to have the chance of working, all other work must be at rock bottom and factors of recuperation in 100% good order. Something to consider trying for a month or so.

How much and what type of work do you do for the body part to be specialized upon? Enough but not too much. How much is enough and how much is too much? The general recommendation is to choose less but do it harder, rather than to do more but do it easier. The only work you'll be doing that's flat-out is for the area to be specialized upon. Therefore, you can do more sets than usual for a single area without lowering the intensity of effort.

Keeping up full-bore effort for squats, bench presses, deadlifts, rows and overhead presses is a darned sight more difficult than keeping up full-bore effort for a list of four arm exercises. If you really pour yourself into the arm exercises, doing 2-3 top sets for each exercise, you might surprise yourself with just how hard you can do the exercises and how much systemic fatigue you can generate.

Note that the specialization exercises chosen are basic building ones, not mere "detail" movements. This is vital if you're to have a chance of *growing*.

Raising the intensity

Ultra–intense techniques *may* be productive during a specialization program, but, as made clear in Chapter 10, they have their disadvantages.

Prudent use of some of these techniques can modify the initial arm specialization program:

Monday
   A light and a medium warmup set of curls and pushups gets the arms ready for what follows.
   1. Seated barbell curl – the seated position makes the movement a partial one and enables you to rest the bar on your thighs to get out extra reps rest–pause style.
   2. Parallel bar dip
   3. Barbell curl to failure
   4. Close–grip bench press to failure
   Rest for ten minutes.
   5. Squat
   6. Donkey calf raise
   7. Stiff–legged deadlift or bent–over row
   8. Bench press
   9. Press behind neck
   10. Crunch style situp
   (Exercises 5–10 will suffer due to the arms having been trained first. This doesn't matter if the arms are the priority. Generally speaking though, arms are trained at the end of the workout.)

Friday
   A light and a medium warmup set of curls and pushups serves to get the arms ready for what follows.
   1. Seated barbell curl
   2. Parallel bar dip
   3. Reverse curl to failure, a 50% weight drop and more reps to failure again
   4. Close–grip bench press to failure plus two forced reps
   5. Parallel bar dip – super slow (see Chapter 13)
   6. Barbell curl – super slow

Other variables

Be consistent with rest periods between sets. Whatever you fix, stick with it. Be it no rest (when doing a single set of each exercise done back-to-back) or be it one minute or ninety seconds, or whatever else if you're doing multiple sets. How many sets per exercise? The harder you train the less you can do. The more sets you do the more you must economize on intensity.

Try it different ways. One set to absolute, total and no-doubt-about-it failure plus (not every workout though) beyond-failure reps. Or, multiple sets *almost* to utter failure. This reads as three or four sets done in a very hard fashion but not the absolute intensity of the "blood and guts" former interpretation.

This doesn't read as six, eight, twelve or more wishy-washy sets. You have to stimulate growth through effort. Effort can't possibly come through large numbers of sets.

Don't stick to one rep range all the time. Conversely, be wary of changing your target reps too often so that you don't get into a good routine. Perhaps use 6-8 reps for one cycle or program, 10-12 for another, and maybe something different for the next. Or, alternate two ranges from workout to workout, adjusting the poundages accordingly. Always remember, how you do the reps is far more important than the number of reps. Avoid getting stuck in a rut with training days, exercises, reps or sets.

Use variations in rep cadence and speed too. If you've been conditioned to taking a breath or more between reps, do your reps in a cheating-free, non-stop fashion for the specialization period. Or, alternate workouts of the different styles.

Keep in mind that what might work for a few weeks during a single body part specialization program can be a disaster if applied to the whole body.

"Softening-up" period

Suppose, in a total body equal-priority program, you've been training your biceps very hard, doing three sets of specific bicep work. Or, you've really been pushing yourself hard on three sets of heel raises to utter failure. Now wouldn't be the right time to specialize on either the biceps or calves.

If you've "hardened" the muscles, you've not set up the best conditions for making the specialization period productive. Better to soften up the areas to be specialized upon before the specialization period starts.

If you plan to specialize upon the biceps soon, drop specific work for the biceps for a couple of months. Let your back work suffice. If you plan to focus on your calves soon, stop direct calf work for a month or so first.

"Softening up" in this way will make your to-be-specialized-upon area more responsive. Break back into the hard work over a couple of weeks and then go full-bore for four weeks or more. You might then add half an inch or more to your previous best girth. If you hold your previous best size and strength right up to the specialization period, you might not even add an eighth of an inch.

Pre-exhaustion

As stated in Robert Kennedy's Savage Sets, the pre-exhaust technique was invented and promoted by Robert Kennedy. The first article on it was published in Iron Man, in 1968. Later, Arthur Jones and Mike Mentzer also promoted the technique.

Of the "beyond regular failure" techniques, you may find that pre-exhaustion (and super slow) can be used more continuously than can the others without burning you out. It can be a productive technique to use if you have problems "getting into" training a certain area. Used prudently, it may help you when specializing.

Pre-exhaustion works by following a single-joint isolation exercise with a multi-joint compound exercise. For example, work the lateral raise to failure and immediately follow it with the press behind neck to failure. The lateral raise works the lateral head of the deltoid. Then, the rest of the deltoid together with the triceps take your lateral head to a greater point of fatigue in the press behind neck. Your press behind neck poundage will suffer but the effect upon your shoulders will be very intense.

You must have the weight set up for the compound exercise before you start on the isolation exercise. You must rush between the two exercises so that the pause is but a few seconds. Have a spotter standing by, or a safety device of some sort, in case – due to fatigue – you lose control while doing the compound movement.

Use pre-exhaustion as one of the tools available to you in a specialization routine. Other common pre-exhaustion combinations are leg extensions and squats, curls and pullups or pulldowns, pushdowns and dips.

One of the drawbacks with pre-exhaustion is that it's very difficult to do in a crowded gym. You need more than one piece of equipment available at the same time. You don't want someone to take the piece of equipment you've set up for the second exercise of the compound.

Consecutive days and twice-a-day training

A technique that will shock a single body part, and perhaps shock it into growth if *used very prudently*, is training on consecutive days. Using the example of the arm specialization routine given earlier, train it three consecutive days and then rest your arms for the rest of the week. You could even do it four consecutive days and then take four or even five days off before training the arms again. This is a very severe training method. With the arms receiving such a battering, stick to training the rest of the body once a week and on one of the arm training days. In this way, all the non-arm days are days of total rest.

Another suggestion applies to the day of the week when you train both the arms and the rest of the body. If it's possible for you to do so – do the arm work in the morning and rest of the work in the afternoon. Then no thought – subconscious or conscious – should be given to exercises to be done immediately after the arm work. Intensity while training the arms can be sustained at its highest because nothing needs to be saved for immediately after.

Another extremely intense *short-term* approach is to train the area to be specialized upon twice each day rather than the normal one session per day. So, for arms, you could train them twice daily for 2 or 3 days per week. The afternoon battering could use a different rep and set scheme to the morning battering. Whether or not you repeat the same workout, the arms will get an almighty shock being trained twice a day for a few weeks. It might just be the shock needed to put half an inch on your upper arms in a month. Ensure you do little work for the rest of the body, and really apply yourself to getting plenty of rest and an adequate diet.

Back-to-back sets

Doing exercises back-to-back is a technique to experiment with during a single body part specialization period. Get your arms warmed up and ready. Then set up the weights for all the arm exercises to follow, setting them up as near to one another as possible. Keep your rep target for each exercise at about eight. Once the first exercise of the run of exercises is started, you get no rest until the final rep of the final exercise is done. The poundages used for the exercises will suffer the deeper you get into the run of exercises. You have to consider this when you set up the poundages to begin with. You'll need a workout or two to get the poundages correctly determined.

Doing your sets back-to-back is more difficult to do in a crowded gym than is pre-exhaustion. It's almost impossible to do. If you plan to do your sets in this manner, do it when the gym is quiet.

Putting it together

There's no single way to specialize on a lagging body part. There are many ways that can work so long as you don't overtrain and don't under-recover.

You *must* train very hard, with progressive poundages, and fully apply yourself to satisfying all requirements for a successful program, both inside and outside the gym. Remember, bodybuilding success comes from satisfying a package of requirements. Neglect of just one of the requirements can negate all the good done by satisfying the other requirements.

Select one suggestion from this chapter, or a combination of more than one suggestion, and experiment for a month. If it goes well, you've learned of an effective short-term specialization method for you. Try it again after a few months.

If the experiment isn't successful, you've still learned something so it wasn't a wasted experience. Fathom out why it didn't work and learn from your mistakes next time you specialize.

One-day specialization

Peary Rader, in The Rader Master Bodybuilding and Weight Gaining System, wrote about *The One Day Program of Specialization*. The forerunner of this approach was specializing on his arms by training them every ninety minutes (six workouts a day) for seven days. Two sets of two exercises were used, one for the biceps and one for the triceps. He used poundages less than usual and didn't work to his limit. He gained three quarters of an inch from this week's work.

Later, he developed a one-day program. Using the example of the upper arms, he recommended training every hour with two exercises – one for the biceps and one for the triceps. The exercises were worked harder than in the one-week program, but not to failure. Massaging the muscles after each workout was recommended. A lighter workout on the half hour between the hourly and heavier workouts was recommended after having first experimented with the hourly program.

While writing this book, I tried an interpretation of this specialization method. The method involves devoting a day to training. If you don't want to stay in the gym for twelve hours, then you have to train at home. I chose to experiment on my triceps as no weight training equipment was necessary. Also, just training a single muscle would be less demanding of time than training triceps and biceps. I wanted to be able to get some writing done between workouts.

From 9 a.m. until 9 p.m., inclusive, I did three sets of a modified version of dips. Facing a sink (basin) I set my hands quite close on the rim and planted my feet so my body from hands to feet was in a straight line. Without moving my feet, I bent my elbows as far as I could and then pushed back to the starting position. I did three sets of almost–to–failure reps, resting only a minute between sets. The reps dropped with each set. The reps usually went twelve or more the first set, ten the second and seven the last. The nearer the feet are to the sink, the easier the exercise.

Every half hour I did three sets of floor pushups using a close hand spacing, keeping the stress of the exercise on the triceps. I did each set a rep or two easier than the hourly workouts.

Over the twelve hours I did thirteen hourly workouts and twelve half–hourly workouts. A week later I still had a gain of 3/16 of an inch so it appeared to be a permanent gain. Quite worth the effort though a smaller gain than Peary Rader made. Had I worked both biceps and triceps I might have made it nearer the half an inch gain.

If you try this method, be sure your body is familiar with the chosen exercise(s). Don't, for example, use the "sink" tricep exercise for the first time on the actual day of specialization. You want to be sore after the day's work, not crippled and injured. Set aside a whole day when you can avoid all disturbances. Train, rest, consume nutritious drinks every hour or two, and think big.

Making it work

In the next chapter there's further information on sets, reps and how to put routines together. No single training instruction chapter of this book can be seen in isolation. The book must be studied in its *entirety* if you're to obtain the full benefits it offers you. Read it, reread it and reread it again.

Following the example of an arm specialization program, you can devise other specialization programs. Put together your program with great care and seriousness. Learn from experience and "listen" to how your body responds, making adjustments if they seem necessary. These adjustments include choosing different exercises, a different set/rep scheme, a different rep cadence or a different workout frequency.

If, no matter how diligently and conscientiously you followed a soundly–constructed specialization routine, it didn't work, what do you do? Forget about such specialization routines for a good while and focus upon getting the whole body growing as a unit. Focus (specialize) on developing a 25% *minimum* gain in the poundages in the key exercises – squats, deadlifts, bench presses (or parallel bar dips) and an overhead press. Then you'll grow, without a single "little" exercise. Priorities, remember.

Don't be a slave to a routine on paper if it just doesn't suit you in practice. At the same time, don't oscillate from one approach to another, never accurately being able to assess the worth of a single interpretation.

It's *you* who must unite your experience, your physical condition, your lifestyle limitations, your training conditions, your mental state, your motivation, your current understanding, your interest and your goals. Only then can you design the routine that seems most appropriate for you *at present*.

It doesn't matter how much your training may seem out-of-step with what others do. Don't be reluctant to be radical in your experiments. What matters to you is what works for you.

13: More Diversity

As has been stated elsewhere in this book, there's more than one way to pack muscle on a typical bodybuilder. You've been taken through all the factors (but not all the variations) that need to come together to make a successful bodybuilding program, excluding nutrition. Now it's time to do some review work together with delving further into productive variations of the basic formula.

Some bodybuilders progress mainly through the "blood and guts" approach of one set to failure per exercise while others mostly use 3–5 "hard" sets per exercise. Some train the whole body twice a week at most, some train some exercises twice a week and the other exercises once a week. Some people train everything once every fifth or sixth day. Others segregate the whole body workout and spread it over three or even four days per week, training each exercise once a week.

Some use free–weights exclusively, some use machines exclusively, others use a mixture. Some use slow repetition speed and reduced poundages while others prefer a faster cadence – though cheating–free – and much heavier poundages. Some people keep the bar moving throughout the set while others prefer a short pause between reps.

Some prefer to rest well between sets, others prefer to rest a maximum of one minute between sets, and others prefer to do all non–warmup sets back–to–back. Some (those who rest well between sets) are in the gym for two hours at a stretch, others are in and out in under half an hour. Some prefer always to do reps above ten, others mostly do 6–8 reps while others rarely go above five. Some do a handful of exercises only, while others do more.

Some use all these variations at one time or another, some prefer to stick to a single way of doing things.

Some use super slow training for long stretches while others use it for single cycles every now and then. Some can't "get into" super slow training and have never used it other than the initial trial. Some never try super slow, being very content with the progress they are making with other methods.

Some can squat and deadlift with nothing but gain. Others can't do regular squats and deadlifts because of some structural problem, whether congenital or acquired. Some people get great results from the regular bench press while others get much better results from bench presses on a low inclined bench. Some people get terrific results from the parallel bar dip, and even prefer it to the bench press. Others get nothing but shoulder problems from the parallel bar dip.

Some people can't progress much in the pullup to save their lives, others love the exercise and can work up to impressive poundages around their waists. For some, the T-bar row is nothing but a threat to the integrity of their backs. To others, it's one of the great exercises. In all routines, the fine-tuning of exercise selection is an individual matter.

Some can grow on only 3,000 calories and seven hours of sleep a night while others need 4,500 calories and 9-10 hours sleep. Some drink lots of milk, some never touch it. Some people are heavy meat eaters, some don't eat any meat. Some use supplements and swear by them, some never touch supplements and believe them to be useless.

What might appear to be the ideal has to be adjusted according to the realities of everyday living and stresses. You have to be flexible enough to move with changing circumstances so progress is sustained over the long-term. This book presents variations upon a basic theme so as to provide you with sufficient alternatives for you always to be able to find something that's workable for you.

A need for different rep ranges?

There's an opinion in bodybuilding that says it's necessary to do some sets of 6-8 reps and some of 15-20, or reps around these numbers, and do this diversity for every body part. The reasoning? The lower reps are needed to train fast-twitch fibers and the components of muscle cells associated with strength. The higher reps, so the reasoning goes, are needed to work the slow twitch fibers and the components of the muscle associated with endurance.

A counter opinion is emphatic in saying that the higher reps needed to train the slow twitch fibers are in the hundreds, not tens. And, the components of endurance-induced muscle size – capillarization, number of mitochondria and the storage of substances the mitochondria use – can only be increased a small amount at best. In comparison with the size gains on a regular bodybuilding routine mostly using reps below ten, the endurance-induced size gains are small. Better to focus, says this counter opinion, on gaining size the most effective way rather than spending time and effort (likely contributing to overtraining) on a less important approach.

Far more important than just which rep range is "best" is the need for very hard work and progressive poundages. How you do the reps, and how you make your workouts progressive, is the substance of training. Concern with training all fiber types and all components of a muscle may be just another distraction from hard work and progressive poundages. When at the level of "finishing" a physique, when the final details are important, these secondary matters matter. When building the substance of a physique, the primary matters are what matter.

> Don't spend inordinate amounts of time studying the "maybes" of training and forget to put in real effort in the gym. Some bodybuilders are walking textbooks of information but never drive themselves hard in the gym. Better that you're ignorant of all the "maybes" and just focus on delivering the real goods where they matter, in the gym. Priorities.

You can benefit from different rep ranges as long as you train hard and progressively. Some people prefer higher reps than do others. Some exercises, at least for some people, are more suited to higher reps. If your calves grow from sets of twenty reps, fine. If they grow quicker from sets of ten, that's fine as well. Your legs will grow from both 20-rep squats and sets of 6–8. Perhaps your bench press progresses well from sets of 5–7 but trying to add weight to the bar when doing sets of 10–12 is far more difficult. Find your own way.

Single-rep work

Very low rep work – triples, doubles and singles – is often criticized as being only necessary for demonstrating strength. Yes, single-rep maximum poundage lifting is necessary to demonstrate absolute strength. But, single-rep training can be an invaluable training tool in actually building strength, as can doubles and triples. How many of the strongest powerlifters and Olympic weightlifters haven't done a lot of very low rep work?

Very low rep work thickens tendons, ligaments and bone, and trains you to be able to recruit more muscle fibers. This makes you a lot stronger, without necessarily making you bigger. It enables you to translate increased muscle size and strength gained from medium and high rep work into the full demonstration of strength for singles. What's wrong with that? Nothing, as long as you don't abuse this type of training and injure yourself. Caution is the key word.

When using single-rep work as a training tool – as against a means of pure strength demonstration – the poundages used are not actual 100% efforts. They are 90–95% of your absolute limit weights – they aren't "real" singles. The provisos are that you're using the big basic exercises that can be done for singles, that you're not "carrying" any injuries, that you can tolerate very low rep work, that you've been recently training on reps no more than five and have conditioned yourself to handling weights near to your absolute limit, that you're not a teenager, and that you're already either at or very near to the goals given in Chapter 3. In other words, you're advanced. If you're qualified, how do you proceed?

Take 90% of your single best lift. If you don't know what this is, estimate it based on your best five-rep set. Estimate it on the low side rather than the high side. Always better to have a longer cycle than to short-circuit it by starting too heavy. Following your warmup work, do five singles with the 90% poundage, taking a couple of minutes or so between singles. Over a couple of workouts, build up to ten singles. Then, add five pounds and do another ten singles at the next workout. You should be able to keep this progression of five pounds every week going for a month if not a couple of months, so long as you're not training too frequently, are eating and sleeping well, and doing everything else called for in this book.

As the poundages get nearer and nearer to your new absolute single lift, reduce the progression to 2½ pounds per increment and take more rest between each pair of singles. When you can no longer get all ten singles with a given weight, keep adding the small increments each week but reduce the number of singles. You may need to add an extra day or two between workouts as you close in on your absolute maximum lift. Stick at it, over as many workouts as you can keep it going, until you're at your new absolute maximum single. Tight form, excellent recovery, thorough warmups, very abbreviated workouts.

This type of training is very severe, so keep total training to a minimum. Focus on a single lift and only do another handful of exercises in maintenance style, in a regular set and rep scheme. You could use the single-rep training on more than one exercise but, for your first attempt, just use one exercise. Get it all right and you'll be surprised just how much you can gain from this sort of work.

Variety of exercises

Stress is given by many to the need to have a variety of exercises "to train the muscle from all angles." There's something in this, but the usual recommendations take the focus away from the big basic lifts to focus upon the far less productive (for building mass) small isolation exercises. Also, the usual focus is upon getting the variety in the same workout whereas it should be had from cycle to cycle.

Take advantage of a variety of exercises, but make sure the variety is of the big basic lifts. Another way to add variety to a workout, is to keep the actual exercises pretty much constant, but change where you do the exercise and with what. For example, take the military press with a barbell. Instead of perhaps boring yourself with the same standing military press with a regular barbell for cycle after cycle, make some changes. Press from supports in the power rack. Press while seated on a slightly inclined bench. Press from a dead-stop at the bottom. Press using a thicker barbell than usual. Do partial presses for a while. Press using a trap bar.

Much the same sort of comments and suggestions can be made for other exercises. There's so much you can do with the big basic lifts that you can get variety without needing even to consider using the little exercises that won't build you up anyway.

When you're already big and strong, and your focus moves to detail and "finish," then the focus of exercise selection doesn't have to be upon the big, multi-joint exercises. Then you're into advanced training. Before you qualify to do this, you have to have built yourself big enough. Few drug-free hard gainers are big enough.

An instant way to add variety to your training, while keeping your routine the same, is to change gym. The change of environment can do wonders to add zest to your motivation.

Super high intensity training and alternatives

To work medium to high rep squats followed immediately by stiff-legged deadlifts, both done to the point of nigh-on collapse is diligence, motivation and plain will of the highest order. To add on another handful of basic movements, each worked right to the bone, and finish the entire series of exercises in less than thirty minutes, is probably as demanding as training can possibly become. Anyone who doesn't believe this can't have trained as hard as I've just described.

Anyone who can train like this on a sustained basis – assuming some use of intensity cycling, adequate rest between workouts and adequate nutrition – is going to become very big, very strong, superbly conditioned in the heart and lungs, mentally resilient, and do all this within a few years rather than decades. Darned effective it undoubtedly is. Training in this manner is incredibly difficult to do. Doing it for one workout isn't enough. Do it every workout for a couple of months – while satisfying all other important considerations – and then you'll see some big results.

As this style of training is almost unbelievably brutal, and so few can do it on a regular basis, and because it involves supervision, extraordinary individual motivation, and workout conditions that very few people can satisfy, it's rarely done. If you can train in this style, do so. If you can only train in this style now and then, do so. Ultra-high intensity training is the most time and cost effective way to get bigger and stronger as long as you recover between workouts.

If you can't train like this, at least not all the time, what else can you do? Compromise (perhaps) upon your rate of gain and try to compensate for the drop of intensity by moderately increasing the volume of training.

A twist in all this is that I believe it *is* possible to train too hard. If you're simply not conditioned for it, not only is it not necessary to train to the point of collapse from a single set, but it's counter productive.

High intensity training is the direction to go in, but be very prudent how you use the mega-intensity training. It's not just what you do in the gym but also the training frequency, the cycling of intensity, the number of calories consumed, the amount of sleep, and other considerations. Everything has to be in order.

What rational interpretation is there of training outside of mega-intensity work? Do more sets of the same short list of basic exercises. The sets must still be quality ones, taken very close to your limit. The more sets you do, the less intensity you must be putting in. Sets must still be kept on the low side. Nothing is written in stone, so understand that there is flexibility. Just how flexible you can be depends upon you.

Here are illustrations of some of the alternatives:

"Blood and guts" approach, twice a week
All warmup work done to begin with, all exercise weights set up in advance so exercises can be done back-to-back.
1. Squat – to absolute failure, about 20 reps
2. Stiff-legged deadlift – to one rep short of absolute failure, about 15 reps (once a week only for the deadlift)
3. Calf raise – to absolute failure plus breakdowns
4. Parallel bar dips – to absolute failure followed by negatives
5. One-arm row – to absolute failure, about 10 reps
6. Seated press – to absolute failure, about 10 reps
7. Barbell curl – to absolute failure, about 8 reps
8. Crunch-style situp – to absolute failure
Absolute failure means continuing until the bar won't budge an inch despite maximum effort.

"Regular" hard training, twice a week

Each exercise is an entity in itself with warmup and "work" sets being done for each exercise before moving on to the next. Two minutes rest between sets, or less. Each "work" set is taken to the point where another rep can't be performed.

1. Crunch–style situp
2. Squat – 3 sets (once a week or three times every two weeks if twice a week is too much)
3. Calf raise – 4 sets
4. Bench press – 5 sets
5. Stiff–legged deadlift – 2 sets *once* a week
6. Press behind neck – 3 sets
7. Pulldown – 3 sets
8. Barbell curl – 3 sets
9. Parallel bar dip – 2 sets

The sets for individual exercises can either be done with a constant poundage and therefore less reps for each repeat set, or, with reduced poundages per repeat set in order to maintain the same rep target.

"Regular" hard training using a 3–day–a–week split routine

Divide the previous routine into two even halves, keeping the upper–body pushing exercises together, and the pulling exercises together. Alternate the routines – do the first half on Monday, the second half on Wednesday, first half on Friday, second half on Monday, et cetera. The training days can and should be adjusted according to circumstances and recovery, as indeed they should be on any routine.

"Regular" hard training using a different 3–day–a–week split routine

Sunday
Bench press – 5 sets
Barbell curl – 4 sets
Close–grip bench press – 3 sets
Calves – 3–4 sets

Tuesday
Deadlift – 2–3 sets
Bent–over row – 4 sets
Shrug – 2 sets
Neck and grip work

Friday
Squat – 5 sets

Calves – 3–4 sets
Seated press – 4 sets
Barbell curl – 4 sets
Parallel bar dip – 3 sets
Neck and grip work

Concerning rep ranges, get the best of all worlds by using all (reasonable) rep ranges over time, not all at once in the same workout or even in the same cycle. Choose 4–6, 6–8, 8–10, 10–12 and sometimes higher reps for lower–body work – 15–20 and 25–30.

Variety is the spice of training life so long as it's productive variety. Keep up your training enthusiasm by changing your rep schemes (and other variables) occasionally.

No matter how beneficial a given rep range is supposed to be, it won't do a darned thing for you unless you combine it with some sustained effort.

Rep cadence

Reps can be done in a continuous cadence or with rest pauses in between. The rest pause is the break between reps. It can be short or not–so–short. The continuous cadence style restricts the size of the poundages that can be used but shortens the duration of the sets and heightens the ache in the muscle(s) being trained. Using a short pause between reps enables greater poundages to be used. Taken to its extreme of thirty seconds or more between reps (this is usually reserved for pure strength training and necessitates setting the bar down between reps) a single set almost becomes a series of single–rep sets.

Some exercises are more suited to one style. Calf raises are most suited to the continuous style. Squats and bent–leg deadlifts provide an almost overwhelming urge to use a rest–pause style, taking a few deep breaths between reps. Other exercises come in between. The first half of the reps come in a near continuous cadence, the other half come in the rest–pause style of a deep breath or few between reps. The three styles of rep performance each have their merits and stress the body somewhat differently. Each has its place.

This is another consideration for you when devising your routines. Again, you have a lot of training time ahead of you so don't try to use all the alternatives at once. Spread them out over several training cycles. Learn what suits you and what doesn't suit you. Design your later programs based on your findings.

Many people get themselves so concerned with what is the "best" rep cadence (and rep range, pace of training and many other matters) that they forget that of first importance is hard work and progressive poundages. While no single "right" combination exists, let's suppose it does. If you have the right combination but don't marry it with absolute will, determination, planning and effort you'll never progressively build up your poundages. If you don't do this, then you can forget about body*building*.

What matters is what works

You're on your own when designing and performing your training routines. It's you who must unite your experience, your physical condition, your lifestyle limitations, your training conditions, your mental state, your motivation, your current understanding, your interest and your goals in order to design the routine that's most appropriate for you *at present*. What's appears to be best for you now may not be in six months time, or in twelve, or even in three. Always stay in the basic pattern of short routines dominated by the big basic exercises, using low to medium sets, varying rep ranges over time, not too frequent workouts, varying the format over cycles, and having generous rest and sound nutritional contributions. Then you'll grow.

What matters is what works. Whatever productive formula you concoct, fine. It doesn't matter how much it may seem out–of–step with what others do. Don't be reluctant to be radical in your experiments. If you stay in the groove of unproductive but conventional training, you'll get nowhere. Strike out and build a bigger and stronger physique than you may have realistically thought possible. Don't be constrained by the training habits of others. You're training yourself, not others. What matters to you is what works for you.

Bone growth?

There's an opinion that believes that bone structure can be affected, beneficially, especially in teenaged bodybuilders and those in their twenties. This opinion advises the use of high rep squats in combination with "breathing" pullovers or Rader chest pulls to enlarge the rib cage and shoulder girdle. This opinion also believes that pulldowns, pullups, very wide grip shrugs and perhaps the press behind the neck will help enlarge the shoulder girdle.

Getting incontrovertible evidence for this is no simple task. However, I believe all very young, and not–so–young bodybuilders should give the opinion the benefit of any doubt and use the "stretching" exercises.

High rep squats, pullovers, pulldowns or pullups, and the press behind the neck should appear regularly in the programs of all able and serious bodybuilders. Wide grip shrugs – sometimes on an inclined bench – can be included in some cycles too.

Super slow

This method of training has been studied and written about in great detail by Ken Hutchins (The Ultimate Exercise Protocol: Super Slow) and Ellington Darden, Ph.D. (Big). Performing reps slowly isn't something new, but the organization and rationale associated with super slow is new. It's another technique to consider experimenting with. It's another of the *many* potentially effective ways to train.

It's important to remember that all these ways are *not* similarly effective for everyone. What someone raves over, and has the results to back up his enthusiasm, may yield nothing for someone else. What's effective for some is ineffective for others. Individual experimentation is a must, though not with the plain ludicrous.

Super slow has its own set and rep scheme and protocol, different to that given for training with a traditional rep speed. Everything else written in this book though – training frequency, cycling, slow poundage increments, brief routines, et cetera – *applies* to super slow.

Super slow has its critics, critics who are as adamant that super slow *isn't* the best way to train as its advocates are adamant that it's one of if not *the* best way to train. Investigate thoroughly, make a fair experiment, and then come to your own conclusion.

Procedure

Hutchins recommends 3–5 reps per set for advanced trainees, and 4–8 for others. Stephen Wedan – an artist and bodybuilding journalist who has written extensively on super slow – advises reps in the range of about 4–5 or 6 and avoiding maximum contractions during the first 2–3 reps. The positive (concentric) part of the rep (the pull or push part) takes ten seconds and the negative (eccentric) contraction takes five seconds, with speed of movement being *steady*, not erratic. You "ease" into each rep, absolutely no snap of movement.

The "turnarounds" at the top and bottom of the reps take additional seconds and you *don't* rest in the locked-out position of, for example, the squat, or, in the stretched position of, for example, the barbell curl. The "turnaround" is done just *before* the lockout of each rep so that there's no conscious rest for the muscles, not even a fraction of a second. Of course there is a stop, to be able to change direction, but you're to imagine the "turnaround" as being a constant but very slow movement – rather like going around a curve to change direction. (A total super slow rep will take about twenty seconds.) The "turnaround" in the position that has the least resistance – the bottom of the barbell curl, and the top of a squat, as examples – is done quicker than the "turnaround" where the position has high resistance. The stress on the muscles is throughout the set – there are no breaks, hence the agony of execution.

Continue each set, without holding your breath, until the bar stops moving. This will happen somewhere during the positive stage of the rep. Only record completed reps in your training diary. The final partial rep doesn't get in until it becomes a complete rep at a later workout.

When the movement stops, that isn't the end of the set. You must *keep* pushing (or pulling) into the movement for fifteen seconds or more.

Supervision

Without supervision you're likely to have trouble maintaining the timing throughout the set. You could count seconds but then your concentration may be removed from getting out the super slow reps. These reps are massively fatiguing and painful. You'll need a supervisor to prevent you from speeding up to get out the final reps of the set. You may be able to count seconds during each rep, without it affecting your concentration much if at all. However, don't try to count seconds during each rep *and* count reps as well. Having two different things to count *will* mar your focus on the exercise.

If you have no alternative to training by yourself, and you want to experiment with super slow training without having to count seconds, what can you do? Do the exercise as slowly as you can on the positive part, without counting anything. Just push or pull enough to keep the bar from stopping. On the negative part, let the bar move at twice the speed. No matter how painful the reps become, keep up this speed. No cheating by quickening things up.

Practice at home with a broomstick in front of a clock. Do all the exercises you're using in the gym while watching the clock. Do this for a few reps daily and you'll soon get the mental "feel" of super slow reps of ten and five seconds, plus the "turnarounds." This will help you in the gym. Do revision broomstick work as well.

Patience and perseverance

If you've never tried this type of training, the thought of a single set of 4–6 reps for no more than six exercises may strike you as a joke of a way to train. Once you've experienced the humbling and painful experience of super slow reps, you'll think differently.

Learning the method takes a while, so persevere and be patient. You'll need to reduce by about 50% the weight you would normally use (for about five reps), depending on how you "normally" do your reps.

Start with four (perfect) reps. (Do more than four reps if you've cut the weight back enough.)

Your ego might be devastated with the initial small poundages you need to use to get out just four reps in regulation style. If you're going to make a fair experiment, forget about what others might think. Work up to 6–8 reps in perfect super slow form and then add a few pounds and start again at four reps.

You'll build up the poundages greatly relative to where you started, and do it quicker than you may think you will when doing your first grueling session with super slow reps.

Friction

If you use machines, there must be no friction in the apparatus. If there's any friction and you feel the bar is getting stuck and movement isn't steady, change the exercise.

Experiment

For your first trial, use a maximum of six basic exercises, twice a week. For example: squat, stiff–legged deadlift or shrug (once a week each at alternate workouts), bench press, pulldown, overhead press, heel raise. Specific arm work is optional. Don't undermine the potential value of super slow by training too frequently. While you're learning the procedure, and are not actually training full–bore, you can train more frequently than later when you'll be going flat–out.

Be ready to take a few weeks (not just a workout or two) to get "into" super slow, to pick up the poundages and then to start filling out your muscles. Start light and focus on performance rather than seeing how much agony you can endure. The agony can come after a few weeks. You may need to experiment with your choice of exercises to ensure they are safe and best suited to super slow for you.

Other than ten minutes of general warmup work and some abdominal work, you can get straight into the six super slow exercises, one set of each and taking just enough rest between exercises to set up the equipment for the next exercise.

You can be in and out of the gym within thirty minutes, and even faster if you do no pre–workout general warmup work. If you're pushed for time, now's a good time to experiment with super slow.

If you're experiencing some aches and pains, and feel the need for a change of pace, now may be the time to experiment with super slow. Rehabilitate yourself while trying to build some muscle.

Unless you do something absurd, you're not going to get injured with super slow. Be sure you have a spotter or racks to take the bar off you because, remember, you don't finish a set until you've been pushing or pulling against a static bar for more than fifteen seconds. This means you can't get the barbell back in the bench press or squat stands, for example. If you don't have safety bars for the squat and bench press, you'd better substitute the bent-legged deadlift and parallel bar dip.

Super slow involves no momentum. If you use super slow regularly, don't expect to be able to revert to a powerlifting routine and immediately duplicate your previous best lifts. If you want to retain your ability to drive up your biggest poundages, you need to keep doing some of this type of training. Try doing it one workout out of every two or three.

With super slow training demanding a drastic change in approach, you'll probably find it best to start doing all your training in this style. After two months, when you have the procedure down pat, you can probably mix super slow with another rep style. Still keep workouts brief – don't pile one type of training on top of the other. Or, alternate a super slow workout with another style of workout.

Very skeptical?

If you're really skeptical and want to try super slow in a limited way, try it on a single body part and do the super slow work first in your workout. I suggest a small body part. How about two exercises for the upper arms? While it isn't the best way to experiment with super slow, it's a lot better than nothing. Take measurements, start light, get the style right, build up the poundage over three months, give it your *all* no more than three times a week (just twice may be better). Then take your measurements again. Now, is it worth experimenting more?

A different perspective

There are a great many opinions about the best way to train for a given goal, even for hard-gaining typical bodybuilders. Quite often, the different arguments are similarly convincing. You have to select what you think may best suit you and give it a good try. Trial and error is a powerful teacher. Experiment rationally, taking your advice from appropriate sources. Learn what suits you.

This book provides a different perspective on training relative to what you can find in the popular bodybuilding literature. By providing this different interpretation you've been given a broader choice of alternative ways of training. A bigger store of information and opinion can be confusing. Much more important is that a bigger store is a richer source of advice to help you to realize your potential.

Nutrition matters a lot, but forget the notion that it's 80% or even 50% of bodybuilding success. Sitting down and eating and drinking is the easy bit, relatively speaking. Knuckling down in the gym to very intense work is the hard bit.

Too many bodybuilders treat supplements as if they are panaceas. They get distracted from satisfying the fundamentals of sound training and of sound nutrition through *ordinary* food. Instead of looking in the gym and at their training frequency for the primary explanation for their inadequate progress, they look at supplement displays in magazines, gyms and stores.

14: Nutrition

For many people, rigorous organization is needed to be able to consume, over time, progressively larger quantities of nutritious food. Some of you may need to add thousands of calories each day. Doing this involves a fundamental restructuring of your diet and an unusual degree of discipline and fortitude. It doesn't just mean adding a few glasses of milk each day. These people – relative to being in "no gains land" – will need to double their intake of solid food *and* add several quarts of milk. While this isn't going to be a diet for life, it will be needed for a good while in order to get you as big as you want to be.

If your nutrition isn't in reasonable order, then no matter how sound your training program is, it won't make you bigger and stronger. That being said, forget the notion that nutrition is 80% or even 50% of bodybuilding success. Knuckling down in the gym to very intense work on squats, deadlifts and a few other great exercises is the hard bit. That's the over–50% bit. Rest *and* nutrition make up the balance.

Satisfying the nutritional requirements for progress in the gym – no matter how challenging that may be for you – is the easy part of the whole business of getting big and strong, *relatively speaking*.

There are tens of thousands of gym members who sleep well, have jobs that aren't physically stressful, and who have diets generous in calories, protein, carbohydrates and micro–nutrients. Plus, they may take a lot of hyped non–nutritional bits and pieces. They fail to gain muscle simply because they don't train effectively.

Once your diet and rest habits *are* in good order, your bodybuilding progress is *totally* a reflection of what you're doing in the gym. Get your diet in good order without making it into a problem. If you find that getting your diet in good order is difficult, what are you going to think when you're grinding out the reps under a heavy squat bar and your body is protesting but your mind has to drive it on?

Too many people have become confused over diet. During the last couple of decades there has been an astonishing increase in the attention given to diet, both inside and outside the bodybuilding world. It's a shame there hasn't been an astonishing increase in the number of typical bodybuilders realizing their strength and size potentials.

Making the most of milk

For the typical skinny and very young bodybuilder to develop a lot of muscle mass, a lot of food needs to be consumed. The easiest way to add a lot of nutritious calories to a regular diet is to add potent drinks, or a lot of milk by itself. Progressively build up to drinking a lot of milk. Don't jump overnight into drinking 2–4 quarts of milk a day. Take a few weeks.

Milk is the base for bodybuilding drinks, a blender the tool for getting all the ingredients into a palatable concoction. Hence, the traditional reliance upon milk in some quarters of the training world. As long as your digestive system can handle milk, make the most of it. Cold in the summer and warm in the winter.

Some people don't digest milk well, and they too quickly conclude that it's not for suitable them. Before you think of substitutes for milk, be sure you've tried all the ways of modifying it to see if you can digest it without problems. First, try drinking milk by itself – don't mix it with anything and don't drink it until you feel hungry. Don't gulp it down but sip it slowly. If this doesn't work, try the same but with low–fat or non–fat milk.

If this doesn't improve matters, buy a lactose enzyme product from a drugstore (chemist). Using these tablets may compensate for your body's possible inability to deal with the lactose in the milk.

If none of these modifications help, then search for lactose–reduced low–fat milk which some supermarkets sell, at least in the USA.

Some people find that "raw" milk can be digested whereas pasteurized milk gives problems. If you've a good reliable source of raw milk, then experiment with that too.

You may find milk that has been in the blender is more difficult to digest. If so, whether or not you usually have sensitivity to milk, don't put milk in a blender.

If, after trying all the modifications, you still can't handle milk, then you have to use alternatives. This assumes you need to get extra calories in your diet from liquid food. If you don't need to increase your calorie intake considerably, you'll be able to manage by just increasing your solid food intake a little.

Those that need greatly increased food intake – especially hard gainers in their teens or early twenties – are the ones that "suffer" from not being able to tolerate milk.

In these cases, you need to find liquid high–calorie and nutritious ready–made non–milk products or, make your own concoctions. Yogurt, soy milk, egg–based products, very low–fat cottage cheese, and "weight–gain" supplements primarily derived from grains can be experimented with (not all of them together) as the base for your "concoctions."

Food rotation

Some people have overt allergies to some foods and chemicals and many of us have "hidden" allergies. Any food that gives you an immediate reaction should be avoided. (Discomfort from food may not be due to an allergic reaction though.) Avoid foods and combinations that disagree with you. Avoid as much as you can foods that have chemicals in them. If you live in the cities, you probably can't avoid them all but you sure can cut out a lot of the chemicals.

Rotating your foods somewhat, and eating a big variety of foods, helps to avoid your body being worn down by allergens. Don't heavily eat or drink a single food without at least having periodic breaks. For example, if you rely heavily on milk, have a rest from it during layoffs and even during the first 2–3 weeks of a new training cycle. Then get back on the milk again.

Don't have wheat for your breakfast cereal everyday. Have oats or barley. Rotate them. Don't always have potatoes with your evening meal. Have pasta, legumes, bread or some other starch. Don't always drink orange juice. What about grapefruit, pineapple, mandarin and apple juice? Get some variety into your diet. It's not only good for your body but good for your taste buds and enjoyment of food.

Fat and cholesterol

There's a lot of popular concern over fat and cholesterol in the diet. (Cholesterol is not a fatty substance but a sterol – a waxy substance insoluble in water.) This concern may worry bodybuilders who are advised to drink a lot of milk.

Don't turn a concern into a neurosis, and so get paranoic over the thought of having more than a couple of egg yolks a week or more than a quart of full–fat milk a week. As a hard training bodybuilder who is health conscious, dietary fat and cholesterol are not the horror substances some make them out to be.

I don't believe a diet that has quite a lot of fat and cholesterol in it is automatically and universally the bad thing some make it out to be. Such a lot depends on other factors. However, this is absolutely *not* the license to start drinking fifteen quarts of full–fat milk and eating thirty eggs a day.

If you consume generously of dairy products and eggs, but have little or no meat, no "junk" food, consume lots of high–fibre foods, eat lots of fruit and greens, eat fish most days, eat a lot of raw food consume olive oil most days (I live in a Mediterranean country and olive oil is revered here), don't smoke, exercise hard – including target heart rate aerobic training, aren't fat, are young or youngish, take a broad spectrum vitamin and mineral supplement together with additional vitamins C and E, don't use drugs, aren't a big worrier, and have don't have a genetic tendency towards unusually high blood cholesterol levels, then how on earth is a year or few on a moderately heavy diet going to do you any harm? Let's keep things in perspective. Anyway, if you use low–fat or non–fat milk rather than full–fat milk, and low–fat cheeses rather than full–fat hard cheeses, then fat intake can be sharply curtailed.

Compare the above scenario with a bodybuilder who downs, weekly, gallons of full–fat milk, dozens of eggs and lots of full–fat cheese in amongst his generous consumption of "junk" food and a low–fibre, highly refined diet. The same bodybuilder who's very heavy, sometimes takes steroids and perhaps even smokes. For such a person, the heavy use of eggs and dairy products is a recipe for disaster, maybe a fatal one.

Don't get me wrong. *Don't* misinterpret me as saying that you should pay no attention to dietary fat and cholesterol. The more unhealthy your overall lifestyle – which includes your diet – the more that fat and cholesterol intake may influence your health. However, the more healthy your overall lifestyle is, the less the dietary fat and cholesterol probably matter because your body is in good order and functioning efficiently.

Play safe though. Have a periodic check of your blood cholesterol level. If it's high, then investigate your lifestyle and seek medical advice. If it's low, you're doing fine. Even if it *is* a high reading, don't automatically assume that it's your intake of fat (or cholesterol) that's the principal cause. There are *so many* factors at play, don't just pick on the popular scapegoat without investigating other possible causative factors.

Substituting some animal fats with similar or even larger quantities of fats from olive oil, fish, nuts and seeds can reduce cholesterol levels without reducing fat intake.

Also, even if your cholesterol level isn't very low, don't think you're an automatic candidate for a heart attack. There are many risk factors in heart disease – as many as twenty–five or more of them including smoking, genetic inheritance, hypertension, diabetes and inactivity. A high cholesterol level is only one risk factor. Pay attention to diminishing all risk factors, including your cholesterol level, but don't focus on just one or two of them.

Medical report on dietary fat and heart disease

To provide some balance on this topic, not all reports condemn dietary fat. On the BBC World Service's Science in Action program, February 1991, there was an interesting report. It opened by reminding listeners that over recent years we've been warned that consuming a lot of fat, especially animal fat, is bad for our hearts. Heart disease is the most common cause of death in developed countries, killing more people than all the kinds of cancers put together. Then came the report itself:

For the last ten years, a team of the British Medical Research Council's Epidemiology Unit has been monitoring 2,500 middle–aged men to find out what aspects of their physiology, lifestyle and diet might indicate susceptibility to heart disease. While results showed that smoking increases risk, and there's evidence that exercise might decrease it, the controversial finding was that our beliefs about fat are open to question.

The Unit's director, Dr. Peter Ellwood, was questioned and he replied:

> We find no convincing evidence of the relationship between fat intake and subsequent risk of heart disease, and our study enables us actually to look at fat of animal origin. We find absolutely no evidence that men who ate more animal fat have an increased subsequent risk of heart disease.

The interviewer asked if low–fat diets really are good for the heart and if this report provided new findings.

Dr. Ellwood continued:

> There have been observational studies such as ours – there have been six or seven major studies throughout the world and none of these have shown that people in the community who eat more fat have a higher risk. There have also been six or seven major trials where fat intake of people has been reduced. Now, none of these give convincing evidence of any benefit of survival in terms of reduced mortality.

Dr. Ellwood went on to say that while there has been a small decrease in deaths attributed to heart disease, due to a low–fat diet, there's no evidence of any reduction of *total mortality,* or of increasing survival. Those who were no longer dying of heart disease were not surviving any longer because they were dying of something else instead.

The program then interviewed the medical director of the British Heart Foundation, an organization that has been vigorous in advising the eating of less fat. The director was asked how strong the evidence for reducing fat really is:

> It's strong, but the situation is more complex than appears on the surface. Faulty eating habits of one kind might be compensated for by habits of another kind and it may be, for example, that eating a lot of fruit and vegetables may compensate, or more than compensate for what seems an adverse diet in other respects. All the dietary things together make it difficult to pick out a single dietary component.
>
> In studies so far, reduction in heart attacks (from reducing dietary fat) has been quite impressive but reducing the number of deaths, as opposed to reducing heart attacks, is much smaller so it's difficult to prove statistically that there's a benefit.

All this *isn't* license for you to ignore your fat intake. However, it does more than suggest that *singling out* dietary fat as the big factor behind heart and circulatory illness is misplaced. Fat intake is just *one* factor amongst so many. Be concerned about fat intake, keeping it moderate at its upper limit if you're young, and reduce it (and total energy intake) as you get into middle age. Just don't turn a concern into a neurosis. An important reason for not consuming excess fat is that you need to get, daily, a lot of carbohydrates. You must have plenty of space in your diet to consume them.

A final point here is that bodybuilders who use steroids need to follow extremely low-fat diets that are almost devoid of saturated fat. This, together with the protective effects of cardiorespiratory work, help to compensate for the heart-threatening side-effects of steroids. Just because the leading title winners are strongly recommending a very low-fat diet, this doesn't mean that it's a necessity for you too.

Life span

My opinion is that maximum *potential* life span is mostly determined by genetic factors – some people are simply "programmed" to live longer than are others. How near you get to realizing your potential is a result of how well you look after yourself and how fortunate you are to avoid death through accident.

If you've abused yourself for most of your life and then, late in life you overhaul your diet – making it "healthy" by reducing fat intake, among other things – that's rather late. So much damage has already been done. What might appear to make a difference in the health of these abused bodies may have little or no relevance to the health of younger bodies, or, indeed, of older bodies that have been well cared for throughout their lives.

By the way, there's *a lot more* to looking after yourself than what's been written here. There's the realm of the mind–body–spirit connection and esoteric wisdom of the Orient, and other matters that are neither in the common psyche of the West nor in the scope of this book.

Monitoring intake

Get a calorie counter and keep a record of your daily calorie intake. Keep it steady for a few weeks and see what happens to your bodyweight. If you gained nothing, try adding an extra three hundred nutritious calories a day, for a few weeks. Discover the difference it makes. All this assumes that you're in the intense part of your training cycle and that you're using a productive routine and training frequency, and are resting well when out of the gym.

Keep increasing calorie intake until you're gaining at a steady rate without adding noticeable body fat. It's likely you'll have to take more than four thousand calories a day if you're under twenty five, and perhaps more than five thousand. As you get older, you can gain without having to consume so many calories.

If you have to increase your calorie intake greatly – by a thousand or two or three – don't try to do it in a single jump. Do it progressively, like with your training. You go from a 200 pound squat to a 300 pound one by making lots of 5, 2½ and 1 pound jumps. Do the same with your diet. Increase portions by small amounts, and add drinks progressively. Let your body gradually adapt to the increased calorie intake.

You should be consuming your highest calorie intake during the 4–6 or however many weeks of a cycle during which you're training at your highest intensity. During the initial easy part of a cycle, don't consume so much because you don't need so much then. Consume the most when you need the most. The most intense part of a cycle is when you should time your rational use of food supplements (other than basic vitamin and mineral supplements), if you can afford to. This is the time for greatest impact.

Don't go way overboard with weight gain and just pile on the weight no matter what comprises the weight. This is the mentality of the out-dated "bulking up" approach. It's muscle we're after, not fat. Keep a close eye on your waist girth and the pinch of fat and skin on your waist. If they move up quickly, cut back on your calorie intake and investigate whether your training is productive. Converting the extra calories into muscle necessitates very sound training and rest habits.

> To transform into muscle even the "highest" quality
> food and supplements over your basic needs, you've
> got to be training effectively. Otherwise, all you'll
> build is body fat.

Typical bodybuilders can't build substantial size while maintaining a very low body fat level. As long as you're lean, letting a little fat come along with a lot of muscle is fine. Concentrate on getting big and strong – without becoming fat – and *then* concern yourself with definition.

If you don't have an accurate idea of how many calories you're eating each day, how can you know how many you need to pack on the muscle? You need nutritional targets just like you need training targets. Get the calories from a mixture of solid food and milk, and concoctions out of the blender. Use whatever mixture suits you, spreading it over many medium to small feeds rather than cramming it all into two or three very large feeds a day. If you want to add a lot of muscle, aim to consume food five times a day, or even six times. This is a lot relative to non-bodybuilders, but then you're a bodybuilder and so have to direct your life in ways that are strange in the eyes of other people.

Just what balance between solid and liquid food you decide upon depends upon you, your preferences, time available to eat in, digestive efficiency and other things. Personally, my preferred nutritional schedule is to have a large breakfast and evening meal. Between the solid meals I work through juice, fruit, milk and drinks out of the blender in quantities determined by my needs at the time.

I don't have the time or interest to eat during the day. Milk and blender concoctions are convenient ways of getting potent feeds with minimal time and preparation involved. I can consume these feeds every two hours with digestive comfort. If I try to eat meals of solid food (other than fruit) any more than once every 4–5 hours, my digestion won't cooperate.

The typical undersized bodybuilder's diet is a pleasure to deal with. Make the most of it. Get stuck into all those (sometimes low–fat) dairy products, fish, eggs, whole–grain products (not just bread), fruit and vegetables, nuts, seeds and legumes. Consume raw as much of your food as is possible. Open all your solid food meals with something raw, be it just a carrot or a tomato. Devise a diet that's practical for you – one that you can keep to over the long–term. Avoid one that's so strict and uncompromising that you only keep to it for a week or few.

By eating like this, in sufficient quantities, all you have to do is train hard and rest generously, and you'll grow. No fuss needs to be made over diet.

If you compromise by getting more than just a few of your calories from less than quality food, or by quitting on the hard reps, or by regularly missing a bit of sleep, don't be surprised if your gains in the gym are compromised upon too. Remember, bodybuilding is all about a co–ordinated package of factors.

What's being dealt with here is a practical diet to permit gains in the gym. The *fine–tuning* of diet to try to "optimize" it for health and longevity is another matter. There's not the space to go into that here.

Appetite

Your appetite is a useful indicator of how well your training is going. If you find, after your workouts, that your appetite seems to take off, you're doing something good. If you find your appetite is flagging, something is wrong in the· gym and/or your recovery habits. Bret Hittleman made this point in the fourteenth issue of HARDGAINER and it backs up my own personal experiences.

I spent four years on a vegan diet – absolutely no animal products, only plant material. During this time, my ability to train hard evaporated, as did my recovery ability. My appetite diminished. After four years of getting steadily smaller and weaker I added eggs to my diet. What a difference the eggs made. I could train hard once more and my appetite took off. Later, I added milk and my bodyweight increased further.

From then on, the worth of my efforts in the gym could be determined by my appetite. When training was going well, I would be ravenous almost immediately after training. This increase in appetite continued for a couple of days and then decreased a little. I'd train again and up shot my appetite.

When training wasn't going well there would be no shooting up of my appetite. It remained constant. My appetite was flagging, as was my whole body. It was time for a change.

When you want to gain, don't allow yourself to get hungry. As soon as you feel hunger coming, sate it. If you go hungry, you're going to start feeding on yourself and negate your efforts in the gym. When your training is going well, you'll likely need to be consuming food very often to keep hunger at bay. Better to eat smaller meals more often than big meals that need many hours in between to digest them.

Don't wait too long after a meal before training. Otherwise, you're going to get hungry during your workout though you probably won't feel it because you're busy training. A couple of hours after a meal of solid food should be enough. It's better to train an hour or so after a milk–based drink or blender concoction – something that can be digested quicker than a meal of solid food. Once you've finished training, say fifteen minutes after, have a potent drink or blender concoction to get in a big supply of protein and carbohydrates.

The fat hard gainer

While the typical hard gainer is a skinny guy struggling to build himself up, there are fat hard gainers who have a more difficult problem. While being concerned about lack of muscle and strength, they are also concerned with getting rid of excess fat.

These bodybuilders have no problems getting enough calories to gain from. They don't need to consume a lot of calories to increase their weight. The tendency to get fat is a major problem here.

When you know that you don't need to consume large amounts of food, you need to be very careful to derive all your calories from very low–fat sources in order to get a generous supply of all the protein, carbohydrate, vitamins and minerals you need to grow muscle. A quality broad spectrum vitamin and mineral supplement is recommended to help prevent any nutritional deficiencies. The less you eat, the more chance you have of not getting enough nutrients.

While drug–using and genetically superior bodybuilders can build *substantial* muscle while losing a lot of fat, few of the rest of us can do the same. Rather than try to do such a difficult task, focus on losing the excess fat while holding onto whatever muscle you already have. You *must* keep up a short, hard and basic gym routine. Once you're lean enough, increase your calorie intake a little, focus on a gaining routine, and build yourself up s–l–o–w–l–y. (Don't try to get "ripped" until you have enough size to "rip" up. Ripped skeletons are unimpressive.)

Solution

The essence of losing body fat (and keeping it lost) is to design a program for life, not just for the short–term. Less food, more energy output, quality eating, patience and persistence. You must focus primarily on foods that have a low–density of calories. Eat lots of bulk foods to fill you up without filling you out – foods low in fat, low in sugar and with little or no refining. To keep your muscle, you still need to have frequent (small) meals, each with protein in it. Avoid having long periods between meals. You need to keep your energy levels from flagging and to prevent your body from feeding on its own muscle.

You need to increase your energy output through activities you can do over the long–term. It's not just a case of doing the activities to mobilize the body's fat stores to lose the weight. You need to keep doing the activities once the fat is off in order to keep it off. On top of your weight training you need to do exercise that's not going to make serious inroads into your recovery ability. Just walking is a good first choice. At about a hundred calories a mile, you can use up a lot of calories without burning yourself out.

Not just calorie consumption

While the calories used up during exercise comprise an important part of a fat–loss program, that's not the only contribution. The increase in metabolism during exercise may continue after the period of exercise. This allows you to burn calories at a higher rate than normal for a while after the exercise.

Intense exercise builds muscle. Muscle tissue requires energy to maintain itself. By increasing your muscular mass you increase your resting metabolic rate.

The higher your resting metabolic rate, the more calories (energy) you need to stay alive. The more calories you need as your minimum, the less you have to cut back your dietary intake to get yourself in an energy deficit. Dietary measures don't need to be severe, so successful dieting becomes more practical and likely.

"Burning" body fat

The body "burns" fat when the cells oxidize it to release energy. If the exercise you do is sustained for long enough – more than ten consecutive minutes – then your body begins to take a big part of its energy from body fat.

The cells that release the energy aren't specifically from the area you're exercising. The energy comes from the general breakdown of fat cells all over the body. Except for surgery, you *can't* focus fat loss on a specific area of the body (spot–reduction).

Refer to Chapter 10, under the section *Aerobic work*, for target heart rate work. You need to work at a level that you can sustain for long enough. Five minutes at 80% isn't what you need. You want to be doing twenty minutes a session minimum, without it exhausting you and "killing" your enthusiasm.

It's better to work moderately, and do it three times every week for life, rather than drive yourself to exhaustion five times a week for a month and then never do target heart rate work again.

I suggest you follow the guidelines given under *Aerobic work* for twenty minutes three times a week. Additional to this you should walk daily, or at least on the four days you're not doing target heart rate work. Work up to 45–60 minutes of walking daily. You're then going to be burning a lot of calories from your fat stores.

Combine this with a diet that has just 250–500 calories below your maintenance levels (no need for crash dieting extremes) and you can lose 1–2 pounds of body fat every week. That's 26 pounds in six months and 52 in a year. Think long–term, remember.

If you find the weight loss slowing down or stopping, increase your walking pace a little or walk over hilly terrain. Cut back your calorie intake a little, increase your energy output, be patient and you'll lose weight again.

Mix up your aerobic activities in the gym. Working on the exercise bike for month after month can exhaust even the most determined. Use the bike, treadmill, climber, skipping, bench stepping, rower and whatever other equipment may be available to you. Doing your aerobic work with company, making it into a social event, helps many people to maintain their training enthusiasm.

Once you're lean enough, cut back on your aerobic work a little, increase your energy intake a little and focus on a body*building* training program. Change your mental outlook and s–l–o–w–l–y build up the muscle and strength. If you get hasty, the fat will find its way back.

Food combinations

I've followed both the pure interpretation of food combining and a modified version. The pure interpretation has simple meals in which different types of food are focused upon – fruit–only meals, concentrated protein meals and concentrated starch meals. Green salads are eaten with either of the latter two meals. Fruit isn't mixed with other foods. Starch foods such as potatoes and breads are not mixed with protein rich foods such as eggs and fish. Meals are well spread out through the day – 4–5 hours between them, or even more.

From this very *basic* description you'll quickly see why it's nigh on impossible to eat a high calorie, protein rich "bodybuilding" diet while keeping to strict food combinations.

I've followed a modified version for about ten years. It improves my digestion relative to the regular mixed way of eating, and makes me feel better. While I'm not saying that everyone will benefit as much as I have, I do believe that many people would benefit considerably. If you find digestion heavy–going, and you're not satisfied with how you feel, experiment with a modified version of food combinations to see if it makes a difference. Remember, it's what we digest and assimilate that matters, not just what we eat.

I never drink milk with meals. I either have it an hour before a meal or at least three hours after a meal of solid food. I can drink milk–based drinks every two hours and be ready for each – no digestive discomfort. I do have concentrated proteins (eggs, cheese, fish) and concentrated starch food (bread, grains, potatoes) at the same meal, but *divide* the meal into two courses, usually eating raw vegetables during the "break." I have the protein food first and then have a "break" for twenty minutes or more, before having the starch foods. I find this division makes my digestion feel as efficient if not *more* efficient than if I have hours between the two courses.

For the bodybuilder who is trying to gain size and strength, and needs to consume a lot of calories, strict adherence to food combining isn't practical. The modification I've suggested works well for me. Also, like milk, I don't mix fruit (and juice) with other foods. The exception to this is the tomato. I treat tomatoes as if they are vegetables and salad items which is how they are commonly used anyway.

Dietary fiber

A diet that provides generous amounts of dietary fiber is protective in many ways. This doesn't mean getting the fiber from a bag of bran but, rather, getting it from an abundance of unrefined, natural foods – grains, potatoes, legumes, nuts, seeds and fruit. A diet high in fiber automatically gets a number of important factors in sound, healthy order.

I've read numerous books over the years connected with diet and health. Of the few that remain vivid in my memory, the ones focusing on the importance of dietary fiber remain the clearest. In particular, Dr. Denis Burkitt's Don't Forget Fiber in Your Diet and A. Stanway's Taking the Rough with the Smooth.

If you've been consuming a low fiber diet for a long time, don't jump straight into a high fiber diet. As with so many other things, do it progressively so you can adjust to it without negative side–effects.

Supplements

How so much is promised by the supplement manufacturers and their distributors. And how so little is delivered.

I have no axe to grind against rational and prudent use of food supplements. If your diet is lacking in diversity and balance, and especially if you don't need to consume a lot of food in order to gain, supplements can help to plug the gaps left by the imbalances or shortages. You should, of course, do your best to get your basic diet as sound and as balanced as possible. Never get sloppy about your diet with the reasoning that you can make up for shortcomings by swallowing a collection of tablets.

Food first, remember, *quality* food. Quality food in sufficient quantities to enable you to gain. Three thousand calories each day from "perfect" sources, prepared in the "optimum" way and supplemented in the most ideal way will do nothing for your gains in the gym if you need 3,500 or more calories a day to gain on.

Too many bodybuilders treat supplements as if they are panaceas. They get distracted from satisfying the fundamentals of sound training and of sound nutrition through *ordinary* food. Instead of looking in the gym and at their training frequency for the primary explanation for their inadequate progress, they look at supplement displays in magazines, gyms and stores.

The advertising barrage to encourage us to use food supplements heavily, is intense. There's nothing new, however, about dietary supplements being advertised in bodybuilding magazines.

The promotion of food supplements has got to such a pitch that a neophyte can be forgiven for believing it's impossible to progress in the gym without taking some combination of supplements. We easily forget there was a different world not so long ago. A world where serious and motivated bodybuilders – with neither supplements nor steroids – could gain twenty, thirty or even forty pounds or more of muscle in less than a year. A world where hard and progressive training on the basics, lots of quality food and milk, together with plenty of rest and sleep was the only "technology" needed for building impressive size and strength.

Human beings haven't changed – they still respond to what they responded to decades ago.

Some food supplements are undoubtedly highly nutritious and useable items. No one is going to doubt this. Though there's no doubt that such food supplements are nutritious, what there *is* doubt about is whether they can do anything that regular food can't do.

Accompanying the obviously nutritious food supplements are the non–nutritious and non–essential items. Over recent years we've had octacosanol, cytochrome C, creatine, beta–sitosterol, smilax officianalis, gamma oryzanol, dimethylglycine, inosine, yohimbe bark extract, cyclofenil, dibencozide, ferulic acid, clenbuterol, GHB, diosgenin and many others. Some of the same items change their form, and new products push the old names out of the way. Items formerly much publicized often quickly disappear from the market. Some of the products are soft drugs and become unavailable without prescription.

Never, I repeat *never*, allow yourself to get caught up in the hype that dominates food supplements, whether of the nutritional or non-nutritional kind.

Food supplements are just that, supplements. They have grown to become almost priority items in the eyes of many – not just among those who use weights. Ordinary food has almost become the secondary item. Let's not get skewed priorities.

It's just astonishing how the sophistication, commercialization and the general awareness of training – both related to food supplements and other matters – has gotten people to focus on the marginal and even irrelevant factors at the expense of the factors of substance.

Double blind objective proof

It would cost food supplement companies large amounts of money to try to provide the double–blind cast–iron objective scientific studies needed to prove the efficacy of the products. We're very unlikely to see this sort of proof. We're left with pseudo–proof from poorly designed studies. They are poorly designed because they use small numbers of inappropriate subjects (perhaps nutritionally depleted children or old people, or not even humans) and for too short periods of time. Or, we're left with anecdotal "proof." While the latter can be interesting, and sometimes useful, it can lead to many expensive dead ends.

Not only is the cost of providing irrefutable evidence likely to be prohibitive, just the thought that the results could *disprove* the efficacy of the products is enough to frighten off the companies from carrying out the necessary studies.

When to use supplements

Food supplements should never be seen as the means by which to try to make an unproductive training program into a productive one. If you can't make progress using the combination of training, rest and ordinary food, the cause of this lack of progress doesn't rest in insufficient use of supplements. The reason rests somewhere in the basic combination of training, rest and food. Get that sorted out and working *before* you experiment with the fine tuning that might come from rational and prudent use of supplements. For goodness sake, maintain the right priorities.

Enough genetically typical bodybuilders have made fantastic progress without ever taking food supplements other than a basic vitamin and mineral product. This shows us that if we can't make substantial progress without supplements, then we must be doing something fundamentally wrong with the basics of getting bigger and stronger.

The best time to experiment with supplements (other than basic vitamin and mineral formulae) is during the part of your training cycle when you're pushing yourself to the limit and need all the help you can get. During these high intensity weeks, try some of the quality nutritious supplements (especially a good protein supplement), perhaps together with one or two non-nutritious items. No need to use the supplements all the time though – keep them for special purposes, for short-term impact. The exception to this is the use of a broad spectrum vitamin and mineral product with perhaps some additional vitamin C and E, and any other product thought to influence health and longevity – take these year round.

The latter are especially recommended for those people who know they simply aren't following the "balanced diet." If you can't or won't eat a more balanced diet, you're better off with basic vitamin and mineral supplements than without. Of course, you're best off with as balanced a diet as you can get, with a wide variety of fresh and unrefined food. Vitamin and mineral supplements may then be wasted, but who can really say for 100% sure?

What to use

While there is an abundance of charlatan food supplements on the market – with the non-nutritional items having more guilty items than the nutritional supplements – there are some very nutritious and quickly assimilated products available. Products free of refined sugar and high in carbohydrates and protein are quality foods. They can be digested easier than regular food and be assimilated more efficiently, allowing you to consume nutrient-dense calories without feeling bloated.

Some supplements provide a lot of concentrated calories without much fat. This is just what the ultra hard-gaining young ectomorph needs, especially if he can't handle milk. (The disadvantage is that they may be expensive relative to obtaining the same nutrients through regular food.) These supplements may, when used in the intense part of a training cycle, provide the nutritional boost you need to keep the gaining momentum going and the gains coming.

To summarize

By all means experiment with rational use of food supplements. Perhaps they will help you along. Mind you, perhaps they won't make a blind bit of difference if your basic diet is in good order. The only conditions are that you're already on a productive routine and are seeing the supplements as a means to improve gains (rather that initiate them), and that you can afford them without cutting out something that you shouldn't cut out.

The bodybuilding world looks forward to the day when there will be a cheap, completely safe, prescription–free, non–placebo effect product that will have a cast iron, 100% proven, quickly demonstrated capability to increase progress in the gym. It hasn't arrived yet but let's avoid the cynicism that says the day will never come.

With the right perspective and set of priorities, the rational use of quality food supplements may help you to speed up progress from an already productive program. With the wrong perspective and set of priorities, food supplements will only fuel frustration as more is spent for the same deficiency of results.

Take your nutrition very seriously. It's a major factor contributing to your health and well–being, *and* to your progress in the gym.

GAIN, GAIN & GAIN AGAIN!

If you get frustrated about the amount of energy you invest in your weight training, for a measly amount of return, a remedy *is* available. There are two publications loaded with exactly what you need to know, in order to get *much* bigger and stronger. One is the book you've just bought, BRAWN. This book will teach you how to overhaul your training and show you that there's much more to weight training than conventional training routines. A one-off book isn't enough though to keep most people on the training "straight and narrow," so we publish the bimonthly HARDGAINER to keep you "on the rails." And, the magazine will further increase your grasp of training by providing you with a variety of opinions from our many authors on the different interpretations of "basics, 'breviated and best" training.

Stuart McRobert, author of BRAWN, publishes and edits HARDGAINER, the magazine in the mould of BRAWN. HARDGAINER, like BRAWN, is published and printed in Cyprus by CS Publishing Ltd. It's been published since 1989, and is sold worldwide only by subscription. Here's some of what you can expect by subscribing to HARDGAINER:

* Truthful information. Instruction based on fact, experience and reality; **not** hyped-up, imaginary claims created to boost circulation.

* Practical training methods suitable for **typical** drug-free people. Methods that have transformed runts into brutes; providing detailed and step-by-step training routines for beginners, intermediates and advanced men.

* Fifty pages in every issue, very little advertising, and crammed with practical instruction—a near-total focus upon teaching you how to train.

So many people that take up weight training end up eventually throwing in the towel. And if they don't give up, they struggle using the same small to moderate poundages, for years on end. It doesn't have to be that way! Here at CS Publishing we have one major cause and goal. To educate as many people as possible on training sensibly, without the use of drugs, and according to individual genetic makeup.

We want to keep you properly informed, so we're offering one or two training courses **FREE**, as an incentive to subscribe. These aren't just useless dust collectors. Each one is 16 pages long, attractively covered, and jam-packed with step-by-step, result-producing and practical instruction. They cater for beginners as well as veteran trainees, and usually sell for $8.50 each.

If you'd rather see a sample of HARDGAINER before being convinced to subscribe, please write to the address below, requesting a free copy.

FREE COURSES

CLIP AND MAIL TODAY

Success Reservation Form

☐ Yes! Count me in on these bargains you're offering. I've checked off the deal that suits me best. Here's the correct payment too. So please rush my package deal to keep me going and growing.

☐ Order a one-year subscription to HARDGAINER (six bimonthly issues) and receive your choice of one of the two training courses below, **FREE**. Just check off your choice. A $38.45 value for only **$29.95** (or £18.95 in the UK).

☐ Order *two* years of HARDGAINER for $54.95 and we'll toss in *both* courses, absolutely **FREE**. A $69.95 value for only **$54.95** (or £34.95 in the UK).

☐ Arm Course   ☐ Bench Press Course
If you just want to order either, or both courses, they are
$8.50 for one or $15.00 for both, P&H included.

Name _____

Address _____

City _____ State _____ Zip _____ Country _____

Please make checks or money orders payable to CS Publishing Ltd., in US dollars.
(In the UK, please pay in Sterling by cheque/postal order.)

Send, air mail, to: CS Publishing Ltd. Dept. 14, P.O. Box 390, CY-2151 Nicosia, Cyprus

Index

The index enables you to review specific points *after* you've first studied the whole book. If you dip into the book, just picking out bits of immediate interest, you won't get the most from **BRAWN**. You need to study every paragraph of every page, preferably reading the chapters in the order they are presented.

The appalling irony of bodybuilding is that the training methods most popular today are utterly unfit for drug-free and genetically typical people. Additionally, these popular training methods are excessively time-consuming and impractical for busy people.

BRAWN provides the instruction needed to put an end to the waste.